# THE POCKET WADSWORTH HANDBOOK

Sixth Edition

# The Pocket Wadsworth Handbook

**Laurie G. Kirszner**
University of the Sciences, Emeritus

**Stephen R. Mandell**
Drexel University

CENGAGE
Learning·

Australia • Brazil • Japan • Korea • Mexico • Singapore •
Spain • United Kingdom • United States

CENGAGE
Learning·

**The Pocket Wadsworth Handbook: Sixth Edition**
**Laurie G. Kirszner and Stephen R. Mandell**

Product Director: Monica Eckman

Product Manager: Margaret Leslie

Product Assistant: Marjorie Cross

Content Coordinator: Danielle Warchol

Content Developer: Karen Mauk

Senior Content Developer: Leslie Taggart

Managing Content Developer: Megan Garvey

Media Developer: Cara Douglass-Graff

Marketing Manager: Lydia Lestar

Market Development Manager: Erin Parkins

Content Project Manager: Corinna Dibble

Art Director: Marissa Falco

Manufacturing Planner: Betsy Donaghey

Rights Acquisition Specialist: Ann Hoffman

Design and Production Services: Cenveo® Publisher Services

Cover Designer: Wing Ngan, Ink Design

Compositor: Cenveo® Publisher Services

Library of Congress Control Number: 2013946491

ISBN-13: 978-1-285-42661-7
ISBN-10: 1-285-42661-4

**Cengage Learning**
200 First Stamford Place, 4th Floor
Stamford, CT 06902
USA

Cengage Learning is a leading provider of customized learning solutions with office locations around the globe, including Singapore, the United Kingdom, Australia, Mexico, Brazil and Japan. Locate your local office at **international.cengage.com/region.**

Cengage Learning products are represented in Canada by Nelson Education, Ltd.

For your course and learning solutions, visit **www.cengage.com.**
Purchase any of our products at your local college store or at our preferred online store **www.cengagebrain.com.**
**Instructors:** Please visit **login.cengage.com** and log in to access instructor-specific resources.

Printed in the U.S.A.
2  3  4  5  6  7  17  16  15  14

# How to Use This Book

We would like to introduce you to *The Pocket Wadsworth Handbook,* Sixth Edition, a quick reference guide for college students. This book was designed to be a truly portable handbook that can fit easily in a backpack or pocket. Despite its compact size, *The Pocket Wadsworth Handbook* covers all the topics you'd expect to find in a much longer book: the writing process (illustrated by a model student paper); sentence grammar and style; punctuation and mechanics; the research process (illustrated by four model student research papers); and MLA, APA, Chicago, and CSE documentation styles. In addition, the book devotes a full chapter to writing an argumentative essay—and a full section to practical assignments (including writing in a digital environment, document design, writing for the workplace, oral presentations, and writing in the disciplines). Finally, it includes an entire section that addresses the concerns of ESL writers.

The explanations and examples of writing in *The Pocket Wadsworth Handbook* can guide you not just in first-year courses but throughout your college career and beyond. Our goal throughout is to make the book clear, accessible, useful, and—most of all—easy to navigate. To achieve this goal, we incorporated distinctive design features throughout to make information easy to find and easy to use.

## Design Features

- **Numerous checklists** summarize key information that you can quickly access as needed.
- **Close-up boxes** provide an in-depth look at some of the more perplexing writing-related issues you will encounter.
- **Part 3 (easily identified with a new "Documenting Sources" tab)** includes the most up-to-date documentation and format guidelines from the Modern Language Association, the American Psychological Association, the University of Chicago Press, and the Council of Science Editors.

- **Specially designed documentation directories** make it easy to locate models for various kinds of sources, including those found in online databases such as *Academic Search Premier* and *LexisNexis*. In addition, annotated diagrams of sample works-cited entries clearly illustrate the elements of proper documentation.
- **Marginal cross-references** throughout the book allow you to flip directly to other sections that treat topics in more detail.
- **Marginal ESL cross-references** throughout the book direct you to sections of Part 9, "Resources for Bilingual and ESL Writers," where concepts are presented as they apply specifically to second-language writers.
- **ESL tips** are woven throughout the text to explain concepts in relation to the unique experiences of bilingual students.

## Acknowledgments

We thank the following reviewers for their advice, which helped us develop the sixth edition:

Eileen Abrams, *Community College of Philadelphia*
Iris Baxter, *California State University, Dominguez Hills*
Paul Benson, *Mountain View College*
Vicki Besaw, *College of Menominee Nation*
Beth Penney, *Monterey Peninsula College*
Gael Sweeney, *Syracuse University*
James Taylor, *University of North Texas*
Rebecca Weber, *University of Illinois, Urbana-Champaign*
Robert Wilson, *Cedar Crest College*

As we have worked to develop a book that would give you the guidance you need to become a self-reliant writer and to succeed in college and beyond, we have had the support of an outstanding team of creative professionals at Cengage Learning: Product Director Monica Eckman; Product Manager Margaret Leslie; Senior Content Developer Leslie Taggart; Product Assistant Maggie Cross; and Senior Content Project Manager Corinna Dibble.

We have also had the good fortune to work with an equally strong team outside Cengage Learning: our outstanding Content Developer Karen Mauk; the staff of Cenveo Publisher Services; our very talented Project Manager and Copyeditor, Susan McIntyre; and Carie Keller, who adapted this book's clear and inviting design. To these people, and to all the others who worked with us on this project, we are very grateful.

Laurie Kirszner
Steve Mandell
January 2014

# Teaching and Learning Resources

## InSite® *InSite*

**Instant Access Code (2 semester):** 978-1-285-44676-9
**Printed Access Card (2 semester):** 978-1-285-44677-6
**Instant Access Code (1 semester):** 978-1-285-44680-6
**Printed Access Card (1 semester):** 978-1-285-44681-3

Better writing starts with **InSite™**. From a single easy-to-navigate site, easily create, assign, and grade writing assignments with **InSite for Composition.** You and your students can manage the flow of papers online, check for originality, and conduct peer reviews. Access a fully customizable, interactive and true-to-page eBook (YouBook), writing prompts for each chapter, private tutoring options, and resources for writers that include anti-plagiarism tutorials and downloadable grammar podcasts. InSite™ provides the tools and resources you and your students need plus the training and support you want. Learn more at http://www.cengage.com/insite. Access code required.

## writ⊗xperience *Write Experience*

**Printed Access Card:** 978-1-285-44695-0
**Instant Access Code:** 978-1-285-44694-3

Students need to learn how to write well in order to communicate effectively and think critically. Cengage Learning's **Write Experience** provides students with writing practice accompanied by automated, real-time feedback and scoring and allows you to assess written communication skills without adding to your workload. Write Experience utilizes artificial intelligence not only to score student grammar and mechanics instantly and accurately, but also to provide students with detailed revision goals and feedback on their writing to help them improve.

Write Experience is the first product designed and created specifically for the higher education market through an exclusive partnership with McCann Associates, and powered by e-Write IntelliMetric Within™—the gold standard for automated scoring of writing, used to score the Graduate Management Admissions Test® (GMAT®) analytical writing assessment.

Better Writing. Better Outcomes. Write Experience. Visit www.cengage.com/writeexperience to learn more.

**aplia** Engage. Prepare. Educate.   *Aplia for Grammar*
**Printed Access Card:** 978-1-428-27756-4
**Instant Access Code:** 978-1-428-27427-3
**Aplia™ for Grammar** provides an eBook, assignable, highly relatable content, and autograded activities that keep students engaged and help them understand that writing is integral to success in academia and beyond. Students learn to master the writing process by working through various stages of the writing process—such as how to come up with a topic, consider their audience, and practice proper integration of source material. Time-saving tools such as customizable, autograded homework assignments with randomized questions help ensure students' accountability, preparation, and effort. Aplia's assessment analytics track student participation, progress, and performance in real-time graphical reports and its flexible gradebook tools are compatible with other learning management systems. Visit www.aplia.com/englishcomposition for more details.

*Merriam-Webster e-Dictionary*
**Printed Access Card:** 978-1-285-05431-5
**Instant Access Code:** 978-1-285-05436-0
Available only when packaged with a Cengage Learning text, this high-quality, economical language reference covers the core vocabulary of everyday life with over 70,000 definitions.

# Writing Essays and Paragraphs

# CHAPTER 1

# Reading Critically

Reading is an essential part of learning. Before you can become an effective writer and a successful student, you need to know how to get the most out of the texts you read.

Central to developing strong reading skills is learning the techniques of **active reading:** physically marking the text in order to identify parallels, question ambiguities, distinguish important points from not-so-important ones, and connect causes with effects and generalizations with specific examples. The understanding you gain from active reading prepares you to think (and write) critically about a text.

> **ESL TIP**
>
> When you read a text for the first time, don't worry about understanding every word. Instead, just try to get a general idea of what the text is about and how it is organized. Later on, you can use a dictionary to look up any unfamiliar words.

## 1a Previewing a Text

Before you actually begin reading a text, you should **preview** it—that is, skim it to get a general sense of its content and emphasis.

When you preview a **periodical article,** scan the introductory and concluding paragraphs for summaries of the author's main points. (Journal articles in the sciences and social sciences often begin with summaries called **abstracts.**) Thesis statements, topic sentences, repeated key terms, transitional words and phrases, and transitional paragraphs can also help you to identify the key points a writer is making. In addition, look for the visual cues—such as <u>headings and lists</u>—that writers use to emphasize ideas.

See 40b–c

When you preview a **book,** start by looking at its table of contents, especially at the sections that pertain to your topic. Then, turn to its index to see how much coverage the book gives to subjects that may be important to you. As you leaf through the chapters, look at any pictures, graphs, and tables, and read the captions that appear with them.

**CHECKLIST**

## Previewing a Text

When you preview a text, try to answer these questions:

- ❑ What is the text's general subject?
- ❑ What are the writer's main points?
- ❑ How much space does the writer devote to topics relevant to your interests or research?
- ❑ What other topics are covered?
- ❑ Who is the author of the text? What do you know about this writer?
- ❑ Is the text current?
- ❑ Does the text strike you as interesting, accessible, and useful?

## Close-Up  VISUAL CUES

When you preview a text, don't forget to note its use of color and of various typographical elements—such as typeface and type size, boldface and italics—to emphasize ideas.

## 1b  Highlighting a Text

When you have finished previewing a work, you should **highlight** it—that is, use a system of symbols and underlining to identify the writer's key points and their relationships to one another. (If you are working with library material, photocopy the pages you need before you highlight them.)

**CHECKLIST**

## Using Highlighting Symbols

- ❑ Underline to indicate information you should read again.
- ❑ Box or circle key words or important phrases.
- ❑ Put question marks next to confusing passages, unclear points, or words you need to look up.
- ❑ Draw lines or arrows to show connections between ideas.
- ❑ Number points that appear in sequence.
- ❑ Draw a vertical line in the margin to set off an important section of text.
- ❑ Star especially important ideas.

## 1c    Annotating a Text

After you have read through a text once, read it again—this time, more critically. At this stage, you should **annotate** the pages, recording your responses to what you read. This process of recording notes in the margins or between the lines will help you understand the writer's ideas and your own reactions to those ideas.

**ESL TIP**
You may find it useful to use your native language when you annotate a text.

Some of your annotations may be relatively straightforward. For example, you may define new words, identify unfamiliar references, or jot down brief summaries. Other annotations may reflect your personal reactions to the text. For example, you may identify a parallel between your own experience and one described in the reading selection, or you may record your opinion of the writer's position.

As you start to **think critically** about a text, your annotations may identify points that confirm (or dispute) your own ideas, question the appropriateness or accuracy of the writer's support, uncover the writer's biases, or even question (or challenge) the writer's conclusion.

The following passage illustrates a student's highlighting and annotations of a passage from Michael Pollan's book *The Omnivore's Dilemma.*

*People drank 5x as much as they do today*

In the early years of the nineteenth century, Americans began drinking more than they ever had before or since, embarking on a collective bender that confronted the young republic with its first major public health crisis—the obesity epidemic of its day. Corn whiskey, suddenly superabundant and cheap, became the drink of choice, and in 1820 the typical American was putting away half a pint of the stuff every day. That comes to more than five gallons of spirits a year for every man, woman, and child in America. The figure today is less than one.

As the historian W. J. Rorabaugh tells the story in *The Alcoholic Republic,* we drank the hard stuff at breakfast, lunch, and dinner, before work and after and very often during. Employers were expected to supply spirits over the course of the workday; in fact, the modern coffee break began as a late-morning whiskey break called "the elevenses." (Just to pronounce it makes you sound tipsy.) Except for a brief respite Sunday morning in church, Americans simply did not gather—whether for a barn raising or quilting bee, corn husking or political rally—without passing the whiskey jug. Visitors from Europe—hardly models of sobriety themselves—marveled at the free flow of American spirits. "Come on then, if you love toping," the journalist William Cobbett wrote his fellow Englishmen in a dispatch from America. "For here you may drink yourself blind at the price of sixpence."

*?*

The results of all this toping were entirely predictable: a rising tide of public drunkenness, violence, and family abandonment, and a spike in alcohol-related diseases. Several of the Founding Fathers—including George Washington, Thomas Jefferson, and John Adams—denounced the excesses of "the Alcoholic Republic," inaugurating an American quarrel over drinking that would culminate a century later in Prohibition.

*✳*

*Did the gov't take action?*

But the outcome of our national drinking binge is not nearly as relevant to our own situation as its underlying cause. Which, put simply, was this: American farmers were producing far too much corn. This was particularly true in the newly settled regions west of the Appalachians, where fertile, virgin soils yielded one bumper crop after another. A mountain of surplus corn piled up in the Ohio River Valley. Much as today, the astounding productivity of American farmers proved to be their own worst enemy, as well as a threat to public health. For when yields rise, the market is flooded with grain, and its price collapses. What happens next? The excess biomass works like a vacuum in reverse: Sooner or later, clever marketers will figure out a way to induce the human omnivore to consume the surfeit of cheap calories.

*Why?*

*✳*

*Examples from contemporary US farming?*

*This is his point*

**CHECKLIST**

## Reading Texts

As you read a text, keep the following questions in mind:

❏ Does the writer provide any information about his or her background? If so, how does this information affect your reading of the text?

❏ What is the writer's **purpose**? How can you tell?

❏ What **audience** is the text aimed at? How can you tell?

❏ What is the most important idea? What support does the writer provide for that idea?

❏ What information can you learn from the introduction and conclusion?

❏ What information can you learn from the **thesis statement** and topic sentences?

❏ What key words are repeated? What does this repetition tell you about the writer's purpose and emphasis?

❏ How would you characterize the writer's tone?

❏ Where do you agree with the writer? Where do you disagree?

❏ What, if anything, is not clear to you?

See
Ch. 2

See
3b

## 1d    Reading Electronic Texts

Even when electronic documents physically resemble print documents (as they do in online newspaper articles), the way they present information can be very different. Print documents are **linear;** that is, readers move in a straight line from the beginning of a document to the end. Print documents are also self-contained, including all the background information, explanations, supporting details, and visuals necessary to make their point.

Electronic documents, however, are usually not linear. They often include advertising, marginal commentary, and graphics, and they may also include sound and video. In addition, links embedded in the text encourage readers to go to other sites for facts, statistical data, visuals, or additional articles that supplement the discussion. For example, readers of the electronic discussion of gun control pictured in Figure 1.1 could link to FBI data about the connection between "concealed carry laws" and violent crime. Once they access this material, they can choose to read it carefully, skim it, or ignore it.

**FIGURE 1.1** Excerpt from "Do More Guns Mean Less Crime?" A *Reason Online* Debate. Reprinted by permission of Reason.

The format of electronic texts presents challenges to readers. First, because links to other material interrupt the document's flow, it may be hard for readers to focus on a writer's main idea and key points or to follow an argument's logic. In addition, pages may be very busy, crowded with distracting marginalia, visuals, and advertisements. For these reasons, it makes sense to use a slightly different process when you apply active reading strategies to an electronic text.

*Previewing*  During the previewing stage, you will probably want to skim the text online, doing your best to ignore visuals, marginal commentary, advertising, and links. If the text looks like something you will want to read more closely, you should print it out (taking care to choose the "printer-friendly" version, which will usually omit the distracting material and enable you to focus on the text's content).

*Highlighting and Annotating*  Once you have hard copy of an electronic text, you can proceed to highlight and annotate it just as you would a print text. Reading on hard copy will enable you to follow the writer's main idea instead of clicking on every link. However, you should be sure to circle any links that look promising so you can explore them later on.

<u>Note:</u>  You can also highlight and annotate Web-based texts with a program like *Diigo*, which makes it possible for you to highlight and write self-stick notes on electronic documents.

## 1e    Writing a Critical Response

Once you have previewed, highlighted, and annotated a text, you should have the understanding (and the material) you need to write a **critical response** that *summarizes, analyzes,* and *interprets* the text's key ideas and perhaps *evaluates* them as well. It can also *synthesize* the ideas in the text with ideas in other texts.

---

**CHECKLIST**

**Elements of a Critical Response**

When you write a critical response, you may include some or all of the following elements:

❑ **Summary:** What is the writer saying?

❑ **Analysis:** What elements is the text made up of?

❑ **Interpretation:** What does the text mean?

❑ **Synthesis:** How is the text like and unlike other texts? How are its ideas like and unlike ideas in other texts?

❑ **Evaluation:** Is the text accurate and reliable? Do its ideas seem reasonable?

---

The following is a student's critical response to the passage from *The Omnivore's Dilemma* on pages 4–5.

Author and title identified · In an excerpt from his book *The Omnivore's Dilemma*, Michael Pollan discusses the drinking habits of nineteenth-century Americans and makes a connection between the cause of this "national drinking binge" and Summary · the factors behind our twenty-first-century unhealthy diets. In both cases, he blames the overproduction of grain by American farmers. He links nineteenth-century overproduction of corn with "a rising tide of public drunkenness, violence, and family abandonment, and a spike in alcohol-related deaths," and he also links the Analysis and interpretation · current overproduction of grain with a "threat to public health." Although there are certainly other causes of our current problems with obesity, particularly among young children, Pollan's analogy makes sense. As long as Evaluation · farmers need to sell their overabundant crops, consumers will be presented with a "surfeit of cheap calories"—with potentially disastrous results.

---

**CHECKLIST**
### Writing a Critical Response

As you read a text, keep the following questions in mind:

❑ Does the text provide any information about the writer's background? If so, how does this information affect your reading of the text?

❑ What is the writer's purpose? How can you tell?

❑ What audience is the text aimed at? How can you tell?

❑ What is the text's most important idea? What support does the writer provide for that idea?

❑ What information can you learn from the text's introduction and conclusion?

❑ What information can you learn from the thesis statement and topic sentences?

❑ What key words are repeated? What does this repetition tell you about the writer's purpose and emphasis?

❑ How would you characterize the writer's tone?

❑ Are there parallels between the writer's experiences and your own?

❑ Where do you agree with the writer? Where do you disagree?

❑ What, if anything, is not clear to you?

---

**Note:** For information on writing a summary, **see 6f3.** For information on synthesizing sources, **see 6f4.** For information on evaluating texts, **see Chapter 8.**

CHAPTER 2

# Understanding Purpose and Audience

Everyone who sets out to write confronts a series of choices. In the writing you do in school, on the job, and in your personal life, your understanding of **purpose** and **audience** is essential, influencing the choices you make about content, emphasis, organization, style, and tone.

## 2a   Determining Your Purpose

In simple terms, your **purpose** for writing is what you want to accomplish:

- **Writing to Reflect**   In diaries and journals, writers explore private ideas and feelings to make sense of their experiences; in autobiographical memoirs, personal blog posts, and online course sites, they communicate their emotions and reactions to others.
- **Writing to Inform**   In newspaper articles, writers report information, communicating factual details to readers; in reference books, instruction manuals, textbooks, and the like (as well as on Web sites sponsored by government agencies or nonprofit organizations), writers provide definitions and explain concepts or processes, trying to help readers see relationships and understand ideas.

*Note:*   In your personal writing, you may write to convey information in *Facebook* updates, text messages, tweets, and instant messages.

- **Writing to Persuade**   In proposals and editorials, as well as in advertising and on political Web sites and blogs, writers try to convince readers to accept their positions on various issues.
- **Writing to Evaluate**   In reviews of books, films, or performances and in reports, critiques, and program evaluations, writers assess the validity, accuracy, and quality of information, ideas, techniques, products, procedures, or services, perhaps assessing the relative merits of two or more things.

Although writers write to reflect, to inform, to persuade, and to evaluate, these purposes are not mutually exclusive, and writers may have other purposes as well. And, of course, in any piece of writing, a writer may have a primary aim and one or more secondary purposes; in fact, a writer may even have different purposes in different sections—or different drafts—of a single document.

**CHECKLIST**

## Determining Your Purpose

In any piece of writing, you can have one or more of the following purposes:

- ❏ to express emotions
- ❏ to inform
- ❏ to persuade
- ❏ to explain
- ❏ to amuse or entertain
- ❏ to evaluate
- ❏ to discover
- ❏ to analyze
- ❏ to debunk
- ❏ to draw comparisons
- ❏ to make an analogy
- ❏ to define
- ❏ to criticize
- ❏ to motivate
- ❏ to satirize
- ❏ to speculate
- ❏ to warn
- ❏ to reassure
- ❏ to take a stand
- ❏ to identify problems
- ❏ to propose solutions
- ❏ to identify causes
- ❏ to predict effects
- ❏ to reflect
- ❏ to interpret
- ❏ to instruct
- ❏ to inspire

## 2b   Identifying Your Audience

Most of the writing you do is directed at an **audience,** a particular reader or group of readers.

### 1   Writing for an Audience

At different times, in different roles, you address a variety of audiences:

- **In your personal life,** you may write notes, emails, or texts to friends and family members.
- **As a citizen,** a consumer, or a member of a community, civic, political, or religious group, you may respond to pressing social, economic, or political issues by writing emails or letters to a newspaper, a public official, or a representative of a special interest group.
- **As an employee,** you may write letters, memos, and reports to your superiors, to staff members you supervise, or to coworkers; you may also be called on to address customers or critics, board members or stockholders, funding agencies, or the general public.

See Ch. 44

See 2b2

- **As a student,** you write reflective statements and response papers as well as essays, reports, exams, and research papers directed at your instructors in various academic **disciplines**. You may also participate in **peer review**, writing evaluations of classmates' essays and responses to their comments about your own work.

As you write, you shape your writing in terms of what you believe your audience needs and expects. Your assessment of your readers' interests, educational level, biases, and expectations determines what information you include, what you emphasize, and how you arrange your material.

## 2 The College Writer's Audience

*Writing for Your Instructor*   As a student, you usually write for an audience of one: the instructor who assigns the paper. Instructors want to know what you know about your subject and whether you can express what you know clearly and accurately. They assign written work to encourage you to use **critical thinking** skills—to ask questions and form judgments—so the way you organize and express your ideas can be as important as the ideas themselves.

Because they are trained as careful readers and critics, your instructors expect accurate information, standard grammar and correct spelling, logically presented ideas, and a reasonable degree of stylistic fluency. They also expect you to define your terms and to support your generalizations with specific examples. Finally, every instructor also expects you to draw your own conclusions and to provide full and accurate **documentation** for ideas that are not your own.

See Pt. 3

*Writing for Other Students*   Before you submit a paper to an instructor, you may have an opportunity to participate in **peer review,** sharing your work with your fellow students and responding in writing to their work.

- **Writing Drafts**   If you know that other students will read a draft of your paper, you need to consider how they might react to your ideas. For example, are they likely to agree with you? To challenge your ideas? To be shocked or offended by your paper's language or content? To be confused, or even mystified, by any of your references? Even if your readers are your own age, you cannot assume that they share your values or your cultural frame of reference. It is therefore very important that you maintain a neutral tone and use moderate language in your paper and that you explain any historical, geographical, or cultural references that might be unfamiliar to your audience.

● **Writing Comments**  When you respond in writing to another student's paper, you need to take into account how your reader will react to your comments. Here, too, your tone is important: you want to be encouraging and polite, offering constructive comments that can help your classmate write a stronger essay.

---

**CHECKLIST**

**Audience Concerns for Peer-Review Participants**

To get the most out of a peer-review session, keep the following guidelines in mind:

❑ **Know the material.** To be sure you understand what kind of comments will be most helpful, read the paper several times before you begin writing your response.

❑ **Focus on the big picture.** Try not to get bogged down by minor problems with punctuation or mechanics or become distracted by a paper's proofreading errors.

❑ **Look for the strongest feature.** Try to zero in on what you think is the paper's greatest strength.

❑ **Be positive throughout.** Try to avoid words like *weak, poor,* and *bad;* instead, try using a compliment before delivering the "bad news": "Paragraph 2 is really well developed; can you add this kind of support in paragraph 4?"

❑ **Show respect.** It is perfectly acceptable to tell a writer that something is confusing or inaccurate, but don't go on the attack.

❑ **Be specific.** Avoid generalizations like "needs more examples" or "could be more interesting"; instead, try to offer helpful, focused suggestions: "You could add an example after the second sentence in paragraph 2"; "Explaining how this process operates would make your discussion more interesting."

❑ **Don't give orders.** Ask questions, and make suggestions.

❑ **Include a few words of encouragement.** In your summary, try to emphasize the paper's strong points.

CHAPTER **3**

# Writing an Essay

Writing is a constant process of decision making—of selecting, deleting, and rearranging material as you plan, shape, draft and revise, and edit and proofread your paper.

## 3a   Planning Your Essay

See
Ch. 2  Once you understand your <u>purpose</u> and <u>audience</u>, you are ready to begin planning your essay—thinking about what you want to say and how you want to say it.

### 1  Understanding Your Assignment

Before you start writing, be sure you understand the exact requirements of your **assignment,** and keep those guidelines in mind as you write and revise. Don't assume anything; ask questions, and be sure you understand the answers.

---

**CHECKLIST**

### Understanding Your Assignment

To help you understand your assignment, consider the following questions:

❑ Has your instructor assigned a specific topic, or can you choose your own?

❑ What is the word or page limit?

❑ How much time do you have to complete your assignment?

See
2b2  ❑ Will you get feedback from your instructor? Will you have an opportunity to participate in <u>peer review</u>?

❑ Does your assignment require research?

See
Ch. 11  ❑ What format (for example, <u>MLA</u>) are you supposed to follow? Do you know what its conventions are?

❑ If your assignment has been given to you in writing, have you read it carefully and highlighted key words?

---

14

## 2 Finding a Topic

Sometimes your instructor will allow you to choose your own topic; more often, however, you will be given a general assignment, which you will have to narrow to a **topic** that suits your purpose, audience, and page limit.

**Finding a Topic**

| Course | Assignment | Topic |
|---|---|---|
| Composition | Write an essay about a challenge students face in their college classes | Learning how to evaluate research sources |

## 3 Finding Something to Say

Once you have a topic, you can begin to collect ideas for your essay, using one (or several) of the strategies listed below:

- **Reading and Observing** As you read textbooks, magazines, and newspapers and browse the Internet, as you engage in conversation with friends and family, and as you watch films and TV shows, look for ideas you can use.
- **Keeping a Journal** Try recording your thoughts about your topic in a print or electronic journal, where you can explore ideas, ask questions, and draw tentative conclusions.
- **Freewriting** Try doing timed, unstructured writing. Writing informally for five to ten minutes without stopping may unlock ideas and encourage you to make free associations about your topic.
- **Brainstorming** On an unlined sheet of paper, record everything you can think of about your topic—comments, questions, lists, single words, and even symbols and diagrams.
- **Asking Questions** If you prefer an orderly, systematic way of finding material to write about, apply the familiar journalistic questions—*who? what? why? where? when?* and *how?*—to your topic.
- **Doing Research** Many college assignments require you to do library or Internet research. **See Part 2** for information on writing with sources.

**ESL TIP**

Don't waste time worrying about writing grammatically correct sentences. Remember, the purpose of writing is to communicate ideas. If you want to write an interesting, well-developed essay, you will need to devote plenty of time to the planning activities described in this section.

## 3b Using a Thesis to Shape Your Essay

Once you have collected material for your essay, your next step is to **shape** your material into a thesis-and-support structure.

A **thesis-and-support essay** includes a **thesis statement** (which expresses the **thesis,** or main idea, of the essay) and the specific information that explains and develops that thesis.

As the diagram below shows, the essay you write will consist of an **introductory paragraph**, which opens your essay and includes your thesis; a number of **body paragraphs,** which provide the support for your thesis statement; and a **concluding paragraph**, which gives your essay a sense of closure, perhaps summing up your main points or restating your thesis.

See 4d

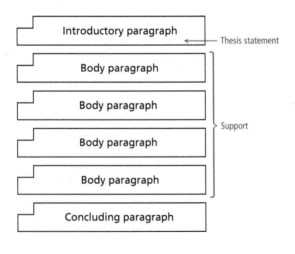

## Close-Up WRITING EFFECTIVE THESIS STATEMENTS

An effective thesis statement has four characteristics:

1. **An effective thesis statement clearly communicates your essay's main idea.** It tells your readers not only what your essay's topic is but also how you will approach that topic and what you will say about it. Thus, your thesis statement reflects your essay's purpose. See 2a

2. **An effective thesis statement is more than a general subject, a statement of fact, or an announcement of your intent.**

   **Subject:** *Wikipedia*

   **Statement of Fact:** Many college students rely on *Wikipedia* for basic information.

   **Announcement:** The essay that follows will show why *Wikipedia* is not a trustworthy source for a research paper.

   **Thesis Statement:** For college-level research, *Wikipedia* is most valuable not as an end in itself but as a gateway to more reliable research sources.

3. **An effective thesis statement is carefully worded.** Your thesis statement—usually expressed in a single concise sentence—should be direct and straightforward. Avoid vague phrases, such as *centers on*, *deals with*, *involves*, *revolves around*, or *is concerned with*. Do not include phrases like *As I will show*, *I plan to demonstrate*, and *It seems to me*, which weaken your credibility by suggesting that your conclusions are based on opinion rather than on reading, observation, and experience.

4. **Finally, an effective thesis statement suggests your essay's direction, emphasis, and scope.** Your thesis statement should not make promises that your essay will not fulfill. It should suggest the major points you will cover and the order in which you will introduce them.

*Note:* As you write and rewrite, you may modify your essay's direction, emphasis, and scope; if you do so, you must also reword your thesis statement.

## 3c    Constructing an Informal Outline

Once you have a thesis statement, you may want to construct an informal outline to guide you as you write. An **informal outline** is an organizational plan that arranges your essay's main points and major supporting ideas in an orderly way.

The following is an informal outline for the model student essay in **3f**.

*Informal Outline*

Thesis statement: For college-level research, *Wikipedia* is most valuable not as an end in itself but as a gateway to more reliable research sources.

Definition of wiki and explanation of *Wikipedia*

- Fast and easy
- Range of topics

*Wikipedia*'s benefits

- Internal links
- External links
- Comprehensive abstracts
- Current and popular culture topics
- "Stub" articles to be expanded

*Wikipedia*'s potential

- Current quality control
- Future enhancements?

*Wikipedia*'s drawbacks

- Not accurate
- Bias
- Vandalism
- Lack of citations

Financial accountancy example: benefits

- Clear, concise
- Internal links
- External links

Financial accountancy example: drawbacks

- No citations
- Limited in scope

## 3d Drafting and Revising

### 1 Writing a Rough Draft

When you write a rough draft, your goal is to get ideas down on paper so you can react to them. You will generally do several drafts of your essay, and you should expect to add or delete words, reword sentences, rethink ideas, and reorder paragraphs as you write. You should also be open to discovering new ideas—or even to taking an unexpected detour.

At this point, concentrate on the body of your essay, and don't waste time writing the "perfect" introduction and conclusion. To make revision easier, leave extra space between lines. Print out every draft, and edit by hand on hard copy, typing in your changes on subsequent drafts.

---

**ESL TIP**

Using your native language occasionally as you draft your paper may keep you from losing your train of thought. However, writing most or all of your draft in your native language and then translating it into English is generally not a good idea. This process will take a long time, and the translation into English may sound awkward.

---

### 2 Revising Your Drafts

When you revise, you "re-see" what you have written and write additional drafts. Everyone's revision process is different, but the following specific strategies can be helpful at this stage of the process:

- <u>Outline</u> **your draft.** A formal outline can help you check the logic of your paper's structure. See 6h1
- **Use word-processing tools.** Use tools like *Microsoft Word*'s **Track Changes** and **Compare Documents** to help you see how your revisions change your essay-in-progress.
- **Participate in peer review.** Ask a classmate for feedback on your draft.
- **Use instructors' comments.** Study your instructor's comments on your draft, and arrange a conference if necessary.
- **Schedule a writing center conference.** A writing center tutor can give you additional feedback on your draft.

- **Use a revision checklist.** Revise in stages, first looking at the whole essay and then turning your attention to the individual paragraphs, sentences, and words. You can use the revision checklist that follows to guide you through the process.

---

**CHECKLIST**

## Revising Your Essay

### The Whole Essay

❑ Are your thesis and support logically related, with each body paragraph supporting your thesis statement? **(See 3b.)**

❑ Is your thesis statement clearly and specifically worded? **(See 3b.)**

❑ Have you discussed everything promised in your thesis statement? **(See 3b.)**

### Paragraphs

❑ Does each body paragraph focus on one main idea, expressed in a clearly worded topic sentence? **(See 4a.)**

❑ Are the relationships of sentences within paragraphs clear? **(See 4b.)**

❑ Are your body paragraphs fully developed? **(See 4c.)**

❑ Does your introductory paragraph arouse interest and prepare readers for what is to come? **(See 4d1.)**

❑ Does your concluding paragraph sum up your essay's main idea? **(See 4d2.)**

### Sentences

❑ Have you used correct sentence structure? **(See Chapters 15 and 16.)**

❑ Are your sentences varied? **(See Chapter 21.)**

❑ Have you eliminated wordiness and unnecessary repetition? **(See 22a–b.)**

❑ Have you avoided overloading your sentences with too many words, phrases, and clauses? **(See 22c.)**

❑ Have you avoided potentially confusing shifts in tense, voice, mood, person, or number? **(See 23a.)**

❑ Are your sentences constructed logically? **(See 23b–c.)**

❑ Have you strengthened your sentences by using parallel words, phrases, and clauses? **(See 24a.)**

❑ Have you placed modifiers clearly and logically? **(See Chapter 25.)**

### Words

❑ Have you eliminated jargon, pretentious diction, clichés, and offensive language from your writing? **(See 26b–c.)**

# Close-Up   CHOOSING A TITLE

When you are ready to decide on a title for your essay, keep these criteria in mind:

- A title should convey your essay's focus, perhaps using key words and phrases from your essay or echoing the wording of your assignment.
- A title should arouse interest, perhaps with a provocative question, a quotation, or a controversial position.

**Assignment:** Write an essay about a challenge students face in their college classes.

**Topic:** Learning how to evaluate research sources.

**Possible Titles:**

Evaluating Research Sources: A Challenge for College Students (echoes wording of assignment and uses key words from essay)

*Wikipedia*: "Making Life Easier" (quotation)

Blocking *Wikipedia* on Campus: The Only Solution to a Growing Problem (controversial position)

*Wikipedia*: Friend or Foe? (provocative question)

## 3e   Editing and Proofreading

When you **edit,** you concentrate on grammar, spelling, punctuation, and mechanics. When you **proofread,** you reread every word carefully to make sure you did not introduce any errors as you typed.

# Close-Up   PROOFREADING STRATEGIES

To help you proofread more effectively, try using these strategies:

- Read your paper aloud.
- Have a friend read your paper aloud to you.
- Read silently, word by word, using your finger or a sheet of paper to help you keep your place.
- Read your paper's sentences in reverse order, beginning with the last sentence.

As you edit, use the Search or Find command to look for usage errors you commonly make—for instance, confusing *it's* with *its, lay* with *lie, effect* with *affect, their* with *there,* or *too* with *to.* You can also uncover <u>sexist language</u> by searching for words like *he, his, him,* or *man.*

See
26c2

Keep in mind that neatness does not equal correctness. The clean text that your computer produces can mask flaws that might otherwise be apparent; for this reason, it is up to you to make sure no spelling errors or typos slip by. When you have finished proofreading, check to make sure the final typed copy of your paper conforms to your instructor's format requirements.

## Close-Up  USING SPELL CHECKERS AND GRAMMAR CHECKERS

Although spell checkers and grammar checkers can make the process of editing and proofreading your papers easier, they have limitations. Remember, spell checkers and grammar checkers are no substitutes for careful editing and proofreading.

- **Spell Checkers**  A spell checker simply identifies strings of letters it does not recognize; it does not distinguish between homophones or spot every typographical error. For example, it does not recognize *there* in "They forgot there books" as incorrect, nor does it identify a typo that produces a correctly spelled word, such as *word* for *work* or *thing* for *think.* Moreover, a spell checker may not recognize every technical term, proper noun, or foreign word you may use.
- **Grammar Checkers**  Grammar checkers scan documents for certain features (the number of words in a sentence, for example); however, they are not able to read a document to see if it makes sense. As a result, grammar checkers are not always accurate. For example, they may identify a long sentence as a run-on when it is, in fact, grammatically correct, and they generally advise against using passive voice—even in contexts where it is appropriate. Moreover, grammar checkers do not always supply answers; often, they ask questions—for example, whether *which* should be *that* or whether *which* should be preceded by a comma—that you must answer. In short, grammar checkers can guide your editing and proofreading, but you must be the one who decides when a sentence is (or is not) correct.

## 3f Model Student Paper

Rebecca James

Professor Burks

English 101

14 November 2012

*Wikipedia*: Friend or Foe?

When given a research assignment, students [Introduction] often turn first to *Wikipedia*, the popular free online encyclopedia. With over 20,000,000 articles, *Wikipedia* is a valuable source for anyone seeking general information on a topic. For college-level [Thesis statement] research, however, *Wikipedia* is most valuable when it is used not as an authoritative source but as a gateway to more reliable research sources.

A wiki is an open-source Web site that allows [Background on wikis and *Wikipedia*] users to edit and add to its content. Derived from a Hawaiian word meaning "quick," the term *wiki* conveys the swiftness and ease with which users can access information on such sites as well as contribute content ("Wiki"). Since its creation in 2001 by Jimmy Wales, *Wikipedia* has grown into a huge database of articles on topics ranging from contemporary rock bands to obscure scientific and technical concepts. In accordance with the site's policies, users can edit existing articles and add new articles using *Wikipedia*'s editing tools, which do not require specialized programming knowledge or expertise.

*Wikipedia* offers several benefits to [Benefits of *Wikipedia*] researchers seeking information on a topic. Longer *Wikipedia* articles often include comprehensive abstracts that summarize their content. Articles

James 2

also often include links to other *Wikipedia* articles. In fact, *Wikipedia*'s internal links, or "wikilinks," are so prevalent that they significantly increase *Wikipedia*'s Web presence. According to Alison J. Head and Michael B. Eisenberg, college students conducting a *Google* search often click first on the *Wikipedia* link, which usually appears on the first page of *Google*'s list of search results. Head and Eisenberg quote a student from their study as saying, "I don't really start with *Wikipedia*; I *Google* something and then a *Wikipedia* entry usually comes up early on, so I guess I use both in kind of a two-step process." In addition, many *Wikipedia* articles contain external links to other print and online sources, including reliable peer-reviewed sources. Finally, because its online format allows users to update its content at any time from any location, *Wikipedia* offers up-to-the-minute coverage of political and cultural events as well as information on popular culture topics that receive little or no attention in other reference sources. Even when the available information on a particular topic is limited, *Wikipedia* allows users to create "stub" articles, which provide basic information that other users can expand over time. In this way, *Wikipedia* offers an online forum for a developing bank of information on a range of topics.

Benefits of
*Wikipedia*

      Another benefit of *Wikipedia* is that it has the potential to become a reliable and comprehensive database of information. As *Wikipedia*'s "About" page explains, the site's articles "are never

James 3

considered complete and may be continually edited and improved." This ongoing editing improves quality and helps to ensure "a neutral representation of information." Using the criteria of accuracy, neutrality, completeness, and style, *Wikipedia* classifies its best articles as "featured" and its second-best articles as "good." In addition, *Wikipedia*'s policy statements indicate that the information in its articles must be verifiable and must be based on documented, preexisting research. Although no professional editorial board oversees the development of content within *Wikipedia*, experienced users may become editors, and this role allows them to monitor the process by which content is added and updated. Users may also use the "Talk" page to discuss an article's content and make suggestions for improvement. With these control measures in place, some *Wikipedia* articles are comparable to articles in professionally edited online resources.

Despite its numerous benefits and its enormous potential, *Wikipedia* is not an authoritative research source. As the site's "Researching with *Wikipedia*" page concedes, "not everything in *Wikipedia* is accurate, comprehensive, or unbiased." Because anyone can create or edit *Wikipedia* articles, they can be factually inaccurate or biased—and they can even be vandalized. Many *Wikipedia* articles, especially those that are underdeveloped, do not supply citations to the sources that support their claims. This absence

Limitations of
*Wikipedia*

of source information should lead users to question the articles' reliability. Of course, many underdeveloped *Wikipedia* articles include labels to identify their particular shortcomings—for example, poor grammar or missing documentation. Still, users cannot always determine the legitimacy of information contained in the *Wikipedia* articles they consult.

Strengths of "Financial Accountancy" *Wikipedia* article

For college students, *Wikipedia* can provide useful general information and links to helpful resources. For example, accounting students will find that the *Wikipedia* article "Financial Accountancy" defines this field in relation to basic accounting concepts and offers a visual breakdown of the key terms within the discipline. This article can help students in accounting classes to understand the basic differences between this and other types of accounting. The article contains several internal links to related *Wikipedia* articles and some external links to additional resources. In comparison, the wiki *Citizendium* does not contain an article on financial accountancy, and the "Financial Accounting" article in the professionally edited *Encyclopaedia Britannica Online* consists only of a link to a related *EB Online* article.

Weaknesses of "Financial Accountancy" *Wikipedia* article

Although the *Wikipedia* article on financial accountancy provides helpful general information about this accounting field, it is limited in terms of its reliability and scope. The top of the article displays a warning label that identifies the article's shortcomings. The article's problems

James 5

include a lack of cited sources. The limitations
of the financial accountancy article reinforce the
sense that Wikipedia is best used not as a source
but as a path to more reliable and comprehensive
research sources.

Like other encyclopedia articles, *Wikipedia*    Conclusion
articles should be used only as a starting point
for research and as a link to more in-depth
sources. Moreover, users should keep in mind that
*Wikipedia* articles can include more factual errors,
bias, and inconsistencies than professionally
edited encyclopedia articles. Although future
enhancements to the site may make it more
reliable, *Wikipedia* users should understand the
current shortcomings of this popular online tool.

James 6

Works Cited

Head, Alison J., and Michael B. Eisenberg. "How
College Students Use the Web to Conduct
Everyday Life Research." *First Monday* 16.4
(2011): n. pag. *Google Scholar*. Web. 27 Oct.
2012.

"Wiki." *Encyclopaedia Britannica Online*.
Encyclopaedia Britannica, 2012. Web. 27
Oct. 2012.

"*Wikipedia*: About." *Wikipedia*. Wikimedia
Foundation, 2012. Web. 28 Oct. 2012.

"*Wikipedia*: Researching with *Wikipedia*."
*Wikipedia*. Wikimedia Foundation, 2012. Web.
28 Oct. 2012.

## 3g Creating a Writing Portfolio

A **writing portfolio,** a collection of coursework in print or
electronic form, offers a unique opportunity for you to present your intellectual track record, showing where you've
been and how you've developed as a writer. Increasingly,
colleges have been using portfolios as a way to assess individual students' performance—and sometimes to see if the
student body as a whole is meeting university standards.

While compiling individual items (usually called **artifacts**) to include in their portfolios, students reflect on their
work and measure their progress; as they do so, they may
improve their ability to evaluate their own work.

### 1 Assembling Your Portfolio

Many academic disciplines are moving toward electronic
portfolios because, when posted on the Internet, they are

immediately accessible to peers and instructors (as well as to prospective employers).

---

**CHECKLIST**
## Suggested Content for Portfolios
The following material might be included in a portfolio:

- ❑ **Table of contents or home page with internal hyperlinks** to artifacts in the portfolio
- ❑ A <u>reflective statement</u> in the form of a cover memo, letter, or essay, with internal hyperlinks to portfolio content
- ❑ **Writing assignments** that provide context for portfolio content
- ❑ **Planning material,** such as journal or blog entries and brainstorming notes
- ❑ **Shaping material,** such as thesis statements and outlines
- ❑ **Rough drafts with revisions** made by hand or with Track Changes
- ❑ **Scanned rough drafts with comments** made by peer reviewers, instructors, and writing center tutors
- ❑ **Photocopies of source material**
- ❑ **Final drafts**
- ❑ **External hyperlinks** to online source material and other Web sites that support the portfolio
- ❑ **Visuals** that enhance your documents
- ❑ **Audio and video clips of oral presentations**
- ❑ *PowerPoint* slides
- ❑ **Collaborative work,** with your own contributions clearly marked
- ❑ **A print or electronic résumé,** if the portfolio will be submitted to a prospective employer

See 3g2

---

2  Writing a Reflective Statement

Instructors usually require students to introduce their portfolios with a **reflective statement**—a memo, letter, or essay in which students assess their writing improvement and achievements over a period of time.

*Excerpt from Reflective Statement*

What has always scared me even more than staring at a blank computer screen is working hard on an essay only to have it returned covered in red ink. The step-by-step *Wikipedia* essay assignment helped me to confront my fear of revision and realize that revision—including outside feedback—is essential to writing.

Comments I received in peer review showed me that feedback could be constructive. I was relieved to see my classmates' comments were tactful and not too critical of my paper's flaws. I think the electronic format was easier for me than face-to-face discussions would have been because I tend to get discouraged and start apologizing when I hear negative comments.

CHAPTER 4

# Writing Paragraphs

A **paragraph** is a group of related sentences. A paragraph may be complete in itself or part of a longer piece of writing.

## CHECKLIST
### When to Begin a New Paragraph
- ❑ Begin a new paragraph whenever you move from one major point to another.
- ❑ Begin a new paragraph whenever you move your readers from one time period or location to another.
- ❑ Begin a new paragraph whenever you introduce a major new step in a process.
- ❑ Begin a new paragraph when you want to emphasize an important idea.
- ❑ Begin a new paragraph every time a new person speaks.
- ❑ Begin a new paragraph to signal the end of your introduction and also the beginning of your conclusion.

## 4a Writing Unified Paragraphs

A paragraph is **unified** when it develops a single main idea. The **topic sentence** states the main idea of the paragraph, and the other sentences in the paragraph support that idea.

> I was a listening child, careful to hear the very different Topic sounds of Spanish and English. Wide-eyed with hearing, I'd sentence listen to sounds more than words. First, there were English (*gringo*) sounds. So many words were still unknown that when the butcher or the lady at the drugstore said something Support to me, exotic polysyllabic sounds would bloom in the midst of their sentences. Often the speech of people in public seemed to me very loud, booming with confidence. The man behind the counter would literally ask, "What can I do for you?" But by being so firm and so clear, the sound of his voice said that he was a *gringo;* he belonged in public society. (Richard Rodriguez, *Aria: Memoir of a Bilingual Childhood*)

*Aria: Memoir of a Bilingual Childhood* by Richard Rodriguez. Copyright © 1980 by Richard Rodriguez. Originally appeared in *The American Scholar*. Reprinted by permission of Georges Borchardt, Inc., on behalf of the author.

**Note:** A topic sentence usually comes at the beginning of a paragraph, but it may appear in the middle or at the end—or even be implied.

## 4b Writing Coherent Paragraphs

A paragraph is **coherent** when all its sentences clearly relate to one another. **Transitional words and phrases** establish coherence by reinforcing the spatial, chronological, and logical connections among the sentences in a paragraph.

> Napoleon certainly made a change for the worse by leav- Topic ing his small kingdom of Elba. After Waterloo, he went back sentence to Paris, and he abdicated for a second time. A hundred days after his return from Elba, he fled to Rochefort in hope Transitional of escaping to America. Finally, he gave himself up to the words and English captain of the ship *Bellerophon*. Once again, he sug- phrases gested that the Prince Regent grant him asylum, and once establish again, he was refused. In the end, all he saw of England was chronology the Devon coast and Plymouth Sound as he passed on to the of events remote island of St. Helena. After six years of exile, he died on May 5, 1821, at the age of fifty-two. (Norman Mackenzie, *The Escape from Elba*)

## Using Transitional Words and Phrases

**To Signal Sequence or Addition**

again, also, besides, first . . . second . . . third, furthermore, in addition, moreover, one . . . another, too

**To Signal Time**

after, afterward, as soon as, at first, at the same time, before, earlier, finally, in the meantime, later, meanwhile, next, now, since, soon, subsequently, then, until

**To Signal Comparison**

also, in comparison, likewise, similarly

**To Signal Contrast**

although, but, despite, even though, however, in contrast, instead, meanwhile, nevertheless, nonetheless, on the contrary, on the one hand . . . on the other hand, still, whereas, yet

**To Introduce Examples**

for example, for instance, namely

**To Signal Narrowing of Focus**

after all, indeed, in fact, in other words, in particular, specifically, that is

**To Introduce Conclusions or Summaries**

as a result, consequently, in conclusion, in other words, in summary, therefore, thus, to conclude

**To Signal Concession**

admittedly, certainly, granted, naturally, of course

**To Introduce Causes or Effects**

accordingly, as a result, because, consequently, hence, since, so, then, therefore

See
24a **Note:** **Parallel** words, phrases, and clauses ("He was a patriot. . . . He was a reformer. . . . He was an innovator. . . .") and repeated key words and phrases ("He invented a new type of printing press. . . . This printing press. . . .") can also help writers achieve coherence.

## 4c   Writing Well-Developed Paragraphs

A paragraph is **well developed** when it includes the support—examples, statistics, expert opinion, and so on—that readers need to understand and accept its main idea.

From Thanksgiving until Christmas, children are bombarded with ads for violent toys and games. Toy manufacturers persist in thinking that only toys that appeal to children's aggressiveness will sell. One television commercial praises the merits of a commando team that attacks and captures a miniature enemy base. Toy soldiers wear realistic uniforms and carry automatic rifles, pistols, knives, grenades, and ammunition. Another commercial shows laughing children shooting one another with plastic rocket fighters and tank-like vehicles. Despite claims that they (unlike action toys) have educational value, video games have increased the level of violence. The most popular video games—such as *Grand Theft Auto V* and *Resident Evil 6*—depict graphic violence, criminal behavior, and other objectionable material. One game allows players to hack up and destroy zombies with a variety of weapons, such as swords, picks, and chainsaws as well as guns and grenades. Other best-selling games graphically simulate hand-to-hand combat on city streets. The real question is why parents buy these violent toys and games for their children. (student writer)

*Topic sentence*

*Specific examples*

*Specific examples*

*Note:* Length alone does not determine whether a paragraph is well developed. The amount and kind of support you need depend on your audience, your purpose, and the scope of your paragraph's main idea.

## 4d Writing Introductory and Concluding Paragraphs

### 1 Introductory Paragraphs

An **introductory paragraph** prepares readers for the essay to follow and makes them want to read further. Typically, it introduces the subject, narrows it, and then states the essay's thesis.

Although it has now faded from view, the telegraph lives on within the communications technologies that have subsequently built upon its foundations: the telephone, the fax machine, and, more recently, the Internet. And, ironically, it is the Internet—despite being regarded as a quintessentially modern means of communication—that has the most in common with its telegraphic ancestor. (Tom Standage, *The Victorian Internet*)

*Thesis statement*

An introductory paragraph may also arouse readers' interest with a relevant quotation, a compelling question, a definition, or a controversial statement.

*Note:* Avoid introductions that simply announce your subject ("In my paper I will talk about Lady Macbeth") or that under-cut your credibility ("I don't know much about alternative energy sources, but I would like to present my opinion").

---

**CHECKLIST**
### Revising Introductions

- ❑ Does your introductory paragraph include a thesis statement?
- ❑ Does it lead naturally into the body of your essay?
- ❑ Does it arouse your readers' interest?
- ❑ Does it avoid statements that simply announce your subject or that undercut your credibility?

---

### 2 Concluding Paragraphs

A **concluding paragraph** reminds readers what they have read. Typically, it begins with specifics—for example, a review of the essay's main points—and then moves to more general comments. If possible, it should end with a statement that readers will remember.

> As an Arab-American, I feel I have the best of two worlds. I'm proud to be part of the melting pot, proud to contribute to the tremendous diversity of cultures, customs and traditions that make this country unique. But Arab-bashing—public acceptance of hatred and bigotry—is something no American can be proud of. (Ellen Mansoor Collier, "I Am Not a Terrorist")

A concluding paragraph may also include a prediction, a warning, a recommendation, or a relevant quotation.

*Note:* Avoid conclusions that just repeat your introduction in different words, offer apologies, or undercut your credibility ("Of course, I am not an expert" or "At least this is my opinion").

---

**CHECKLIST**
### Revising Conclusions

- ❑ Does your concluding paragraph sum up your essay, perhaps by reviewing the essay's main points?
- ❑ Does it do more than just repeat the introduction?
- ❑ Does it avoid apologies?
- ❑ Does it end memorably?

CHAPTER **5**

# Writing an Argumentative Essay

## 5a Organizing an Argumentative Essay

An **argumentative essay** takes a stand on an issue and uses logic and evidence to change the way readers think or to move them to action. When you write an argumentative essay, you follow the same process you use when you write any <u>essay</u>. However, argumentative essays use special strategies to win audience approval and to overcome potential opposition.

See Ch. 3

 ELEMENTS OF AN
ARGUMENTATIVE ESSAY

### Introduction

The <u>introduction</u> of your argumentative essay acquaints readers with your subject. Here you show how your subject concerns your audience and establish common ground with your readers.

See 4d1

### Thesis Statement

The <u>thesis statement</u> of an argumentative essay should be **debatable**—that is, it should take a side on an issue. Most often, you present your thesis statement in your introduction. However, if you are presenting a highly controversial position, you may postpone stating your thesis until later in your essay.

See 3b

### Background

In this section, you can summarize others' opinions on the issue, give definitions of key terms, or review basic facts.

### Arguments in Support of Your Thesis

Here you present your points along with the **evidence**—facts, examples, and expert opinion—to support them. Most often, you begin with your weakest argument and work up to your strongest.

## ELEMENTS OF AN ARGUMENTATIVE ESSAY (continued)

### Refutation of Opposing Arguments

In an argumentative essay, you should summarize and **refute**—disprove or call into question—the major arguments against your thesis.

### Conclusion

See 4d2

The conclusion of your argumentative essay often restates the major points in support of your thesis. Your conclusion can also summarize key points, restate your thesis, or remind readers of the weaknesses of opposing arguments. Many writers like to end with a statement that sums up their argument.

## 5b Model Argumentative Essay

The following argumentative essay includes many of the elements discussed in the Close-up box above. The student, Samantha Masterton, was asked to write an argumentative essay on a topic of her choice, drawing her supporting evidence from her own knowledge and experience as well as from other sources.

Masterton 1

Samantha Masterton

Professor Egler

English 102

14 April 2013

The Returning Student: Older Is Definitely Better

After graduating from high school, young
people must decide what they want to do with
the rest of their lives. Many graduates (often
without much thought) decide to continue
their education uninterrupted, and they go
on to college. This group of teenagers makes
up what many see as typical first-year college
students. Recently, however, this stereotype has
been challenged by an influx of older students,
including myself, into American colleges and
universities (Palmer). Not only do these students
make a valuable contribution to the schools they
attend, but they also offer an alternative to
young people who go to college simply because
they do not know what else to do. A few years
off between high school and college can give
many students the life experience they need to
appreciate the value of higher education and to
gain more from it.

The college experience of an eighteen-
year-old is quite different from that of an older
"nontraditional" student. The typical high school
graduate is often concerned with things other
than studying—for example, going to parties,
dating, and testing personal limits. However,
older students—those who are twenty-five years

*Introduction*

*Thesis statement*

*Background*

Masterton 2

of age or older—are serious about the idea of returning to college. Although many high school students do not think twice about whether or not to attend college, older students have much more to consider when they think about returning to college. For example, they must decide how much time they can spend getting their degree and consider the impact that attending college will have on their family and their finances.

Background (continued)

In the United States, the makeup of college students is changing. According to the US Department of Education report *Nontraditional Undergraduates,* the percentage of students who could be classified as "nontraditional" has increased over the last decade (7). So, despite the challenges that older students face when they return to school, more and more are choosing to make the effort.

Argument in support of thesis

Most older students return to school with clear goals. The *Nontraditional Undergraduates* report shows that more than one-third of nontraditional students decided to attend college because it was required by their job, and 87% enrolled in order to gain skills (10). Getting a college degree is often a requirement for professional advancement, and older students are therefore more likely to take college seriously. In general, older students enroll in college with a definite course of study in mind. For older students, college is an extension of work rather than a place to discover what they want to

Masterton 3

be when they graduate. An influential study by psychologists R. Eric Landrum, Je T'aime Hood, and Jerry M. McAdams concluded, "Nontraditional students seemed to be more appreciative of their opportunities, as indicated by their higher enjoyment of school and appreciation of professors' efforts in the classroom" (744).

Older students also understand the actual benefits of doing well in school; as a result, they take school seriously. The older students I know rarely cut classes or put off studying. This is because older students are often balancing the demands of home and work and because they know how important it is to do well. The difficulties of juggling school, family, and work force older students to be disciplined and focused—especially concerning their schoolwork. This pays off: older students tend to spend more hours per week studying and tend to have a higher GPA than younger students do (Landrum, Hood, and McAdams 742-43).

*Argument in support of thesis*

My observations of older students have convinced me that many students would benefit from delaying entry into college. Eighteen-year-olds are often immature and inexperienced. They cannot be expected to have formulated definite goals or developed firm ideas about themselves or about the world in which they live. In contrast, older students have generally had a variety of real-life experiences. Most have worked for several

*Argument in support of thesis*

Masterton 4

years, many have started families. Their years in the "real world" have helped them become more focused and more responsible than they were when they graduated from high school. As a result, they are better prepared for college than they would have been when they were younger.

Of course, postponing college for a few years is not for everyone. Certainly some teenagers have a definite sense of purpose and these individuals would benefit from an early college experience. Charles Woodward, a law librarian, went to college directly after high school, and for him the experience was positive. "I was serious about learning, and I loved my subject," he said. "I felt fortunate that I knew what I wanted from college and from life." Many younger students, however, are not like Woodward; they graduate from high school without any clear sense of purpose. For this reason, it makes sense for them to postpone college until they are mature enough to benefit from the experience.

Granted, some older students have difficulties when they return to college. Because they have been out of school so long, these students may have problems studying and adapting to academic life. As I have seen, though, most of these problems disappear after a period of adjustment. Of course, it is true that many older students find it difficult to balance the needs of their family with college and to deal with the financial burden of tuition. However, this challenge is becoming easier with the growing

Masterton 5

number of online courses, the availability of distance education, and the introduction of governmental programs, such as educational tax credits (Agbo 164-65).

All things considered, higher education is often wasted on the young, who are either too immature or too unfocused to take advantage of it. Taking a few years off between high school and college would give these students the time they need to make the most of a college education. The increasing number of older students returning to college seems to indicate that many students are taking this path. According to a US Department of Education report, *Digest of Education Statistics, 2007,* 31.3% of students enrolled in American colleges in 2005 were twenty-five years of age or older (273). Older students such as these have taken time off to serve in the military, to gain valuable work experience, or to raise a family. In short, they have taken the time to mature. By the time they get to college, these students have defined their goals and made a firm commitment to achieve them.

Conclusion

Concluding statement

Masterton 6

## Works Cited

Agbo, S. "The United States: Heterogeneity of the Student Body and the Meaning of 'Nontraditional' in U.S. Higher Education." *Higher Education and Lifelong Learners: International Perspectives on Change*. Ed. Hans G. Schuetze and Maria Slowey. London: Routledge, 2000. 149-69. Print.

Landrum, R. Eric, Je T'aime Hood, and Jerry M. McAdams. "Satisfaction with College by Traditional and Nontraditional College Students." *Psychological Reports* 89.3 (2001): 740-46. Print.

Palmer, Corburn. "Older Workers Head Back to College." *USA Today College*. USA Today, 27 Jan. 2012. Web. 6 Apr. 2013.

United States. Dept. of Educ. Office of Educ. Research and Improvement. Natl. Center for Educ. Statistics. *Digest of Education Statistics, 2007*. By Thomas D. Snyder, Sally A. Dillow, and Charlene M. Hoffman. 2008. *National Center for Education Statistics*. Web. 5 Apr. 2013.

---. ---. ---. ---. *Nontraditional Undergraduates*. By Susan Choy. 2002. *National Center for Education Statistics*. Web. 7 Apr. 2013.

Woodward, Charles B. Personal interview. 21 Mar. 2013.

Works-cited list begins new page

Four sets of three unspaced hyphens indicate that *United States, Dept. of Educ., Office of Educ. Research and Improvement,* and *Natl. Center for Educ. Statistics* are repeated from the previous entry

# PART

# CHAPTER 6

# Writing a Research Paper

**Research** is the systematic investigation of a topic outside your own knowledge and experience. However, doing research means more than just reading about other people's ideas. When you undertake a research project, you become involved in a process that requires you to **think critically:** to evaluate and interpret the ideas explored in your sources and to formulate ideas of your own. Whether you are working with print sources (books, journals, magazines) or electronic sources (online catalogs, databases, the Internet), in the library or on your own computer, your research will be most efficient if you follow a systematic process. (As an added benefit, such a process will help you avoid unintentional **plagiarism.**)

See
Ch. 10

---

**CHECKLIST**

## The Research Process

❑ Move from an assignment to a topic. **(See 6a.)**

❑ Do exploratory research and formulate a research question. **(See 6b.)**

❑ Assemble a working bibliography. **(See 6c.)**

❑ Develop a tentative thesis. **(See 6d.)**

❑ Do focused research. **(See 6e.)**

❑ Take notes. **(See 6f.)**

❑ Fine-tune your thesis. **(See 6g.)**

❑ Outline your paper. **(See 6h1.)**

❑ Draft your paper. **(See 6h2.)**

❑ Revise your paper. **(See 6h3.)**

❑ Prepare a final draft. **(See 6i.)**

## 6a Moving from Assignment to Topic

The first step in the research process is to make sure you understand your assignment: when your paper is due, how long it should be, and what manuscript guidelines and documentation style you are to follow. Once you understand the basic requirements and scope of your assignment, you need to find a topic to write about.

In many cases, your instructor will help you to choose a topic, either by providing a list of suitable topics or by suggesting a general subject area—for example, a famous trial, an event that happened on the day you were born, a social problem on college campuses, or an issue related to the Internet. Even in these cases, you will still need to choose one of the topics or narrow the subject area—deciding, for example, on one trial, one event, one problem, or one issue.

If your instructor prefers that you select a topic on your own, you should consider a number of possible topics and weigh both their suitability for research and your interest in them. You decide on a topic for your research paper in much the same way as you decide on a topic for a short essay: you read, brainstorm, talk to people, and ask questions.

Specifically, you talk to friends and family members, coworkers, and perhaps your instructor; you read magazines and newspapers; you take stock of your interests; you consider possible topics suggested by your other courses—historical events, scientific developments, and so on; and, of course, you browse the Internet. (The **subject guides** in your See 7b2 **search engine** and in your library's **online catalog** can be See 7a1 particularly helpful as you look for a promising topic or narrow a broad subject.)

## 6b Doing Exploratory Research and Formulating a Research Question

Doing **exploratory research**—searching the Internet and looking through general reference works, such as encyclopedias, bibliographies, and specialized dictionaries (either in print or online)—helps you to get an overview of your topic. Your goal at this stage is to formulate a **research question,** the question you want your research paper to answer. A research paper helps you to decide which sources to seek out, which to examine first, which to examine in depth, and which to skip entirely. (The answer to your research question will be your paper's <u>thesis statement</u>.)

See 3b

## 6c    Assembling a Working Bibliography

During your exploratory research, you begin to assemble a **working bibliography** of the sources you consult. (This working bibliography will be the basis for your <u>works-cited list</u>, which will include all the sources you cite in your paper.)

See 11a2

### 1  Recording Bibliographic Information

Keep records of interviews (including telephone and email interviews), meetings, lectures, films, and electronic sources as well as of books and articles. For each source, include not only basic identifying details—such as the date of an interview, the call number of a library book, the URL of an Internet source and the date you downloaded it (and perhaps the search engine you used to find it as well), or the author of an article accessed from a library's subscription database—but also a brief **evaluation** that includes comments about the kind of information the source contains, the amount of information offered, its relevance to your topic, and its limitations.

## Close-Up    ASSEMBLING A WORKING BIBLIOGRAPHY

Make sure you have the following information for your sources:

**Article**  Author(s); title of article (in quotation marks); title of journal (italicized in computer file, underlined on index card); volume and issue numbers; date; inclusive page numbers; medium; date downloaded (if applicable); URL (if applicable); brief evaluation

**Book**  Author(s); title (italicized in computer file, underlined on index card); call number (for future reference); city of publication; publisher; date of publication; medium; brief evaluation

You can record this information in a computer file designated "Bibliography" or, if you prefer, on individual index cards.

### Information for Working Bibliography (in Computer File)

| | |
|---|---|
| Author — | Badke, William |
| Title — | "What to Do with *Wikipedia*" |
| Publication information and medium — | *Online* Mar.-Apr. 2008: 48-50. *Academic Search Elite.* Web. Accessed April 7, 2013. |
| URL — | <http://www.infotoday.com/online/mar08/Badke.shtml> |
| Evaluation — | Argues that it's important for the academic community to be involved in *Wikipedia*'s development. |

### Information for Working Bibliography (on Index Card)

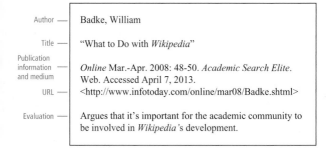

| | |
|---|---|
| Author — | Bauerlein, Mark |
| Title — | The Dumbest Generation: How the Digital Age Stupefies Young Americans and Jeopardizes Our Future (or, Don't Trust Anyone Under 30) |
| Publication information — | NY: Penguin, 2008. |
| Medium — | Print |
| Evaluation — | Book is several years old, so information may be dated. Chapter 4, "Online Learning and Non-Learning," includes useful discussion of poor writing in Wikipedia articles. |

As you go about collecting sources and building your working bibliography, monitor the quality and relevance of all the materials you examine, and download or print all the sources you plan to use. Making informed choices early in the research process will save you a lot of time in the long run. (For information on evaluating sources, **see Chapter 8.**)

### 2 Preparing an Annotated Bibliography

Some instructors require an **annotated bibliography,** a list of all your sources accompanied by a brief summary and evaluation of each source.

*Annotated Bibliography (Excerpt)*

Zickuhr, Kathryn, and Lee Rainie. *"Wikipedia,* Past and
    Present." *Pew Internet & American Life Project.* Pew
    Research Center, 13 Jan. 2011. Web. 7 Apr. 2013.
    <pewinternet.org/Reports/2011/Wikipedia.aspx>.

    This report discusses the kinds of people who most
    commonly consult *Wikipedia*, considering factors such as
    age, race and ethnicity, income level, and education level.
    It includes a table that gives percentages of *Wikipedia*
    users within various categories.

    This report provides important data on *Wikipedia*
    users. It shows that the majority of American *Wikipedia*
    users are educated adults.

## 6d    Developing a Tentative Thesis

Your **tentative thesis** is a preliminary statement of the main
point you think your research will support. This statement,
which you will eventually refine into a <u>thesis statement</u>,
should be the tentative answer to your research question.

See
6g

### Developing a Tentative Thesis

**Subject Area**
Issue related to the Internet
**Topic**
Using *Wikipedia* for college-level research
**Research Question**
What effect has *Wikipedia* had on academic research?
**Tentative Thesis**
The debate surrounding *Wikipedia* has helped people in the
academic community to consider how college-level research
has changed in recent years.

Because your tentative thesis suggests the specific direction your research will take as well as the scope and empha-

sis of your argument, it can help you generate a list of the key points you plan to develop in your paper. This list can help you narrow the focus of your research so you can zero in on a few specific areas to explore as you read and take notes.

### Listing Your Key Points

<u>Tentative thesis:</u> The debate surrounding *Wikipedia* has helped people in the academic community to consider how college-level research has changed in recent years.

- Give background about *Wikipedia*; explain its benefits and drawbacks.
- Talk about who uses *Wikipedia* and for what purposes.
- Explain possible future enhancements to the site.
- Explain college professors' resistance to *Wikipedia*.
- Talk about efforts made by librarians and others to incorporate *Wikipedia* into academic research.

 ## 6e    Doing Focused Research

Once you have decided on a tentative thesis and made a list of the main points you plan to discuss in your paper, you are ready to begin your focused research. During exploratory research, you look at general reference works to get an overview of your topic. During **focused research,** however, you look for the specific information—facts, examples, statistics, definitions, quotations—you need to support your points.

### 1  Reading Sources

As you look for information, try to explore as many sources and as many different viewpoints as possible. It makes sense to examine more sources than you actually intend to use. This strategy will enable you to proceed even if one or more of your sources turns out to be biased, outdated, unreliable, superficial, or irrelevant—in other words, not suitable. Exploring different viewpoints is just as important. After all, if you read only those sources that agree on a particular issue, you will have difficulty understanding the full range of opinions about your topic.

As you explore various sources, try to evaluate each source's potential usefulness to you as quickly as possible. For example, if your source is a book, skim the table of contents and the index; if your source is a journal article, read the abstract. Then, if an article or a section of a book seems useful, photocopy it for future reference. Similarly, when you find an online source that looks promising, send yourself the link (or print out the pages you need) so that See Ch. 8 you can <u>evaluate</u> them further later on.

**2** Balancing Primary and Secondary Sources

During your focused research, you will encounter both **primary sources** (original documents and observations) and **secondary sources** (interpretations of original documents and observations).

### Primary and Secondary Sources

| Primary Source | Secondary Source |
|---|---|
| Novel, poem, play, film | Criticism |
| Diary, autobiography | Biography |
| Letter, historical document, speech, oral history | Historical analysis |
| Newspaper article | Editorial |
| Raw data from questionnaires or interviews | Social science article; case study |
| Observation/experiment | Scientific article |

For some research projects, primary sources are essential; however, most research projects in the humanities rely heavily on secondary sources, which provide scholars' insights and interpretations. Remember, though, that the further you get from the primary source, the more chances exist for inaccuracies caused by misinterpretations or distortions.

## 6f Taking Notes

As you locate information in the library and on the Internet, take notes (either by hand or at your computer) to create a record of exactly what you found and where you found it.

# 1 Recording Source Information

Each piece of information you record in your notes (whether <u>summarized</u>, <u>paraphrased</u>, or <u>quoted</u> from your sources) <sub>See 6f3</sub> should be accompanied by a short descriptive heading that indicates its relevance to one of the points you will develop in your paper. Because you will use these headings to guide you as you organize your notes, you should make them as specific as possible. For example, labeling every note for a paper on *Wikipedia* **Wikipedia** or **Internet** will not prove very helpful later on. More focused headings—for instance, **Wikipedia's popularity** or **college instructors' objections**— will be much more useful.

Also include brief comments that make clear your reasons for recording the information. These comments (enclosed in brackets so you will know they are your own ideas, not those of your source) should establish the purpose of your note—what you think it can explain, support, clarify, describe, or contradict—and perhaps suggest its relationship to other notes or to other sources. Any questions you have about the information (or its source) can also be included in your comment.

Finally, be sure each note fully and accurately identifies the source of the information you are recording. You do not have to write out the complete citation, but you do have to include enough information to identify your source. For example, **Zickuhr and Rainie** would be enough to send you back to your working bibliography, where you would be able to find the complete documentation for the authors' article.

## Close-Up  TAKING NOTES

When you take notes, your goal is flexibility: you want to be able to arrange and rearrange information easily and efficiently as your paper takes shape.

**If you take notes at your computer,** type each individual note (accompanied by source information) under a specific heading rather than listing all information from a single source under the same heading, and be sure to divide notes from one another with extra space or horizontal lines, as illustrated on page 52. (As you revise, you can move notes around so notes on the same topic are grouped together.)

*(continued)*

**TAKING NOTES** *(continued)*

**If you take notes by hand,** use the time-tested index-card system, taking care to write on only one side of the card and to use a separate index card for each individual note rather than running several notes together on a single card. (Later, you can enter the information from these notes into your computer file.)

## Notes (in Computer File)

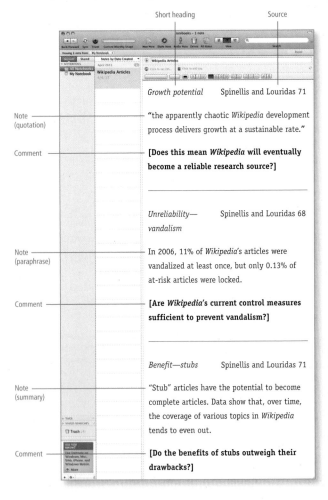

Short heading        Source

Note (quotation)

*Growth potential*        Spinellis and Louridas 71

"the apparently chaotic *Wikipedia* development process delivers growth at a sustainable rate."

Comment

**[Does this mean *Wikipedia* will eventually become a reliable research source?]**

Note (paraphrase)

*Unreliability—*        Spinellis and Louridas 68
*vandalism*

In 2006, 11% of *Wikipedia*'s articles were vandalized at least once, but only 0.13% of at-risk articles were locked.

Comment

**[Are *Wikipedia*'s current control measures sufficient to prevent vandalism?]**

Note (summary)

*Benefit—stubs*        Spinellis and Louridas 71

"Stub" articles have the potential to become complete articles. Data show that, over time, the coverage of various topics in *Wikipedia* tends to even out.

Comment

**[Do the benefits of stubs outweigh their drawbacks?]**

## Notes (on Index Card)

Short heading                               Source

```
Drawback — poor writing              Bauerlein 153-54
     Bauerlein notes that Wikipedia articles are written
in a "flat, featureless, factual style." He goes on to say
that "Wikipedia prose sets the standard for intellectual
style. Students relying on Wikipedia alone, year in and
year out, absorb the prose as proper knowledge discourse,
and knowledge itself seems blank and uninspiring."

[Does Wikipedia's poor writing actually influence
students' writing?]
```

Note

Comment

---

**CHECKLIST**

## Taking Notes

❏ **Identify the source of each piece of information,** including the page numbers of quotations from paginated sources.

❏ **Include everything now that you will need later** to understand your note—names, dates, places, connections with other notes—and to remember why you recorded it.

❏ **Distinguish quotations from paraphrases and summaries and your own ideas from those of your sources.** If you copy a source's words, place them in quotation marks. (If you take notes by hand, circle the quotation marks; if you type your notes, put the quotation marks in boldface.) If you write down your own ideas, enclose them in brackets— and, if you are typing, boldface them as well. These techniques will help you avoid accidental plagiarism in your paper.

See
Ch. 10

❏ **Put an author's ideas into your own words whenever possible,** summarizing and paraphrasing material as well as adding your own observations and analyses.

❏ **Copy quoted material accurately,** using the exact words, spelling, punctuation marks, and capitalization of the original.

❏ **Never paste information from a source directly into your paper.** This practice can lead to plagiarism.

**ESL TIP**

Taking notes in English (rather than in your native language) will make it easier for you to transfer the notes into a draft of your paper. However, you may find it faster and more effective to use your native language when writing your own comments about each note.

**2** Managing Photocopies and Downloaded Material

Much of the information you gather will be in the form of photocopies (of articles, book pages, and so on) and material downloaded (and perhaps printed out) from the Internet or from a library database. Learning to manage this source information efficiently will save you a lot of time.

First, do not use the ease of copying and downloading as an excuse to postpone decisions about the usefulness of your material. If you download or copy every possible source, you can easily accumulate so much information that it will be almost impossible for you to keep track of it.

Also keep in mind that photocopies and downloaded articles are just raw material. You will still have to interpret and evaluate your sources and make connections among their ideas.

Moreover, photocopies and downloaded material do not give you much flexibility: after all, a single page may include information that could be earmarked for several different sections of your paper. This lack of flexibility makes it almost impossible for you to arrange source material into any meaningful order. Just as you would with any source, you will have to take notes on the information you read. These notes will give you the flexibility you need to organize and write your paper.

## Close-Up  AVOIDING PLAGIARISM

See Ch. 10

To avoid the possibility of accidental plagiarism, never paste source material directly into your paper. Instead, keep all downloaded material in a separate file—not in your Notes file. After you read this material and decide how to use it, you can move the information you use into your Notes file (along with full source information).

**CHECKLIST**

**Working with Photocopies and Downloaded Material**

To get the most out of photocopies and material downloaded from the Internet, follow these guidelines:

❑ Be sure you have recorded full and accurate source information, including the inclusive page numbers, electronic address (URL), and any other relevant information, in your working bibliography file.

❑ For printed material, clip or staple together consecutive pages of a single source.

❑ Do not photocopy or download a source without reminding yourself—*in writing*—why you are doing so. In pencil or on removable self-stick notes, record your initial responses to the source's ideas, jot down cross-references to other works or notes, and highlight important sections.

❑ Photocopying can be time-consuming and expensive, so try to avoid copying material that is only marginally relevant to your paper.

❑ Keep all hard copies of source material together in a separate file so you will be able to find them when you need them. Keep all electronic copies of source material together in one clearly labeled file.

*Note:* Many **electronic tools** give you other options for saving and organizing your source material. For example, *Zotero* can help you manage citations and build your bibliography, and a wiki can enable you to share the results of your research with classmates.

**3** Summarizing, Paraphrasing, and Quoting

When you take notes, you can write them in the form of *summary or paraphrase,* or you can *quote* material directly from a source. The kind of note you take depends on how you plan to use the material.

*Summarizing Sources* Summarize when you plan to convey just a general sense of a source's ideas. A **summary** is a brief restatement, *in your own words,* of the main idea of a passage or an article. A summary is always much shorter than the original because it omits the examples, asides, analogies, and rhetorical strategies that writers use to add emphasis and interest.

When you summarize, be very careful not to use the exact language or phrasing of your source. Remember that your summary should include only your source's ideas, not your own interpretations or opinions. Finally, be sure to include documentation.

## Original Source

Today, the First Amendment faces challenges from groups who seek to limit expressions of racism and bigotry. A growing number of legislatures have passed rules against "hate speech"—[speech] that is offensive on the basis of race, ethnicity, gender, or sexual orientation. The rules are intended to promote respect for all people and protect the targets of hurtful words, gestures, or actions.

Legal experts fear these rules may wind up diminishing the rights of all citizens. "The bedrock principle [of our society] is that government may never suppress free speech simply because it goes against what the community would like to hear," says Nadine Strossen, president of the American Civil Liberties Union and professor of constitutional law at New York University Law School. In recent years, for example, the courts have upheld the right of neo-Nazis to march in Jewish neighborhoods; protected cross-burning as a form of free expression; and allowed protesters to burn the American flag. The offensive, ugly, distasteful, or repugnant nature of expression is not reason enough to ban it, courts have said.

But advocates of limits on hate speech note that certain kinds of expression fall outside of First Amendment protection. Courts have ruled that "fighting words"—words intended to provoke immediate violence—or speech that creates a clear and present danger are not protected forms of expression. As the classic argument goes, freedom of speech does not give you the right to yell "Fire!" in a crowded theater. (Sudo, Phil. "Freedom of Hate Speech?")

From *Scholastic Update*, 1992. Copyright © 1992 by Scholastic Inc. Reprinted by permission of Scholastic Inc.

## Summary

Some people think stronger laws against the use of hate speech weaken the First Amendment, but others argue that some kinds of speech remain exempt from this protection (Sudo 17).

# Close-Up  SUMMARIZING

- **A summary is original.** It should use your own language and phrasing, not the language and phrasing of your source.
- **A summary is concise.** It should always be much shorter than the original—sometimes just a single sentence.
- **A summary is accurate.** It should express the main idea of your source.
- **A summary is objective.** It should not include your opinions.
- **A summary is complete.** It should convey a sense of the entire passage, not just part of it.

*Paraphrasing Sources* A summary conveys just the main idea of a source; a **paraphrase**, however, is a *detailed* restatement, in your own words, of a source's key ideas—but not your opinions or interpretations of those ideas. A paraphrase not only indicates the source's main points but also reflects its tone and emphasis. A paraphrase can sometimes be as long as—or even longer than—the source itself. (If you quote distinctive words or expressions from your source, be sure to put them in quotation marks.)

Compare the following paraphrase with the summary of the same source on page 56.

### Paraphrase

Many groups want to limit the right of free speech guaranteed by the First Amendment to the Constitution. They believe this is necessary to protect certain groups of people from "hate speech." Women, people of color, and gay men and lesbians, for example, may find that hate speech is used to intimidate them. Legal scholars are afraid that even though the rules against hate speech are well intentioned, such rules undermine our freedom of speech. As Nadine Strossen, president of the American Civil Liberties Union, says, "The bedrock principle [of our society] is that government may never suppress free speech simply because it goes against what the community would like to hear" (qtd. in Sudo 17). People who support speech codes point out, however, that certain types of speech are not protected by the First Amendment—for example, words that create a "clear and present danger" or that would lead directly to violence (Sudo 17).

## Close-Up PARAPHRASING

- **A paraphrase is original.** It should use your own language and phrasing, not the language and phrasing of your source.
- **A paraphrase is accurate.** It should reflect both the ideas and the emphasis of your source.
- **A paraphrase is objective.** It should not include your own opinions or interpretations.
- **A paraphrase is complete.** It should include all the important ideas in your source.

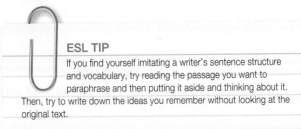

**ESL TIP**

If you find yourself imitating a writer's sentence structure and vocabulary, try reading the passage you want to paraphrase and then putting it aside and thinking about it. Then, try to write down the ideas you remember without looking at the original text.

*Quoting Sources* Quote when you want to use a source's unique wording in your paper. When you **quote,** you copy a writer's statements exactly as they appear in a source, word for word and punctuation mark for punctuation mark, enclosing the borrowed words in quotation marks.

As a rule, you should not quote extensively in a research paper. Numerous quotations interrupt the flow of your discussion and give readers the impression that your paper is just an unassimilated collection of other people's ideas.

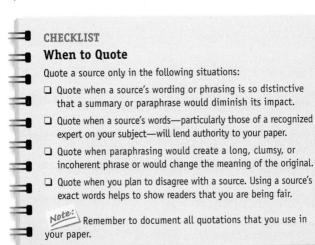

**CHECKLIST**

**When to Quote**

Quote a source only in the following situations:

❑ Quote when a source's wording or phrasing is so distinctive that a summary or paraphrase would diminish its impact.

❑ Quote when a source's words—particularly those of a recognized expert on your subject—will lend authority to your paper.

❑ Quote when paraphrasing would create a long, clumsy, or incoherent phrase or would change the meaning of the original.

❑ Quote when you plan to disagree with a source. Using a source's exact words helps to show readers that you are being fair.

*Note:* Remember to document all quotations that you use in your paper.

## 4 Synthesizing Sources

Summaries and paraphrases rephrase a source's main ideas, and quotations reproduce a source's exact language. Synthesis combines summary, paraphrase, and quotation to create an essay or paragraph that expresses a writer's original viewpoint.

A **synthesis** integrates information from two or more sources. In a synthesis, you weave ideas from your sources together and show how these ideas are similar or different. In the process, you try to make sense of your sources and help readers understand them in some meaningful way. For this reason, knowing how to write a synthesis is an important skill.

The following synthesis, written by a student as part of a research paper, effectively uses paraphrase and quotation to define the term *outsider art* and to explain it in relation to a particular artist's life and work.

## Sample Student Synthesis

Bill Traylor is one of America's leading outsider artists. According to *Raw Vision* magazine, Traylor is one of the foremost artists of the twentieth century (Karlins). Born on a cotton plantation as a slave in the 1850s and illiterate all his life, Traylor was self-taught and did not consider himself an artist. He created work for himself rather than for the public (Glueck). The term *outsider art* refers to works of art created by individuals who are by definition outside society. Because of their mental condition, lack of education, criminal behavior, or physical handicaps, they are not part of the mainstream of society. According to Louis-Dreyfus, outsider artists also possess the following characteristics:

> Few have formal training of any kind. They do their work absent from the self-consciousness that necessarily comes from being an artist in the ordinarily accepted circumstance. The French call it "Art Brut." But here in America, "Outsider Art" also refers to work done by the poor, illiterate, and self-taught African Americans whose artistic product is not the result of a controlling mental or behavioral factor but of their untaught and impoverished social conditions. (iv)

As a Southern African-American man with few resources and little formal training, Traylor fits the definition of an outsider artist whose works are largely defined by the hardships he faced.

*Margin annotations:*

Topic sentence states main point

Summary of Karlins article

Paraphrase from one-page Glueck article

Long quotation from introduction to exhibit pamphlet

Conclusion summarizes main point

As this example demonstrates, an effective synthesis weaves information from different sources into the discussion, establishing relationships between sources and the writer's own ideas.

---

**CHECKLIST**
## Synthesizing Sources
❑ Analyze and interpret your source material.
❑ Blend sources carefully, identifying each source and naming its author(s) and title.
❑ Identify key similarities and differences among your sources.
❑ Provide identifying tags and transitional words and phrases to help readers follow your discussion.
❑ Be sure to clearly differentiate your ideas from those of your sources.
❑ Document all paraphrased and summarized material as well as all quotations.

---

## 6g Fine-Tuning Your Thesis

After you have finished your focused research and note-taking, you are ready to refine your tentative thesis into a carefully worded statement that expresses a conclusion that See 3b your research can support. This <u>thesis statement</u> should be more detailed than your tentative thesis, accurately conveying the direction, emphasis, and scope of your paper.

### Fine-Tuning Your Thesis

**Tentative Thesis**

The debate surrounding *Wikipedia* has helped people in the academic community to consider how college-level research has changed in recent years.

**Thesis Statement**

All in all, the debate over *Wikipedia* has been a positive development because it has led the academic community to confront the challenges of open, collaborative software on the Web.

## 6h Outlining, Drafting, and Revising

Once you have a thesis statement, you are ready to construct an outline to guide you as you draft your paper.

### 1 Outlining

Before you can write your rough draft, you need to make some sense out of all the notes you have accumulated, and you do this by sorting and organizing them. A **formal outline** includes all the ideas you will develop in your paper, indicating not only the exact order in which you will present these ideas but also the relationship between main points and supporting details.

 **Close-Up** CONSTRUCTING A FORMAL OUTLINE

When you construct a formal outline for your research paper, follow these guidelines:

**Structure**

- Outline format should be followed strictly.

    I. First major point of your paper
       A. First subpoint
       B. Next subpoint
          1. First supporting example
          2. Next supporting example
             a. First specific detail
             b. Next specific detail
    II. Second major point

- Headings should not overlap.
- No heading should have a single subheading. (A category cannot be subdivided into one part.)
- Each entry should be preceded by an appropriate letter or number, followed by a period.
- The first word of each entry should be capitalized.

**Content**

- The outline should include the paper's thesis statement.
- The outline should cover only the body of the essay, not the introductory or concluding paragraphs.
- Headings should be concise and specific.

*(continued)*

CONSTRUCTING A FORMAL OUTLINE *(continued)*

**Style**

- Headings of the same rank should be grammatically parallel.
- A **topic outline** should use words or short phrases, with all headings of the same rank using the same parts of speech.
- In a topic outline, entries should not end with periods.
- A **sentence outline** should use complete sentences, with all sentences in the same tense.
- In a sentence outline, each entry should end with a period.

The following is a **topic outline** for the model student research paper in **11c**.

## Topic Outline

<u>Thesis statement:</u> All in all, the debate over *Wikipedia* has been a positive development because it has led the academic community to confront the challenges of open, collaborative software on the Web.

  I. Definition of wiki and explanation of *Wikipedia*

    A. Fast and easy

    B. Range of topics

 II. Introduction to *Wikipedia*'s drawbacks

    A. Warnings on "Researching with *Wikipedia*" page

    B. Criticisms in "Reliability of *Wikipedia*" article

    C. Criticisms by academics

        1. Villanova University

        2. Middlebury College history department

III. *Wikipedia*'s unreliability

    A. Lack of citations

    B. Factual inaccuracy and bias

    C. Vandalism

IV. *Wikipedia*'s poor writing

    A. *Wikipedia*'s coding system

    B. *Wikipedia*'s influence on students' writing (Bauerlein)

   V. *Wikipedia*'s popularity and benefits
      A. Pew report statistic and table
      B. Comprehensive abstracts, links to other sources, and current and comprehensive bibliographies
  VI. *Wikipedia*'s advantages over other online encyclopedias
      A. Very current information
      B. More coverage of popular culture topics
      C. "Stub" articles
 VII. *Wikipedia*'s ongoing improvements
      A. Control measures
      B. Users as editors
      C. "Talk" page
VIII. *Wikipedia*'s content
      A. Spinellis and Louridas's view
      B. Graph showing *Wikipedia*'s topic coverage
  IX. Academic community's reservations about *Wikipedia*
      A. Academics' failure to keep up with technology
      B. Academics' qualifications to improve *Wikipedia*
   X. Librarians' efforts to use and improve *Wikipedia*
      A. Badke's and Bennington's support for *Wikipedia*
      B. Responsibility of academic community
  XI. *Wikipedia* in the classroom
      A. *Wikipedia*'s "classroom coordination project" and "School and University Projects" page
      B. Collaborative and critical thinking assignments
 XII. Academics' changing view of *Wikipedia*
      A. Academics' increasing acceptance
      B. Academics' increasing involvement
      C. Recent *Wikipedia* initiatives
         1. "Rate This Page"
         2. PPI

The following is an excerpt from a **sentence outline** for the model student research paper in **11c**.

*Sentence Outline (Excerpt)*

Thesis statement: All in all, the debate over *Wikipedia* has been a positive development because it has led the academic community to confront the challenges of open, collaborative software on the Web.

I. *Wikipedia* is the most popular wiki.
   A. Users can edit existing articles and add new articles using *Wikipedia*'s editing tools.
   B. *Wikipedia* has grown into a huge database.
II. *Wikipedia* has several shortcomings that limit its trustworthiness.
   A. *Wikipedia*'s "Researching with *Wikipedia*" page acknowledges existing problems.
   B. *Wikipedia*'s "Reliability of *Wikipedia*" page presents criticisms.
   C. Academics have objections.
III. *Wikipedia* is not always reliable or accurate.
   A. Many *Wikipedia* articles do not include citations.
   B. *Wikipedia* articles can be inaccurate or biased.
   C. *Wikipedia* articles can be targets for vandalism.

## 2 Drafting

See 3d1

When you write your **rough draft**, follow your outline, using your notes as needed. As you draft, jot down questions to yourself, and identify points that need further clarification (you can bracket your comments and print them in boldface on your draft, or you can write them on self-stick notes). You can also use *Microsoft Word*'s Comment tool to add notes. Finally, leave space for material you plan to add, and bracket phrases or whole sections that you think you may later decide to move or delete. In other words, lay the groundwork for revision.

As your draft takes shape, be sure to supply transitions between sentences and paragraphs to show how your points are related. Also be careful to copy source information fully and accurately on this and every subsequent draft, placing documentation as close as possible to the material it identifies.

## Close-Up  DRAFTING

You can use a split screen or multiple windows to view your notes as you draft your paper. You can also copy the material that you need from your notes and then insert it into the text of your paper. (As you copy, be especially careful that you do not unintentionally commit plagiarism.)

See 10b

*Shaping the Parts of Your Paper*  Like any other essay, a research paper has an introduction, a body, and a conclusion. In your rough draft, as in your outline, you focus on the body of your paper. You should not spend time planning an introduction or a conclusion at this stage; your ideas will change as you write, and you will want to develop your opening and closing paragraphs later to reflect those changes.

- **Introduction**  In your **introduction,** you identify your topic and establish how you will approach it, perhaps presenting an overview of the problem you will discuss or summarizing research already done on your topic. Your introduction also includes your thesis statement, which presents the position you will support in the rest of the paper.  See 4d1

- **Body**  As you draft the **body** of your paper, you lead readers through your discussion with clear topic sentences that correspond to the divisions of your outline.  See 4a

> Without a professional editorial board to oversee its development, *Wikipedia* has several shortcomings that ultimately limit its trustworthiness as a research source.

You can also use headings if they are a convention of the discipline in which you are writing.  See 40b

### Wikipedia's Advantages

> *Wikipedia* has advantages over other, professionally edited online encyclopedias.

As you write your rough draft, carefully worded topic sentences and headings will help you keep your discussion under control.

- **Conclusion**  In the **conclusion** of your research paper, you may want to restate your thesis. This is especially important in a long paper because by the time your readers get to the end, they may have lost sight of your paper's main idea. Your **conclusion** can also include a summary of your key points, a call for action, or perhaps an apt quotation. (Remember, however, that in your rough draft, your concluding paragraph is usually very brief.)

See 4d2

***Working Source Material into Your Paper***  In the body of your paper, you evaluate and interpret your sources, comparing different ideas and assessing various points of view. As a writer, your job is to draw your own conclusions, blending information from your sources into a paper that coherently and forcefully presents your own original viewpoint to your readers.

See Ch. 9

Be sure to **integrate source material** smoothly into your paper, clearly and accurately identifying the relationships among various sources (and between those sources' ideas and your own). If two sources present conflicting interpretations, you should be especially careful to use precise language and accurate transitions to make the contrast apparent (for instance, **Although some academics believe that** *Wikipedia* **should not be a part of college-level research, Badke argues . . .**). When two sources agree, you should make this clear (for example, **Like Badke, Bennington claims . . .** or **Spinellis and Louridas's findings support Peek's point**). Such phrasing will provide a context for your own comments and conclusions. If different sources present complementary information about a subject, blend details from the sources carefully, keeping track of which details come from which source.

## Close-Up  INTEGRATING VISUALS

See 40d

Photographs, diagrams, graphs, tables, and other visuals can be very useful in your research paper because they can provide additional support for the points you make. You may be able to create a visual on your own (for example, by taking a photograph or creating a bar graph). You may also be able to scan an appropriate visual from a book or magazine or access an image database, such as *Google Images*.

# 3 Revising

*Using Outlines and Checklists* A good way to begin revising is to make an outline of your draft to check the logic of its organization and the relationships among sections of the paper. As you continue to revise, the checklists in **3d2** can help you assess your paper's overall structure and its individual paragraphs, sentences, and words.

*Using Instructor Comments* Your instructor's revision suggestions, which can come in a conference or in handwritten comments on your paper, can also help you revise. Alternatively, your instructor may use *Microsoft Word*'s Comment tool to make comments electronically on a draft that you have emailed to him or her. When you revise, you can incorporate these suggestions into your paper.

*Draft with Instructor's Comments (Excerpt)*

Emory University English professor Mark Bauerlein asserts that *Wikipedia* articles are written in a "flat, featureless, factual style" (153). Even though *Wikipedia* has instituted a coding system in which it labels the shortcomings of its less-developed articles, a warning about an article's poor writing style is likely to go unnoticed by the typical user.

> Comment [JB1]: You need a transition sentence before this one to show that this ¶ is about a new idea. See 4b.

> Comment [JB2]: Wordy. See 22a.

*Revision Incorporating Instructor's Suggestions*

Because they can be edited by anyone, *Wikipedia* articles are often poorly written. Emory University English professor Mark Bauerlein asserts that *Wikipedia* articles are written in a "flat, featureless, factual style" (153). Even though *Wikipedia* has instituted a coding system to label the shortcomings of its less-developed articles, a warning about an article's poor writing style is likely to go unnoticed by the typical user.

*Using Peer Review* Feedback you get from **peer review**—other students' comments, handwritten or electronic—can also help you revise. As you incorporate your classmates' suggestions, as well as your own changes and any suggested

by your instructor, you can use *Microsoft Word*'s Track
Changes tool to help you keep track of the revisions you
make on your draft.

### Draft with Peer Reviewers' Comments (Excerpt)

**Comment [RS1]:** I think you need a better transition here.

Because users can update articles in real
time from any location, *Wikipedia* offers up-to-
the-minute coverage of political and cultural
events as well as timely information on popular
culture topics that receive little or no attention

**Comment [TG2]:** I think some examples here would really help.

in other reference sources. In addition, because
*Wikipedia* has such a broad user base, more topics
are covered in *Wikipedia* than in other online

**Comment [DL3]:** I agree. Maybe talk about a useful *Wikipedia* article you found recently.

resources. Even when there is little information
on a particular topic, *Wikipedia* allows users to
create "stub" articles, which provide minimal
information that users can expand over time.

**Comment [RS4]:** Why?

Thus, *Wikipedia* can be a valuable first step in
finding reliable research sources.

### Revision with Track Changes

*Wikipedia* has advantages over other online
encyclopedias. Because users can update articles in
real time from any location, *Wikipedia* offers up-to-
the-minute coverage of political and cultural events
as well as timely information on popular culture
topics that receive little or no attention in other
reference sources. In addition, because *Wikipedia* has
such a broad user base, more topics are covered in
*Wikipedia* than in other online resources. For example,
a student researching the history of video gaming
would find *Wikipedia*'s "Wii" article, with its numerous
pages of information and hundreds of references, to
be a valuable resource. In contrast, the "Nintendo
Wii" article in the professionally edited *Encyclopaedia*

*Britannica Online* consists of a few paragraphs and a handful of external resources. Even when there is little information on a particular topic, *Wikipedia* allows users to create "stub" articles, which provide minimal information that users can expand over time. Thus, by offering immediate access to information on relatively obscure topics, *Wikipedia* can be a valuable first step in finding reliable research sources on such topics.

Keep in mind that you will probably take your paper through several drafts, changing different parts of it each time or working on one part over and over again. After revising each draft thoroughly, print out a corrected version and label it *First draft, Second draft,* and so on. Then, make additional corrections by hand on that draft before typing in changes for the next version. You should also save and clearly label every electronic draft.

## Close-Up   PREPARING YOUR WORKS-CITED LIST

When you finish revising your paper, copy the file that contains your working bibliography and insert it at the end of your paper. Keep the original file for your working bibliography as a backup in case any data is lost in the process. Delete any irrelevant entries, and then create your works-cited list. (Make sure the format of the entries in your works-cited list conforms to the documentation style you are using.)

If you save multiple drafts of your works-cited list, be sure to name each file with the date or some other label so that it is readily identifiable. Keep all files pertaining to a single project in a folder dedicated to that paper or assignment.

**Note:** You can use a citation tool, such as *Zotero, CiteMe, RefWorks, EndNote,* or *EasyBib,* to create your bibliography and to make sure that all the sources you used—and only those sources—appear in your works-cited list.

---

**CHECKLIST**

## Revising a Research Paper

As you revise your research paper, keep the following questions in mind:

❏ Should you do more research to find support for certain points?

❏ Do you need to reorder the major sections of your paper?

❏ Should you rearrange the order in which you present your points within those sections?

❏ Do you need to add topic sentences? section headings? transitional paragraphs?

See Ch. 9  ❏ Have you integrated your notes smoothly into your paper?

See 9a  ❏ Do you introduce source material with identifying tags?

❏ Are quotations blended with paraphrase, summary, and your own observations and reactions?

See Ch. 10  ❏ Have you avoided plagiarism by carefully documenting all borrowed ideas?

❏ Have you analyzed and interpreted the ideas of others rather than simply stringing those ideas together?

❏ Do your own ideas—not those of your sources—establish the focus of your discussion?

---

## 6i   Preparing a Final Draft

See 3e  Before you print out the final version of your paper, edit and proofread a hard copy of your works-cited list as well as the paper itself. Next, consider (or reconsider) your paper's **title.** It should be descriptive enough to tell your readers what your paper is about, and it should create interest in your sub-

See 2a  ject. Your title should also be consistent with the purpose and tone of your paper. (You would hardly want a humorous title for a paper about famine in sub-Saharan Africa or inequities in the American justice system.) Finally, your title should be engaging and to the point—perhaps even provocative. Often, a quotation from one of your sources will suggest a likely title.

When you are satisfied with your title, read your paper through one last time, proofreading for any grammar, spelling, or typing errors you may have missed. Pay particular attention to parenthetical documentation and works-cited entries. (Remember that every error undermines your credibility.) Finally, make sure your paper's format conforms to your instructor's guidelines. Once you are satisfied that your paper is as accurate as you can make it, print out a final copy. Then, fasten the pages with a paper clip (do not staple the pages or fold the corners together), and hand it in. Some instructors will allow you to email your final draft. (For a model MLA-style research paper, **see 11c.**)

CHAPTER **7**

# Finding Information

## 7a  Finding Information in the Library

If you are like most students, you go right to the Internet when you begin a research project. Certainly, the Internet enables you to quickly access a tremendous amount of information. When it comes to finding trustworthy, high-quality, and authoritative sources, however, nothing beats your college library.

## Close-Up  WHY USE THE LIBRARY?

- Many important publications are available only in print or through the library's databases.
- The information in your college library is cataloged and classified.
- Because the library's databases list only published sources, the information you access will always be available, unlike the information on the Internet.

*(continued)*

See 8a

---

**WHY USE THE LIBRARY?** *(continued)*

- Because librarians screen the resources in your college library, these resources are likely to meet academic standards of reliability. (Even so, you still have to <u>evaluate</u> any information before you use it in a paper.)

- Bibliographic information for the documents in your college library is easy to determine, unlike that of documents on the Internet.

- The library staff is available to answer your questions and to help you find material.

---

**1** Searching the Library's Online Catalog

The best way to start your research is by visiting your college library's **Web site.** The Web site's home page is a gateway to a vast amount of information—for example, the library's catalog, the databases the library makes available, special library services, and general information about the library. Figure 7.1 shows the home page of a library's Web site.

FIGURE 7.1 Home page of an academic library's Web site. © Drexel University.

Your next step is to search the library's **online catalog,** a database that lists all the material held in the library's collections. When you search the online catalog for information, you may do either a *keyword search* or a *subject search.*

*Doing a Keyword Search* When you do a **keyword search,** you enter into the online catalog's Search box a word (or words) associated with your topic. The computer then displays a list of entries (called **hits**) that contain these words. The more precise your keywords, the more specific and useful the information you retrieve will be. For example, *Civil War* will yield many thousands of hits; *The Wilderness Campaign* will yield far fewer.

Another way to limit (or broaden) your search is to carry out a **Boolean search,** which combines keywords with the search operators *and, or,* or *not.*

---

**CHECKLIST**

**Using Search Operators**

When you do a keyword search, follow these guidelines:

❑ Use **quotation marks** to search for a specific phrase: *"Baltimore Economy."*

❑ Use an **asterisk** after a word to retrieve a root word with any ending: *photo\** will yield *photograph, photographer, photojournalist, photoactive,* and so on.

❑ Use a **question mark** to replace a single character inside or at the end of a word: *wom?n* will yield *woman* and *women.*

❑ Use **and** to search for sites that contain both terms: *Baltimore* and *Economy.*

❑ Use **or** to search for sites that contain either term: *Baltimore* or *Philadelphia.*

❑ Use **not** to exclude the term that comes after the *not: Baltimore* and *Economy* not *Agriculture.*

---

*Doing a Subject Search* When you do a **subject search,** you enter a subject heading into the online catalog's search box. The resources in an academic library are classified under specific subject headings. Many online catalogs list these subject headings to help you identify the exact words that you need for your search. Figure 7.2 on page 74 shows the results of a subject search in a university library's online catalog.

**2** Searching the Library's Databases

Through your college library's Web site, you can also access a variety of online databases to which the library subscribes. These **databases** are collections of digital information—such as newspaper, magazine, and journal articles—arranged

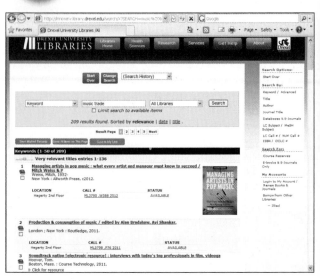

FIGURE 7.2 Online catalog search results for the subject heading *Music Trade*. © Drexel University.

for easy access and retrieval. (You search these databases the same way you search the library's online catalog—by doing a See 7a1 **keyword search** or a **subject search**.)

One of the first things you should do is find out which databases your library subscribes to. You can usually access these databases through the library's Web site, and if necessary, you can ask a reference librarian for more information. Figure 7.3 shows a partial list of databases to which one library subscribes.

College libraries subscribe to information service companies, such as Gale Cengage Learning, which provide access to hundreds of databases not available for free on the Internet. These databases enable you to access current information from scholarly journals, abstracts, books, reports, case studies, government documents, magazines, and newspapers. Some library databases cover many subject areas (*Expanded Academic ASAP Plus* or *LexisNexis Academic*, for example); others cover a single subject area in great detail (*PsycINFO* or *Sociological Abstracts*, for example).

Assuming that your library offers a variety of databases, how do you know which ones will be best for your research? First, you should determine the level of the periodical articles listed in the database. A **periodical** is a scholarly journal, magazine, newspaper, or other publication that appears at regular intervals (weekly, monthly, or quarterly, for example). **Scholarly journals** are often the

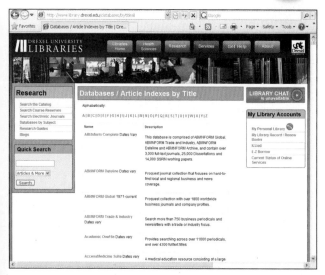

**FIGURE 7.3** Excerpt from list of databases to which one academic library subscribes. © Drexel University.

most reliable sources you can find on a subject. They contain articles written by experts in a field, and because journals focus on a particular subject area, they usually provide in-depth analysis. However, because journal articles are aimed at experts, they can be difficult for general readers to understand. **Popular periodicals** are magazines and newspapers that publish articles aimed at general readers. These periodicals are more accessible, but they are less reliable than scholarly journals because they vary greatly in quality. Some articles might conform to academic standards of reliability, but others may be totally unsuitable as sources.

Next, you should look for a database that is suitable for your topic. Most libraries list databases alphabetically by title or arrange them by subject area. Some offer online study guides that list databases (as well as other resources) that are appropriate for research in a given subject area. If you know what database you are looking for, you can find it in the alphabetical listing. If you don't, go to the subject list and locate your general subject area—*History, Nursing,* or *Linguistics,* for example. Then, review the databases that are listed under this heading.

You can begin with a multisubject **general database** that includes full-text articles. Then, you can move on to more **specialized databases** that examine your specific subject in detail.

**Close-Up** FREQUENTLY USED GENERAL DATABASES

| Database | Description |
| --- | --- |
| *Academic OneFile* | Articles from journals and reference sources in a number of disciplines |
| *Credo Reference* | A database of over two hundred reference books |
| *Expanded Academic Plus* | Articles from journals in the humanities, social sciences, and the natural and applied sciences |
| *FirstSearch* | Full-text articles from many popular and scholarly periodicals |
| *LexisNexis Academic* | Full-text articles from national news publications as well as legal and business publications |
| *Opposing Viewpoints Resource Center* | A library of debates on current topics |
| *ProQuest Research Library* | An index of journal articles in various disciplines, many full text |
| *Readers' Guide Full-Text Mega Edition* | Full-text articles from over two hundred journals from as far back as 1994 and popular periodicals from as far back as 1983 |

## Specialized Databases

**HUMANITIES**

| Database | Description |
| --- | --- |
| **Communication** | |
| *Communication & Mass Media Complete* | Index and abstracts for more than four hundred journals and coverage of two hundred more |
| **History** | |
| *History Reference Center* | Full-text articles and other resources for the study of history |

## Literature

| | |
|---|---|
| *MLA International Bibliography* | An index for books, articles, and Web sites focusing on literature |
| *Gale Literature Criticism Online* | Full-text articles on literary criticism and analysis |

## Philosophy

| | |
|---|---|
| *Philosopher's Index* | Index and abstracts from over five hundred fifty journals from forty countries |

### SOCIAL SCIENCES

| Database | Description |
|---|---|
| **Business** | |
| *ABI/INFORM Global* | A ProQuest collection of over eighteen hundred journals and company profiles |
| *Business Source Premier* | Indexes more than seventy-eight hundred publications |
| **Economics** | |
| *EconLit* | Offers a wide range of economics-related resources |
| **Education** | |
| *Education Research Complete* | The world's largest collection of full-text education journals |
| **Psychology** | |
| *PsycINFO* | Indexes books and journal articles in the psychological and behavioral sciences |
| **Sociology and Social Work** | |
| *Sociological Abstracts* | An index of literature in sociology |
| *Social Work Abstracts* | An index of current research in social work |

### NATURAL AND APPLIED SCIENCES

| Database | Description |
|---|---|
| **Biology** | |
| *Biological Sciences* | Abstracts and citations from a wide range of biological research |
| **Chemistry** | |
| *American Chemical Society Publications* | Articles from over thirty peer-reviewed journals |
| **Computer Science** | |
| *ACM Guide to Computing Literature* | Over 750,000 citations and abstracts of literature about computing |

*continued*

## Specialized Databases *(continued)*

NATURAL AND APPLIED SCIENCES

| Database | Description |
|---|---|
| **Engineering** | |
| *IEEE Xplore* | Full-text access to all IEEE journals, magazines, and conference proceedings |
| **Environmental Science** | |
| *Environmental Science Database* | Information on environmental subjects |
| **Nursing** | |
| *ProQuest Nursing & Allied Health Source* | Resources for nursing and the allied health fields |

CHECKLIST

## Questions for Choosing the Right Database

Before you decide which database to use, ask the following questions:

❑ Is the database suited to your subject? Is it too general or too specialized?

❑ Does the database include scholarly journals, popular periodicals, or both?

❑ Does the database contain the full text of articles or just citations?

❑ Are you able to limit your search—for example, to just scholarly publications or to just peer-reviewed publications?

❑ How easy (or difficult) is the database to use?

❑ Does the database allow you to download and/or email documents?

❑ What years does the database cover?

### 3 Finding Books

The online catalog also gives you the information you need for locating specific books. Catalog entries for books include the author's name, the title, the subject, publication information, and a call number. A **call number** is like a book's address in the library: it tells you exactly where to find the book you are looking for. (Figure 7.4 shows the results of an author search in a university library's online catalog.)

FIGURE 7.4 Online catalog search results for the author *Denis Johnson*.
© Drexel University.

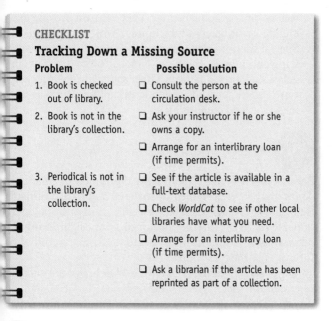

**CHECKLIST**

## Tracking Down a Missing Source

| Problem | Possible solution |
|---------|-------------------|
| 1. Book is checked out of library. | ☐ Consult the person at the circulation desk. |
| 2. Book is not in the library's collection. | ☐ Ask your instructor if he or she owns a copy. |
| | ☐ Arrange for an interlibrary loan (if time permits). |
| 3. Periodical is not in the library's collection. | ☐ See if the article is available in a full-text database. |
| | ☐ Check *WorldCat* to see if other local libraries have what you need. |
| | ☐ Arrange for an interlibrary loan (if time permits). |
| | ☐ Ask a librarian if the article has been reprinted as part of a collection. |

## 4 Consulting General Reference Sources

**General reference sources**—dictionaries, encyclopedias, almanacs, atlases, bibliographies, and so on—can provide an overview of your topic as well as essential background and factual information. Even though they do not discuss your topic in enough depth to be used as research sources, the following general reference works can be useful for gathering information and for focusing your research on the specific issues you want to explore in depth.

- **Encyclopedias**—such as the *Encyclopedia Americana* and *The New Encyclopaedia Britannica*—provide an introduction to your topic and give you a sense of the scholarly debates related to it. Individual encyclopedia entries often contain bibliographies that can lead you to works that you can use as research sources.
- **Bibliographies** are lists of sources on a specific topic. For example, the *MLA International Bibliography* lists books and articles published in literature, and the *Bibliographic Guide to Education* lists published sources on all aspects of education. Bibliographic entries often include abstracts.
- **Biographical reference books**—such as *Who's Who in America, Who's Who,* and the *Dictionary of American Biography*—provide information about people's lives as well as bibliographic listings. They can also provide general information about the times in which people lived.
- **Special dictionaries** focus on topics such as synonyms, slang and idioms, rhyming, symbols, proverbs, sign language, and foreign phrases. Other special dictionaries concentrate on specific academic disciplines, such as law, medicine, and computing.

## 7b  Finding Information on the Internet

Because Web searches can yield thousands of hits, students can be overwhelmed by material and have a difficult time distinguishing valuable research sources from questionable material. Internet documents vary significantly in quality, so it is important to **evaluate** them carefully before you use them as sources.

See 8b

To do a Web search, you need a **Web browser**—such as *Microsoft Internet Explorer, Mozilla Firefox, Safari, Opera,* or *Google Chrome*—that enables you to access the Web.

Once you are connected to the Web, you use a **search engine** such as *Google* or *Yahoo!* to search for and retrieve documents. There are two ways to use search engines to find information: by *doing a keyword search* and by *using subject directories*.

### 1  Doing a Keyword Search

The most common method of locating information is by doing a **keyword search**, entering a keyword (or words) into your search engine's search box. (Figure 7.5 shows a search

See 7a1

engine's keyword search page.) The search engine will identify any site in its database on which the keywords appear.

FIGURE 7.5 *Google* keyword search page in *Google Chrome*.

You can create a list of useful keywords by looking at the subject catalog of your college library and using its headings. You can also find keywords by accessing an online encyclopedia, such as *Wikipedia*, and looking at the category list that follows each article.

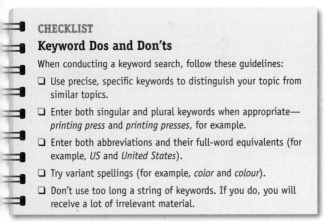

### CHECKLIST
### Keyword Dos and Don'ts
When conducting a keyword search, follow these guidelines:
- ❑ Use precise, specific keywords to distinguish your topic from similar topics.
- ❑ Enter both singular and plural keywords when appropriate—*printing press* and *printing presses*, for example.
- ❑ Enter both abbreviations and their full-word equivalents (for example, *US* and *United States*).
- ❑ Try variant spellings (for example, *color* and *colour*).
- ❑ Don't use too long a string of keywords. If you do, you will receive a lot of irrelevant material.

## 2 Using Subject Directories

Some search engines, such as *Yahoo!* and *About.com,* contain subject directories—lists of general categories from which you can choose. Each general category will lead you to a more specific list of categories and subcategories until you get to the topic you want. For example, clicking on *Society and Culture* could lead you to *Activism* and then to *Animal Rights* and eventually to an article about factory farming. Although using subject guides is not as efficient as keyword searching, it can be a useful tool for finding or narrowing a topic. (Figure 7.6 shows the *About.com* subject directory.)

FIGURE 7.6 *About.com* subject directory page.

## 3 Choosing the Right Search Engine

*General-Purpose Search Engines* The most widely used search engines are **general-purpose search engines** that focus on a wide variety of topics. Some of these search engines are more user-friendly than others; some allow for more sophisticated searching functions; some are updated more frequently; and some are more comprehensive than others. As you try out various search engines, you will probably settle on a favorite that you will turn to first whenever you need to find information.

## Close-Up    POPULAR GENERAL-PURPOSE SEARCH ENGINES

*AltaVista* <altavista.com>: Good, precise engine for focused searches. Fast and easy to use. Large database.

*Ask.com* <ask.com>: Allows you to narrow your search by asking questions, such as *Are dogs smarter than pigs?*

*Bing* <bing.com>: Currently the second most widely used search engine on the Web, *Bing* has a variety of specialized functions that sort responses into categories. By clicking on progressively narrower categories, you get more specific results. In some searches, a single "Best Match" response may appear. Excellent image and video functions.

*Excite* <excite.com>: Good for general topics. Because it searches a vast number of Web sites, you often receive more information than you need.

*Google* <google.com>: Arguably the best search engine available, it accesses a large database that includes both text and graphics. It is easy to navigate, and searches usually yield a high percentage of useful hits. (See pages 84–85 for more information about *Google* resources.)

*HotBot* <hotbot.com>: Excellent, fast search engine for locating specific information. Good search options allow you to fine-tune your searches.

*Lycos* <lycos.com>: One of the oldest search engines on the Web, *Lycos* lets you see results on one side of the page and the actual Web pages on the other. At the bottom of the page, it offers additional search terms as well as a "second opinion" feature that links to another search engine.

*Yahoo!* <yahoo.com>: Good for exploratory research. Enables you to search using either subject headings or keywords. Searches its own indexes as well as the Web.

Because even the best search engines search only a fraction of the material available on the Web, if you use only one search engine, you will most likely miss much valuable information. It is therefore a good idea to repeat each search with several different search engines or to use a **metasearch** or **metacrawler** engine that uses several search engines simultaneously.

## Close-Up  METASEARCH ENGINES

*Dogpile* <dogpile.com>

*Kartoo* <kartoo.com>

*Mamma* <mamma.com>

*MetaCrawler* <metacrawler.com>

*SurfWax* <surfwax.com>

*Vivisimo* <vivisimo.com>

*Specialized Search Engines*  In addition to general-purpose search engines and metasearch engines, there are also **specialized search engines** devoted entirely to specific subject areas, such as literature, business, sports, and women's issues. Hundreds of specialized search engines are indexed at <listofsearchengines.info>.

## Close-Up  GOOGLE RESOURCES

*Google* is the most-used search engine on the Internet. Most people who use *Google,* however, do not actually know its full potential. Following are just a few of the resources that *Google* offers:

- *Blog Search*  Enables users to find blogs on specific subjects
- *Blogger*  A tool for creating and posting blogs online
- *Book Search*  A database that allows users to access millions of books that they can either preview or read for free
- *Google Earth*  A downloadable, dynamic global map that enables users to see satellite views of almost any place on the planet
- *Finance*  Business information, news, and interactive charts
- *News*  Enables users to search thousands of news stories
- *Patent Search*  Enables users to search the full text of US patents

- *Google Scholar*   Searches scholarly literature, including peer-reviewed papers, books, and abstracts
- *Google Translate*   A free online language translation service that instantly translates text and Web pages

You can access these tools by going to the *Google* home page, clicking on MORE in the upper left of your screen, and then clicking on EVEN MORE on the pull-down menu.

---

CHECKLIST

## Tips for Effective Web Searches

❑ **Choose the right search engine.** No single all-purpose search engine exists. Review the list of search engines in the boxes on pages 82–85.

❑ **Choose your keywords carefully.** A search engine is only as good as the keywords you use.

❑ **Include enough terms.** If you are looking for information on housing, for example, search for several variations of your keyword: *housing, houses, home buyer, buying houses, residential real estate,* and so on.

❑ **Use more than one search engine.** Because different search engines index different sites, try several. If one does not yield results after a few tries, try another. Also, don't forget to try a metasearch engine like *MetaCrawler*.

❑ **Add useful sites to your Bookmark or Favorites list.** Whenever you find a particularly useful Web site, **bookmark** it by selecting this option on the menu bar of your browser (with some browsers, such as *Microsoft Internet Explorer*, this option is called Favorites).

---

**4** Using *Wikipedia* as a Research Source

Although no encyclopedia—electronic or print—should be used as a research source, *Wikipedia* requires an extra level of scrutiny.

*Wikipedia* is an open-source, online general encyclopedia created through the collaborative efforts of its users. Anyone (not necessarily experts) registered with the site can write an article, and in most cases, anyone who views the site can edit an article. The theory is that if enough people contribute, over time, entries will become more and more accurate. Many instructors point out, however, that the coverage in

*Wikipedia* is uneven; some articles follow acceptable standards of academic research, but many others do not. Because some articles have little or no documentation, it is difficult to judge their merit. In addition, because *Wikipedia* does not have an editorial staff responsible for checking entries for accuracy, it is not a reliable source of information.

Still, *Wikipedia* does have its strengths. Because its content is constantly being revised, *Wikipedia* can be more up to date than other reference sources. Also, many articles contain bibliographic citations that enable users to link to reliable sources of information. Still, even though you can use *Wikipedia* to get a general overview of your topic, most instructors do not consider it a trustworthy, let alone authoritative, research source.

## 7c  Doing Field Research

In addition to using information you find in the library or on the Internet, you can find your own information by doing **field research**—making observations, conducting interviews, and conducting surveys.

### 1  Making Observations

Some writing assignments are based on your own **observations.** For example, an art history paper can include information gathered during a visit to a museum, and an education paper can include an account of a classroom visit.

---

**CHECKLIST**
**Making Observations**
- ❏ Decide what you want to observe and where you want to observe it.
- ❏ Determine in advance what you hope to gain from your observations.
- ❏ Bring a laptop or tablet so that you can record your observations.
- ❏ Make a record of the time, date, and place of your observations.

---

### 2  Conducting Interviews

**Interviews** (conducted in person, by telephone, or by email) can provide material that you cannot find anywhere else—for example, a first-hand account of an event or an opinion of an expert.

**CHECKLIST**

**Conducting Interviews**

- ❑ Always make an appointment.
- ❑ Prepare a list of questions tailored to the subject matter.
- ❑ Do background reading about your topic. Do not ask for information that you can easily get elsewhere.
- ❑ Have a pen and paper or laptop with you. If you want to record the interview, get your subject's permission in advance.
- ❑ Send an email thanking the subject of the interview.

### 3 Conducting Surveys

If your research project is about a contemporary social, political, or economic issue, a **survey** of attitudes or opinions can give you valuable information.

**CHECKLIST**

**Conducting Surveys**

- ❑ Determine what you want to know.
- ❑ Generate a list of questions.
- ❑ Decide how to distribute your survey. Will you email it? Post a questionnaire on *Facebook*? Use an online tool such as *SurveyMonkey* or *Google Forms*?
- ❑ Collect and analyze the responses.

CHAPTER **8**

# Evaluating Sources

The sources that you use in your research papers help to establish the level of trustworthiness and authority that readers believe you have. If you use high-quality, reliable sources, your readers are likely to assume that you have more than a superficial knowledge of your subject. If, however, you use questionable sources, readers will begin to doubt your authority, and they may dismiss your ideas. For these reasons, it is very important to **evaluate** your research sources to make sure they are trustworthy and reliable.

## 8a    Evaluating Library Sources

Before you decide to use a library source (print or electronic), you should assess its suitability according to the following criteria:

- **Reliability:** *Is the source trustworthy?* Does the writer support his or her conclusions with facts and expert opinion, or does the source rely on unsupported opinion? Is the information accurate and free of factual errors? Does the writer include documentation and a bibliography?
- **Credibility:** *Is the source respected?* A contemporary review of a source can help you make this assessment. *Book Review Digest,* available in print and online, lists popular books that have been reviewed in at least three newspapers or magazines and includes excerpts from representative reviews as well as abstracts. Is the writer well known in his or her field? Can you check the writer's credentials? Is the article **refereed** (that is, chosen by experts in the field)?
- **Objectivity:** *Does the writer strive to present a balanced discussion?* Sometimes a writer has a particular agenda to advance. Compare a few statements from the source with a neutral source—a textbook or an encyclopedia, for example—to see whether the writer seems to be exhibiting bias or slanting facts.
- **Currency:** *Is the source up to date?* The date of publication tells you whether the information in a book or article is current. A source's currency is particularly important for scientific and technological subjects, but even in the humanities, new discoveries and new ways of thinking lead scholars to reevaluate and modify their ideas.
- **Scope of coverage:** *Does the source treat your topic in enough detail?* To be useful, a source should treat your topic comprehensively. For example, a book should include a section or chapter on your topic, not simply a brief reference or a note. To evaluate an article, either read the abstract or skim the entire article for key facts, looking closely at section headings, information set in boldface type, and topic sentences. An article should have your topic as its central subject (or at least one of its main concerns).

In general, **scholarly publications**—books and journals aimed at an audience of expert readers—are more reliable than **popular publications**—books, magazines, and newspapers aimed at an audience of general readers. However, assuming they are current, written by reputable authors, and documented, articles from respected popular publications (such as the *Atlantic* and *Scientific American*) may be appropriate for your research. Check with your instructor to be sure.

## Scholarly versus Popular Publications

FIGURE 8.1 Scholarly (left) and popular (right) publications.

| Scholarly Publications | Popular Publications |
|---|---|
| Report the results of research | Entertain and inform |
| Are often published by a university press or have some connection with a university or other academic organization | Are published by commercial presses |
| Are usually peer reviewed—that is, reviewed by other experts in the author's field before they are published | Are usually not peer reviewed |
| Are usually written by someone who is a recognized authority in the field | May be written by experts in a particular field but more often are written by freelance or staff writers |

*continued*

**Scholarly versus Popular Publications** *(continued)*

| Scholarly Publications | Popular Publications |
| --- | --- |
| Are written for a scholarly audience so often use technical vocabulary and include challenging content | Are written for general readers so tend to use an accessible vocabulary and do not include challenging content |
| Nearly always contain extensive documentation as well as a bibliography of works consulted | Rarely cite sources or use documentation |
| Are published primarily because they make a contribution to a particular field of study | Are published primarily to make a profit |

## 8b  Evaluating Internet Sources

Because anyone can post anything on the Internet, you can easily be overwhelmed by unreliable material. As you sort through and attempt to evaluate this information, the following general guidelines can help you distinguish between acceptable and unacceptable research sources.

 **Close-Up**  ACCEPTABLE VERSUS UNACCEPTABLE INTERNET SOURCES

**Acceptable**
- Web sites sponsored and maintained by reliable organizations
- Articles in established online encyclopedias, such as <britannica.com>
- Web sites sponsored by reputable newspapers and magazines
- Blogs by reputable authors

**Unacceptable**
- Information from anonymous sources
- Information found in chat rooms and on discussion boards
- Articles in e-zines and other questionable online publications

Before you use an Internet source, you should evaluate it for *reliability*, *credibility*, *objectivity*, *currency*, and *scope of coverage*.

*Reliability*  **Reliability** refers to the accuracy of the material itself and to its use of proper documentation.

Factual errors—especially errors in facts that are central to the main idea of the source—should cause you to question the reliability of the material you are reading. To evaluate a site's reliability, ask these questions:

- Is the text free of basic grammatical and mechanical errors?
- Does the site contain factual errors?
- Does the site provide a list of references?
- Are working links available to other sources?
- Can information be verified by print or other sources?

*Credibility*  **Credibility** refers to the credentials of the person or organization responsible for the site.

Web sites operated by well-known institutions (the Smithsonian or the Library of Congress, for example) have a high degree of credibility. Those operated by individuals (personal Web pages or blogs, for example) are often less reliable. To evaluate a site's credibility, ask these questions:

- Does the site list an author (or authors)? Are credentials (for example, professional or academic affiliations) provided for the author?
- Is the author a recognized authority in his or her field?
- Is the site **refereed?** That is, does an editorial board or a group of experts determine what material appears on the Web site?
- Can you determine how long the Web site has existed?

*Objectivity*  **Objectivity** refers to the degree of bias that a Web site exhibits.

Some Web sites strive for objectivity, but others make no secret of their biases. They openly advocate a particular point of view or action, or they clearly try to sell something. Some Web sites may try to hide their biases. For example, a Web site may present itself as a source of factual information when it is actually advocating a political point of view. To evaluate a site's objectivity, ask these questions:

- Does advertising appear in the text?
- Does a business, a political organization, or a special interest group sponsor the site?

- Does the site express a particular viewpoint?
- Does the site contain links to other sites that express a particular viewpoint?

*Currency*  **Currency** refers to how up to date the Web site is.

The easiest way to assess a site's currency is to see when it was last updated. Keep in mind, however, that even if the date on the site is current, the information that the site contains may not be. To evaluate a site's currency, ask these questions:

- Does the site indicate the date when it was last updated?
- Are all the links to other sites still functioning?
- Is the actual information on the page up to date?
- Does the site clearly identify the date it was created?

---

**CHECKLIST**

**Determining the Legitimacy of an Anonymous or Questionable Web Source**

When a Web source is anonymous (or has an author whose name is not familiar to you), you have to take special measures to determine its legitimacy:

❑ **Follow the links.** Follow the hypertext links in a document to other documents. If the links take you to legitimate sources, you know that the author is aware of these sources of information.

❑ **Find out what Web pages link to the site.** You can go to <alexa.com> to find information about a Web site. Type the Web site's URL into *Alexa*'s search box, and you will be given the volume of traffic to the site, the ownership information for the site, and the other sites visited by people who visited the URL. You will also be given a link to the "Wayback Machine" <archive.org/web/web.php>, an archive that shows what the page looked like in the past.

❑ **Do a keyword search.** Do a search using the name of the sponsoring organization or the author as keywords. Other documents (or citations in other works) may identify the author.

❑ **Verify the information.** Check the information you find against a reliable source—a textbook or a reputable Web site, for example. Also, see if you can find information that contradicts what you have found.

- ❑ **Check the quality of the writing.** Review the writing on the Web site to see if there are typos, misspellings, and errors in grammar or word choice. If the writer is careless about these things, he or she has probably not spent much time checking facts.

- ❑ **Look at the URL.** Although a Web site's URL is not a foolproof guide to the site's purpose, it does give you some useful information. The last part of a Web site's URL (immediately following the **domain name**) can often tell you whether the site is sponsored by a commercial entity (*.com*), a nonprofit organization (*.org*), an educational institution (*.edu*), the military (*.mil*), or a government agency (*.gov*). Knowing this information can help you assess its legitimacy.

*Scope of Coverage*  **Scope of coverage** refers to the comprehensiveness of the information on a Web site.

More coverage is not necessarily better, but some sites may be incomplete. Others may provide information that is no more than common knowledge. Still others may present discussions that are not suitable for college-level research. To evaluate the scope of a site's coverage, ask these questions:

- Does the site provide in-depth coverage?
- Does the site provide information that is not available elsewhere?
- Does the site identify a target audience? Does this target audience suggest the site is appropriate for your research needs?

## Close-Up  EVALUATING MATERIAL FROM ONLINE FORUMS

Be especially careful with material posted on discussion boards, blogs, newsgroups, and other online forums. Unless you can adequately evaluate this material—for example, determine its accuracy and the credibility of the author or authors—you should not use it in your paper. In most cases, online forums are not good sources of high-quality information.

# CHAPTER 9

# Integrating Source Material into Your Writing

See 6f

Experienced researchers know that copying down the exact words of a source is the least efficient way of <u>taking notes</u>. A better approach is to take notes that combine summaries, paraphrases, and quotations. This strategy ensures that you understand your source material and see its relevance to your research.

## 9a Integrating Quotations

Be sure to work quotations smoothly into your sentences. Quotations should never be awkwardly dropped into your paper, leaving the exact relationship between the quotation and your point unclear. Be sure to provide a context for the quotation, and quote only those words you need to make your point.

**Unacceptable:** For the Amish, the public school system represents a problem. "A serious problem confronting Amish society from the viewpoint of the Amish themselves is the threat of absorption into mass society through the values promoted in the public school system" (Hostetler 193).

**Improved:** For the Amish, the public school system is a problem because it represents "the threat of absorption into mass society" (Hostetler 193).

Whenever possible, use an **identifying tag** (a phrase that identifies the source) to introduce the quotation.

As John Hostetler points out, the Amish see the public school system as a problem because it represents "the threat of absorption into mass society" (193).

## Close-Up INTEGRATING SOURCE MATERIAL INTO YOUR WRITING

To make sure all your sentences do not sound the same, experiment with different methods of integrating source material into your paper.

- Vary the verbs you use to introduce a source's words or ideas (instead of repeating *says*).

| | | |
|---|---|---|
| acknowledges | discloses | observes |
| admits | explains | predicts |
| affirms | finds | proposes |
| believes | illustrates | reports |
| claims | implies | speculates |
| comments | indicates | suggests |
| concludes | insists | summarizes |
| concurs | notes | warns |

- Vary the placement of the identifying tag, putting it sometimes in the middle or at the end of the quoted material instead of always at the beginning.

  **Quotation with Identifying Tag in Middle:** "A serious problem confronting Amish society from the viewpoint of the Amish themselves," observes Hostetler, "is the threat of absorption into mass society through the values promoted in the public school system" (193).

  **Paraphrase with Identifying Tag at End:** The Amish are also concerned about their children's exposure to the public school system's values, notes Hostetler (193).

## Close-Up PUNCTUATING IDENTIFYING TAGS

Whether or not to use a comma with an identifying tag depends on where you place the tag in the sentence. If the identifying tag immediately precedes a quotation, use a comma.

As Hostetler points out, "The Amish are successful in maintaining group identity" (56).

*(continued)*

PUNCTUATING IDENTIFYING TAGS *(continued)*

If the identifying tag does not immediately precede a quotation, do not use a comma.

> Hostetler points out that the Amish frequently "use severe sanctions to preserve their values" (56).

*Note:* Never use a comma after *that:* Hostetler says that‚ Amish society is "defined by religion" (76).

*Substitutions or Additions within Quotations* Indicate changes or additions that you make to a quotation by enclosing these changes in brackets.

**Original Quotation:** "Immediately after her wedding, she and her husband followed tradition and went to visit almost everyone who attended the wedding" (Hostetler 122).

**Quotation Revised to Make Verb Tenses Consistent:** Nowhere is the Amish dedication to tradition more obvious than in the events surrounding marriage. Right after the wedding celebration, the Amish bride and groom "visit almost everyone who [has] attended the wedding" (Hostetler 122).

**Quotation Revised to Supply an Antecedent for a Pronoun:** "Immediately after her wedding, [Sarah] and her husband followed tradition and went to visit almost everyone who attended the wedding" (Hostetler 122).

**Quotation Revised to Change a Capital to a Lowercase Letter:** The strength of the Amish community is illustrated by the fact that "[i]mmediately after her wedding, she and her husband followed tradition and went to visit almost everyone who attended the wedding" (Hostetler 122).

*Omissions within Quotations* When you delete words from a quotation, substitute an <u>ellipsis</u> (three spaced periods) for the deleted words.

See 32f

**Original:** "Not only have the Amish built and staffed their own elementary and vocational schools, but they have gradually organized on local, state, and national levels to cope with the task of educating their children" (Hostetler 206).

**Quotation Revised to Eliminate Unnecessary Words:**
"Not only have the Amish built and staffed their own elementary and vocational schools, but they have gradually organized . . . to cope with the task of educating their children" (Hostetler 206).

*Note:* If the passage you are quoting already contains ellipses, place brackets around any ellipses you add.

## Close-Up  OMISSIONS WITHIN QUOTATIONS

Be sure that you do not misrepresent quoted material when you delete words. For example, do not say, "the Amish have managed to maintain . . . their culture" when the original quotation is "the Amish have managed to maintain *parts* of their culture."

*Note:* For information on integrating long quotations into your papers, **see 31a3.**

## 9b  Integrating Paraphrases and Summaries

Introduce paraphrases and summaries with identifying tags, and end them with appropriate documentation. By doing so, you differentiate your ideas from those of your sources.

**Misleading (Ideas of Source Blend with Ideas of Writer):** Art can be used to uncover many problems that children have at home, in school, or with their friends. For this reason, many therapists use art therapy extensively. Children's views of themselves in society are often reflected by their art style. For example, a cramped, crowded art style using only a portion of the paper shows their limited role (Alschuler 260).

**Correct (Identifying Tag Differentiates Ideas of Source from Ideas of Writer):** Art can be used to uncover many problems that children have at home, in school, or with their friends. For this reason, many therapists use art therapy extensively. According to William Alschuler in *Art and Self-Image,* children's views of themselves in society are often reflected by their art style. For example, a cramped, crowded art style using only a portion of the paper shows their limited role (260).

CHAPTER **10**

# Avoiding Plagiarism

## 10a Defining Plagiarism

**Plagiarism** occurs when a writer (intentionally or unintentionally) uses the words, ideas, or distinctive style of others without acknowledging their source. For example, you plagiarize when you submit someone else's work as your own or fail to document appropriately.

Most plagiarism is **unintentional plagiarism**—for example, inadvertently pasting a quoted passage into a paper and forgetting to include the quotation marks and documentation.

There is a difference, however, between an honest mistake and **intentional plagiarism**—for example, copying a passage word for word from a journal article or submitting a paper that someone else has written. The penalties for unintentional plagiarism may sometimes be severe, but intentional plagiarism is almost always dealt with harshly: students who intentionally plagiarize can receive a failing grade for the paper (or the course) and can even be expelled from school.

## Close-Up DETECTING PLAGIARISM

The same technology that has made unintentional plagiarism more common has also made plagiarism easier to detect. By doing a *Google* search, an instructor can quickly find the source of a phrase that has been plagiarized from an Internet source. In addition, plagiarism detection services, such as Turnitin.com, can search scholarly databases and identify plagiarized passages in student papers.

## 10b  Avoiding Unintentional Plagiarism

The most common cause of unintentional plagiarism is sloppy research habits. To avoid this problem, start your research paper early. Do not cut and paste text from a Web site or full-text database directly into your paper. If you paraphrase, do so correctly by following the advice in **6f3.**

In addition, take care to manage your sources—especially those you download—so that they do not overwhelm you. Unintentional plagiarism often occurs when students use information from a source thinking that it is their own. For this reason, you should clearly identify all paraphrases, summaries, and quotations, and keep this source material in a labeled file. (For longer papers, create a separate file for each section of your paper.)

Another cause of unintentional plagiarism is failure to use proper <u>documentation</u>. In general, you must document the following information:

See Chs. 11–14

- Direct quotations, summaries, and paraphrases of material in sources (including Web sources)
- Images that you borrow from a source (print or electronic)
- Facts and opinions that are another writer's original contributions
- Information that is the product of an author's original research
- Statistics, charts, graphs, or other compilations of data that are not yours

Material that is considered **common knowledge** (information most readers probably know) need not be documented. This includes facts available from a variety of reference sources, familiar sayings, and well-known quotations. Your own original research (interviews and surveys, for example) also does not require documentation.

So, although you do not have to document the fact that John F. Kennedy graduated from Harvard in 1940 or that he was elected president in 1960, you do have to document information from a historian's evaluation of his presidency. The best rule to follow is, if you have doubts, document.

## 10c  Avoiding Intentional Plagiarism

When students plagiarize *intentionally,* they make a decision to misappropriate the ideas or words of others—and this is no small matter. Not only does intentional plagiarism deprive the student of a valuable educational experience (instructors assign research for a reason), it also subverts the educational goals of other students as well as of the institution as a whole. Because academic honesty is absolutely central to any college or university, intentional plagiarism is taken very seriously.

## 10d Avoiding Other Kinds of Plagiarism

When instructors assign a research paper, they expect it to be your original work and to be written in response to a specific assignment. For this reason, you should not submit a paper that you have written for another course.

Collaborative work is acceptable in the course for which it was assigned. Even so, each member of the group should clearly identify the sections on which he or she worked.

Finally, passages written by a writing center tutor or by a friend or a family member are unacceptable. If you present material contributed by others as if it were your own original work, you are committing plagiarism.

## 10e Revising to Eliminate Plagiarism

You can avoid plagiarism by using documentation wherever it is required and by following these guidelines.

### 1 Enclose Borrowed Words in Quotation Marks

**Original:** DNA profiling begins with the established theory that no two people, except identical twins, have the same genetic makeup. Each cell in the body contains a complete set of genes. (William Tucker, "DNA in Court")

**Plagiarism:** William Tucker points out that DNA profiling is based on the premise that genetic makeup differs from person to person and that each cell in the body contains a complete set of genes (26).

Even though the student writer documents the source of his information, he uses the source's exact words without placing them in quotation marks.

**Correct (Borrowed Words in Quotation Marks):** William Tucker points out that DNA profiling is based on the premise that genetic makeup differs from person to person and that "[e]ach cell in the body contains a complete set of genes" (26).

**Correct (Paraphrase):** William Tucker points out that DNA profiling is based on the premise that genetic makeup differs from person to person and that every cell includes a full set of an individual's genes (26).

---

**CHECKLIST**

**Plagiarism and Internet Sources**

Any time you download text from the Internet, you risk committing plagiarism. To avoid the possibility of unintentional plagiarism, follow these guidelines:

❑ Download information into individual files so that you can keep track of your sources.

❑ Do not cut and paste blocks of downloaded text directly into your paper.

❑ Whether your information is from emails, online discussion groups, blogs, or Web sites, always provide appropriate documentation.

❑ Always document figures, tables, charts, and graphs obtained from the Internet or from any other electronic source.

---

**2 Do Not Imitate a Source's Syntax and Phrasing**

**Original:** If there is a garbage crisis, it is that we are treating garbage as an environmental threat and not what it is: a manageable—though admittedly complex—civic issue. (Patricia Poore, "America's 'Garbage Crisis'")

**Plagiarism:** If a garbage crisis does exist, it is that people see garbage as a menace to the environment and not what it actually is: a controllable—if obviously complicated—public problem (Poore 39).

Although this student does not use the exact words of her source, she closely follows the original's syntax and phrasing, simply substituting synonyms for the author's words.

**Correct (Paraphrase in Writer's Own Words; One Distinctive Phrase Placed in Quotation Marks):** Patricia Poore argues that America's "garbage crisis" is exaggerated; rather than viewing garbage as a serious environmental hazard, she says, we should look at garbage as a public problem that may be complicated but that can be solved (39).

### 3 Document Statistics Obtained from a Source

Although many people assume that statistics are common knowledge, they are usually the result of original research and must be documented.

> **Correct (Documentation Provided):** According to one study of 303 accidents recorded, almost one-half took place before the drivers were legally allowed to drive at eighteen (Schuman et al. 1027).

### 4 Differentiate Your Words and Ideas from Those of Your Source

> **Original:** At some colleges and universities traditional survey courses of world and English literature . . . have been scrapped or diluted. . . . What replaces them is sometimes a mere option of electives, sometimes "multicultural" courses introducing material from Third World cultures and thinning out an already thin sampling of Western writings, and sometimes courses geared especially to issues of class, race, and gender. (Irving Howe, "The Value of the Canon")

> **Plagiarism:** At many universities the Western literature survey courses have been edged out by courses that emphasize minority concerns. These courses are "thinning out an already thin sampling of Western writings" in favor of courses geared especially to issues of "class, race, and gender" (Howe 40).

Because the student writer does not differentiate his ideas from those of his source, it appears that only the quotation in the last sentence is borrowed when, in fact, the first sentence also owes a debt to the original. The writer should have clearly identified the boundaries of the borrowed material by introducing it with an identifying tag and ending with documentation.

> **Correct:** According to critic Irving Howe, at many universities the Western literature survey courses have been edged out by courses that emphasize minority concerns. These courses, says Howe, are "thinning out an already thin sampling of Western writings" in favor of "courses geared especially to issues of class, race, and gender" (40).

## CHECKLIST
## Avoiding Plagiarism

❏ **Take careful notes.** Be sure you have recorded information from your sources carefully and accurately.

❏ **Store downloaded sources in clearly labeled files.** If you are writing a short paper, you can keep your source material in one file. For longer papers, you may find it best to create a separate file for each of your sources.

❏ **In your notes, clearly identify borrowed material.** Always enclose your own comments within brackets. In handwritten notes, put all words borrowed from your sources inside *circled* quotation marks. If you are taking notes on a computer, boldface all quotation marks.

❏ **In your paper, differentiate your ideas from those of your sources** by clearly introducing borrowed material with an identifying tag and by following it with parenthetical documentation.

❏ **Enclose all direct quotations** used in your paper within quotation marks.

❏ **Review all paraphrases and summaries** in your paper to make certain that they are in your own words and that any distinctive words and phrases from a source are quoted.

❏ **Document all quoted material and all paraphrases and summaries** of your sources.

❏ **Document all information** that is open to dispute or that is not common knowledge.

❏ **Document all opinions, conclusions, figures, tables, statistics, graphs, and charts** taken from a source.

❏ **Never submit the work of another person as your own.** Do not buy a paper online or hand in a paper given to you by a friend. In addition, never include in your paper passages that have been written by a friend, relative, or writing tutor.

❏ **Never use sources that you have not actually read (or invent sources that do not exist).**

## 10f Understanding Plagiarism in the Disciplines

Although plagiarism always involves the misappropriation of ideas, words, or research results, different disciplines have different conventions about what constitutes plagiarism. Becoming familiar with the conventions of the discipline in which you are writing will help you avoid the most common causes of plagiarism.

### 1 Plagiarism in the Humanities

In the humanities, plagiarism is often the result of inaccurate summarizing and paraphrasing, failure to use quotation marks where they are required, and confusion between your ideas and those of your sources. You can eliminate these problems by taking accurate notes, avoiding cutting and pasting sources directly into your papers, and documenting all words and ideas that are not your own.

### 2 Plagiarism in the Social Sciences

In the social sciences, you can avoid plagiarism by correctly documenting paraphrases, summaries, and quotations as well as all statistics and visuals that are not your own. Keep in mind that the social sciences are bound by ethical considerations regarding the treatment of research subjects and the protection of privacy as well as the granting of credit to all individuals who contribute to a research project.

### 3 Plagiarism in the Natural and Applied Sciences

In the natural and applied sciences, it is important to acknowledge the contributions of others. Using the experimental results, computer codes, chemical formulas, graphs, images, or ideas or words of others without proper acknowledgment constitutes plagiarism. In addition, falsifying data, fabricating data, or publishing misleading information is considered scientific misconduct and can have serious consequences.

PART **3**

# Documenting Sources

## MLA Entry for a Source from an Online Database

Keillor, Garrison. "Love Me: A Short Story." *Atlantic* July-Aug. 2003: 115-22. *Academic Search Elite*. Web. 2 May 2011.

- Author's last name
- First name
- Title of short story
- Title of periodical
- Date of access
- Date of publication
- Inclusive page numbers
- Name of database
- Publication medium

## APA Entry for a Source from an Internet Site

Yip, T., Gee, G. C., & Takeuchi, D. T. (2008). Radical discrimination and psychological distress: The impact of ethnic identity and age among immigrant and United States-born Asian adults. *Developmental Psychology, 44*(3), 787–800. doi:10.1037/0012-1649.44.3.787

- Author's last name
- Initials
- Year of publication
- Title of article
- Volume number
- Issue number
- Inclusive page numbers
- DOI
- Title of periodical

## Chicago Entry for a Source from an Online Publication

Dekoven, Marianne. "Utopias Limited: Post-Sixties and Postmodern American Fiction." *Modern Fiction Studies* 41, no. 1 (1995). doi:10.1353/mfs.1995.0002.

- Author's last name
- First name
- Title of article
- Title of periodical
- Volume number
- Issue number
- Year of publication
- DOI

## CSE Entry for a Source from an Internet Site

3. Sarra, SA. The method of characteristics with applications to conservation laws. J Online Math and Its Apps. [Internet]. 2003: [cited 2013 Aug 26];3. Available from: http://www.joma.org/vol3/articles/sarra/sarra.html

- Author's last name
- Initials
- Title of article
- Title of periodical
- Number of entry
- Description of medium
- Year of publication
- Date of access
- Semicolon
- Volume number
- URL

# Directory of MLA Parenthetical References

# Directory of MLA Works-Cited List Entries

## PRINT SOURCES: *Entries for Articles*

### Articles in Scholarly Journals

### Articles in Magazines and Newspapers

## PRINT SOURCES: *Entries for Books*

### Authors

CHAPTER 11

# MLA Documentation Style

**Documentation** is the formal acknowledgment of the sources you use in your paper. This chapter explains and illustrates the documentation style recommended by the Modern Language Association (MLA). Chapter 12 discusses the documentation style of the American Psychological Association (APA), Chapter 13 gives an overview of the format recommended by *The Chicago Manual of Style,* and Chapter 14 presents the format recommended by the Council of Science Editors (CSE) and the formats used by organizations in other disciplines.

## Close-Up    CITATION GENERATORS

A number of Web sites can help you generate properly formatted citations for the most commonly used documentation styles. The most popular are *CiteMe* <citeme.com>, *EasyBib* <easybib.com>, *Zotero* <zotero.org>, and *Son of Citation Machine* <citationmachine.net>.

Although these sites can save you time and effort, most have limitations. For this reason, you still have to proofread bibliographic entries carefully before you submit your paper.

## 11a    Using MLA Style

**MLA style**\* is required by instructors of English and other languages as well as by many instructors in other humanities disciplines. MLA documentation has three parts: *parenthetical references in the body of the paper (also known as in-text citations), a works-cited list,* and *content notes.*

### 1  Parenthetical References

MLA documentation uses parenthetical references in the body of the paper keyed to a works-cited list at the end of the paper. A typical parenthetical reference consists of the author's last name and a page number.

The colony appealed to many idealists in Europe (Kelley 132).

If you state the author's name or the title of the work in your discussion, do not also include it in the parenthetical reference.

Penn's political motivation is discussed by Joseph J. Kelley

in *Pennsylvania, The Colonial Years, 1681-1776* (44).

To distinguish two or more sources by the same author, include a shortened title after the author's name. When you shorten a title, begin with the word by which the work is alphabetized in the list of works cited.

---

\*MLA documentation style follows the guidelines set in the *MLA Handbook for Writers of Research Papers*, 7th ed. (New York: MLA, 2009).

Penn emphasized his religious motivation (Kelley, *Pennsylvania* 116).

## Close-Up  PUNCTUATING WITH MLA PARENTHETICAL REFERENCES

**Paraphrases and Summaries**  Parenthetical references are placed *before* the sentence's end punctuation.

Penn's writings epitomize seventeenth-century religious thought (Dengler and Curtis 72).

**Quotations Run In with the Text**  Parenthetical references are placed *after* the quotation but *before* the end punctuation.

As Ross says, "Penn followed his conscience in all matters" (127).

According to Williams, "Penn's utopian vision was informed by his Quaker beliefs . . ." (72).

**Quotations Set Off from the Text**  When you quote more than four lines of prose or more than three lines of poetry, parenthetical references are placed one space after the end punctuation.

See 31a3

According to Arthur Smith, William Penn envisioned a state based on his religious principles:

> Pennsylvania would be a commonwealth in which all individuals would follow God's truth and develop according to God's law. For Penn, this concept of government was self-evident. It would be a mistake to see Pennsylvania as anything but an expression of Penn's religious beliefs. (314)

## Sample MLA Parenthetical References

### 1. A Work by a Single Author

Fairy tales reflect the emotions and fears of children (Bettelheim 23).

### 2. A Work by Two or Three Authors

The historian's main job is to search for clues and solve mysteries (Davidson and Lytle 6).

With the advent of behaviorism, psychology began a new phase of inquiry (Cowen, Barbo, and Crum 31-34).

### 3. A Work by More Than Three Authors

List only the first author, followed by **et al.** ("and others").

Helping each family reach its goals for healthy child development and overall family well-being was the primary approach of Project EAGLE (Bartle et al. 35).

Or, list the last names of all authors in the order in which they appear on the work's title page.

Helping each family reach its goals for healthy child development and overall family well-being was the primary approach of Project EAGLE (Bartle, Couchonnal, Canda, and Staker 35).

### 4. A Work in Multiple Volumes

If you list more than one volume of a multivolume work in your works-cited list, include the appropriate volume and page number (separated by a colon followed by a space) in the parenthetical citation.

Gurney is incorrect when he says that a twelve-hour limit is negotiable (6: 128).

### 5. A Work without a Listed Author

Use the full title (if brief) or a shortened version of the title (if long), beginning with the word by which it is alphabetized in the works-cited list.

The group later issued an apology ("Satire Lost" 22).

### 6. A Work That Is One Page Long

Do not include a page reference for a one-page article.

Sixty percent of Arab Americans work in white-collar jobs (El-Badru).

### 7. An Indirect Source

If you use a statement by one author that is quoted in the work of another author, indicate that the material is from an indirect source with the abbreviation **qtd. in** ("quoted in").

> According to Valli and Lucas, "the form of the symbol is an
> icon or picture of some aspect of the thing or activity being
> symbolized" (qtd. in Wilcox 120).

### 8. More Than One Work

Cite each work as you normally would, separating one citation from another with a semicolon.

> The Brooklyn Bridge has been used as a subject by many
> American artists (McCullough 144; Tashjian 58).

*Note:* Long parenthetical references distract readers. Whenever possible, present them as **content notes**.

See 11a3

### 9. A Literary Work

When citing a work of **fiction**, it is often helpful to include more than the author's name and the page number in the parenthetical citation. Follow the page number with a semicolon, and then include any additional information that might be helpful.

> In *Moby-Dick*, Melville refers to a whaling expedition funded
> by Louis XIV of France (151; ch. 24).

Parenthetical references to **poetry** do not include page numbers. In parenthetical references to *long poems,* cite division and line numbers, separating them with a period.

> In the *Aeneid,* Virgil describes the ships as cleaving the
> "green woods reflected in the calm water" (8.124).

(In this citation, the reference is to book 8, line 124 of the *Aeneid.*)

When citing *short poems,* identify the poet and the poem in the text of the paper, and use line numbers in the citation.

> In "My mistress' eyes are nothing like the sun," Shakespeare's
> speaker says, "I have seen roses damasked red and white, /
> But no such roses see I in her cheeks," (lines 5-6).

*Note:* When citing lines of a poem, include the word **line** (or **lines**) in the first parenthetical reference; use just the line numbers in subsequent references.

When citing a **play,** include the act, scene, and line numbers (in arabic numerals), separated by periods. Titles of classic literary works (such as Shakespeare's plays) are often abbreviated (**Mac. 2.2.14-16**).

## 10. Sacred Texts

When citing sacred texts, such as the Bible or the Qur'an, include the version (italicized) and the book (abbreviated if longer than four letters, but not italicized or enclosed in quotation marks), followed by the chapter and verse numbers (separated by a period).

> The cynicism of the speaker is apparent when he says, "All
>
> things are wearisome; no man can speak of them all" (*New*
>
> *English Bible*, Eccles. 1.8).

*Note:* The first time you cite a sacred text, include the version in your parenthetical reference; after that, include only the book. If you are using more than one version of a sacred text, however, include the version in each in-text citation.

## 11. An Entire Work

When citing an entire work, include the author's name and the work's title in the text of your paper rather than in a parenthetical reference.

> Lois Lowry's *Gathering Blue* is set in a technologically
>
> backward village.

## 12. Two or More Authors with the Same Last Name

To distinguish authors with the same last name, include their initials in your parenthetical references.

> Increases in crime have caused thousands of urban
>
> homeowners to install alarms (L. Cooper 115). Some of these
>
> alarms use sophisticated sensors that were developed by the
>
> army (D. Cooper 76).

## 13. A Government Document or a Corporate Author

Cite such works using the organization's name (usually abbreviated) followed by the page number (**Amer. Automobile Assn. 34**). You can avoid long parenthetical references by working the organization's name (not abbreviated) into your discussion.

> According to the President's Commission for the Study
>
> of Ethical Problems in Medicine and Biomedical and

Behavioral Research, the issues relating to euthanasia
are complicated (76).

### 14. A Legal Source

Titles of acts or laws that appear in the text of your paper or
in the works-cited list should not be italicized or enclosed
in quotation marks. In the parenthetical reference, titles are
usually abbreviated, and the act or law is referred to by sections. Include the USC (United States Code) and the year the
act or law was passed (if relevant).

> Such research should include investigations into the
>
> cause, diagnosis, early detection, prevention, control, and
>
> treatment of autism (42 USC 284q, 2000).

Names of legal cases are usually abbreviated (**Roe v. Wade**).
They are italicized in the text of your paper but not in the
works-cited list.

> In *Goodridge v. Department of Public Health*, the court
>
> ruled that the Commonwealth of Massachusetts had not
>
> adequately provided a reasonable constitutional cause for
>
> barring homosexual couples from civil marriages (2003).

### 15. An Electronic Source

If a reference to an electronic source includes paragraph
numbers rather than page numbers, use the abbreviation **par.**
or **pars.** followed by the paragraph number or numbers.

> The earliest type of movie censorship came in the form of
>
> licensing fees, and in Deer River, Minnesota, "a licensing
>
> fee of $200 was deemed not excessive for a town of 1000"
>
> (Ernst, par. 20).

If the electronic source has no page or paragraph numbers, cite the work in your discussion rather than in a parenthetical reference. By consulting your works-cited list,
readers will be able to determine that the source is electronic and may therefore not have page numbers.

> In her article "Limited Horizons," Lynne Cheney observes
>
> that schools do best when students read literature not for
>
> practical information but for its insights into the human
>
> condition.

## 2 Works-Cited List

The **works-cited list,** which appears at the end of your paper, is an alphabetical listing of all the research materials you cite. Double-space within and between entries on the list, and indent the second and subsequent lines of each entry one-half inch. (**See 11b** for full manuscript guidelines.)

### MLA PRINT SOURCES Entries for Articles

Article citations include the author's name; the title of the article (in quotation marks); the title of the periodical (italicized); the volume and issue numbers (when applicable; see page 118); the year or date of publication; the pages on which the full article appears, without the abbreviation *p.* or *pp.*; and the publication medium (**Print**). Figure 11.1 on page 118 shows where you can find this information.

*Articles in Scholarly Journals*

#### 1. An Article in a Scholarly Journal

MLA guidelines recommend that you include both the volume number and the issue number (separated by a period) for all scholarly journal articles that you cite, regardless of whether they are paginated continuously throughout an annual volume or separately in each issue. Follow the volume and issue numbers with the year of publication (in parentheses), the inclusive page numbers, and the publication medium.

> Siderits, Mark. "Perceiving Particulars: A Buddhist Defense."
>
> *Philosophy East and West* 54.3 (2004): 367-83. Print.

*Articles in Magazines and Newspapers*

#### 2. An Article in a Weekly Magazine (Signed)

For signed articles, start with the author, last name first. In dates, the day precedes the month (abbreviated except for May, June, and July).

> Corliss, Richard. "His Days in Hollywood." *Time* 14 June 2004:
>
> 56-62. Print.

#### 3. An Article in a Weekly Magazine (Unsigned)

For unsigned articles, start with the title of the article.

> "Ronald Reagan." *National Review* 28 June 2004: 14-17. Print.

Publication medium (print)

Author — Patricia Harkin

Title — **The Reception of Reader-Response Theory**

This essay offers a historical explanation for the place of reader-response theory in English studies. Reader-response was a part of two movements: the (elitist) theory boom of the 1970s and the (populist) political movements of the 1960s and 1970s. If the theory boom was to remain elitist, it had to deauthorize reader-response. If reader-response was to remain populist, it had to consent to and participate in that deauthorization. In the 1980s reader-response was popular among compositionists, even as it began to lose currency among theorists. Later, however, compositionists professionalized themselves by deemphasizing, or even ignoring, reading. Now, as the profession again considers including explicit instruction in reading in the introductory writing course, the thinkers who could help us most have faded from the discussion.

I begin with an anomaly. In an issue of *Reader* focused on "Reading the Profession," Gary Ettari and Heather C. Easterling wonder why, even though reading is "one of the central activities" (12) of English studies, their graduate preparation has omitted explicit discussion of "making sense [. . .] of what happens when we read" (13).[1] Ettari and Easterling, who identify themselves at the time of writing as graduate students at the University of Washington, raise a wise and well-founded question. For me and for others who remember the heyday of reader-response theory during the 1970s and 1980s, the question also evokes

Journal title, volume number, issue number, and date of publication —

CCC 56:3 / FEBRUARY 2005

410 — Page number

FIGURE 11.1 First page of a journal article showing the location of the information needed for documentation. © College Composition and Communication/National Council of Teachers of English.

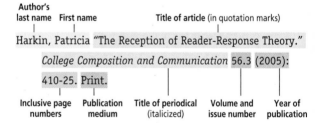

Author's last name · First name · Title of article (in quotation marks)

Harkin, Patricia "The Reception of Reader-Response Theory."

*College Composition and Communication* 56.3 (2005):

410-25. Print.

Inclusive page numbers · Publication medium · Title of periodical (italicized) · Volume and issue number · Year of publication

### 4. An Article in a Monthly Magazine

Thomas, Evan. "John Paul Jones." *American History*

Aug. 2003: 22-25. Print.

### 5. An Article That Does Not Appear on Consecutive Pages

When, for example, an article begins on page 120 and then skips to page 186, include only the first page number, followed by a plus sign.

Di Giovanni, Janine. "The Shiites of Iraq." *National*

*Geographic* June 2004: 62+. Print.

### 6. An Article in a Newspaper (Signed)

Krantz, Matt. "Stock Success Not Exactly Unparalleled."

*Wall Street Journal* 11 June 2004: B1+. Print.

### 7. An Article in a Newspaper (Unsigned)

"A Steadfast Friend on 9/11 Is Buried." *New York Times*

6 Aug. 2002, late ed.: B8. Print.

*Note:* Omit the article *the* from the title of a newspaper even if the newspaper's actual title includes the article.

### 8. An Editorial in a Newspaper

"The Government and the Web." Editorial. *New York Times*

25 Aug. 2009, late ed.: A20. Print.

### 9. A Letter to the Editor of a Newspaper

Chang, Paula. Letter. *Philadelphia Inquirer* 10 Dec. 2013,

suburban ed.: A17. Print.

### 10. A Book Review in a Newspaper

Straw, Deborah. "Thinking about Tomorrow." Rev. of *Planning

for the 21st Century: A Guide for Community Colleges,* by

William A. Wojciechowski and Dedra Manes. *Community

College Week* 7 June 2004: 15. Print.

### 11. An Article with a Title within Its Title

If the article you are citing contains a title that is normally enclosed in quotation marks, use single quotation marks for the interior title.

Zimmerman, Brett. "Frantic Forensic Oratory: Poe's 'The Tell-

Tale Heart.'" *Style* 35 (2001): 34-50. Print.

If the article you are citing contains a title that is normally italicized, use italics for the title in your works-cited entry.

Lingo, Marci. "Forbidden Fruit: The Banning of *The Grapes of

Wrath* in the Kern County Free Library." *Libraries and

Culture* 38 (2003): 351-78. Print.

**MLA PRINT SOURCES** Entries for Books

Book citations include the author's name; book title (italicized); and publication information (place, publisher, date, publication medium). Figures 11.2 and 11.3 show where you can find this information.

Author's last name | First name and middle initial | Italicized title (all major words and first word of subtitle capitalized)

Kleiner, Fred S. *Gardner's Art through the Ages: A Global History.*

Enhanced 13th ed. Boston: Wadsworth, 2011. Print.

Edition | City | Publisher's name (abbreviated) | Year of publication | Publication medium

FIGURE 11.2 Title page from a book showing the location of the information needed for documentation. © Cengage Learning, 2011.

Publication medium (print)

GARDNER'S
ART
THROUGH THE
AGES

Title

Subtitle — A GLOBAL HISTORY

Edition — ENHANCED THIRTEENTH EDITION

Author

FRED S. KLEINER

WADSWORTH
CENGAGE Learning

Publisher

Copyright year

City of publication

FIGURE 11.3 Copyright page from a book showing the location of the information needed for documentation. © Cengage Learning, 2011.

## Close-Up    PUBLISHERS' NAMES

MLA requires that you use abbreviated forms of publishers' names in the works-cited list. In general, omit articles; abbreviations, such as *Inc.* and *Corp.*; and words such as *Publishers, Books,* and *Press.* If the publisher's name includes a person's name, use the last name only. Finally, use standard abbreviations whenever you can—*UP* for University Press and *P* for Press, for example.

| Name | Abbreviation |
| --- | --- |
| Basic Books | Basic |
| Government Printing Office | GPO |
| The Modern Language Association of America | MLA |
| Oxford University Press | Oxford UP |
| Alfred A. Knopf, Inc. | Knopf |
| Random House, Inc. | Random |
| University of Chicago Press | U of Chicago P |

In each works-cited entry, capitalize all major words of the book's title except articles, coordinating conjunctions, prepositions, and the *to* of an infinitive (unless such a word is the first or last word of the title or subtitle). Do not italicize the period that follows a book's title.

### *Authors*

### 12. A Book by One Author

> Bettelheim, Bruno. *The Uses of Enchantment: The Meaning and Importance of Fairy Tales.* New York: Knopf, 1976. Print.

### 13. A Book by Two or Three Authors

List the first author with last name first. List subsequent authors with first name first in the order in which they appear on the book's title page.

> Peters, Michael A., and Nicholas C. Burbules. *Poststructuralism and Educational Research.* Lanham: Rowman, 2004. Print.

### 14. A Book by More Than Three Authors

List the first author only, followed by **et al.** ("and others").

> Badawi, El Said, et al. *Modern Written Arabic.* London: Routledge, 2004. Print.

Or, include all the authors in the order in which they appear on the book's title page.

> Badawi, El Said, Daud A. Abdu, Mike Carfter, and Adrian Gully.
>
> *Modern Written Arabic*. London: Routledge, 2004. Print.

## 15. Two or More Books by the Same Author

List books by the same author in alphabetical order by title. After the first entry, use three unspaced hyphens followed by a period in place of the author's name.

> Ede, Lisa. *Situating Composition: Composition Studies and the*
>
> *Politics of Location*. Carbondale: Southern Illinois UP,
>
> 2004. Print.
>
> ---. *Work in Progress*. 6th ed. Boston: Bedford, 2004. Print.

**Note:** If the author is the editor or translator of the second entry, place a comma and the appropriate abbreviation after the hyphens (**---, ed.**). See entry 17 for more on edited books and entry 25 for more on translated books.

## 16. A Book by a Corporate Author

A book is cited by its corporate author when individual members of the association, commission, or committee that produced it are not identified on the title page.

> American Automobile Association. *Western Canada and*
>
> *Alaska*. Heathrow: AAA, 2012. Print.

## 17. An Edited Book

An edited book is a work prepared for publication by a person other than the author. If your focus is on the *author's* work, begin your citation with the author's name. After the title, include the abbreviation **Ed.** ("Edited by"), followed by the editor or editors.

> Twain, Mark. *Adventures of Huckleberry Finn*. Ed. Michael
>
> Patrick Hearn. New York: Norton, 2001. Print.

If your focus is on the *editor's* work, begin your citation with the editor's name followed by the abbreviation **ed.** ("editor") if there is one editor or **eds.** ("editors") if there is more than one. After the title, give the author's name, preceded by the word **By**.

> Hearn, Michael Patrick, ed. *Adventures of Huckleberry Finn*.
>
> By Mark Twain. New York: Norton, 2001. Print.

*Editions, Multivolume Works, Graphic Narratives,*
*Forewords, Translations, and Sacred Works*

### 18. A Subsequent Edition of a Book

When citing an edition other than the first, include the edition number that appears on the work's title page.

> Wilson, Charles Banks. *Search for the Native American*
>
> > *Purebloods.* 3rd ed. Norman: U of Oklahoma P, 2000.
> >
> > Print.

### 19. A Republished Book

Include the original publication date after the title of a republished book—for example, a paperback version of a hardcover book.

> Wharton, Edith. *The House of Mirth.* 1905. New York:
>
> > Scribner's, 1975. Print.

### 20. A Book in a Series

If the title page indicates that the book is a part of a series, include the series name, neither italicized nor enclosed in quotation marks, and the series number, followed by a period, after the publication information. Use the abbreviation **Ser.** if *Series* is part of the series name.

> Davis, Bertram H. *Thomas Percy.* Boston: Twayne, 1981. Print.
>
> > Twayne's English Authors Ser. 313.

### 21. A Multivolume Work

When all volumes of a multivolume work have the same title, include the number of the volume you are using.

> Fisch, Max H., ed. *Writings of Charles S. Peirce: A*
>
> > *Chronological Edition.* Vol. 4. Bloomington: Indiana UP,
> >
> > 2000. Print.

If you use two or more volumes that have the same title, cite the entire work.

> Fisch, Max H., ed. *Writings of Charles S. Peirce: A*
>
> > *Chronological Edition.* 6 vols. Bloomington: Indiana UP,
> >
> > 2000. Print.

When the volume you are using has an individual title, you may cite the title without mentioning any other volumes.

> Mareš, Milan. *Fuzzy Cooperative Games: Cooperation with*
>
> > *Vague Expectations.* New York: Physica-Verlag, 2001.
> >
> > Print.

If you wish, however, you may include supplemental information, such as the number of the volume, the title of the entire work, the total number of volumes, or the inclusive publication dates.

### 22. An Illustrated Book or a Graphic Narrative

An **illustrated book** is a work in which illustrations accompany the text. If your focus is on the *author's* work, begin your citation with the author's name. After the title, include the abbreviation **Illus.** ("Illustrated by") followed by the illustrator's name and then the publication information.

> Frost, Robert. *Stopping by Woods on a Snowy Evening*. Illus.
>
> Susan Jeffers. New York: Dutton-Penguin, 2001. Print.

If your focus is on the *illustrator's* work, begin your citation with the illustrator's name followed by the abbreviation **illus.** ("illustrator"). After the title, give the author's name, preceded by the word **By**.

> Jeffers, Susan, illus. *Stopping by Woods on a Snowy Evening*.
>
> By Robert Frost. New York: Dutton-Penguin, 2001. Print.

A **graphic narrative** is a work in which text and illustrations work together to tell a story. Cite a graphic narrative as you would cite a book.

> Bechdel, Alison. *Fun Home: A Family Tragicomic*. Boston:
>
> Houghton, 2006. Print.

### 23. The Foreword, Preface, or Afterword of a Book

> Campbell, Richard. Preface. *Media and Culture: An*
>
> *Introduction to Mass Communication*. By Bettina Fabos.
>
> Boston: Bedford, 2005. vi-xi. Print.

### 24. A Book with a Title within Its Title

If the book you are citing contains a title that is normally italicized (a novel, play, or long poem, for example), do not italicize the interior title.

> Fulton, Joe B. *Mark Twain in the Margins: The Quarry Farm*
>
> *Marginalia and* A Connecticut Yankee in King
>
> Arthur's Court. Tuscaloosa: U of Alabama P,
>
> 2000. Print.

If the book you are citing contains a title that is normally enclosed in quotation marks, keep the quotation marks.

> Hawkins, Hunt, and Brian W. Shaffer, eds. *Approaches to*
> *Teaching Conrad's "Heart of Darkness" and "The Secret*
> *Sharer."* New York: MLA, 2002. Print.

### 25. A Translation

> García Márquez, Gabriel. *One Hundred Years of Solitude*. Trans.
> Gregory Rabassa. New York: Avon, 1991. Print.

### 26. The Bible

> *The New English Bible with the Apocrypha.* Oxford Study ed.
> New York: Oxford UP, 1976. Print.

### 27. The Qur'an

> *Holy Qur'an.* Trans. M. H. Shakir. Elmhurst: Tahrike Tarsile
> Qur'an, 1999. Print.

*Parts of Books*

### 28. A Short Story, Play, Poem, or Essay in a Collection of an Author's Work

> Bukowski, Charles. "lonely hearts." *The Flash of Lightning*
> *behind the Mountain: New Poems*. New York: Ecco, 2004.
> 115-16. Print.

*Note:* The title of the poem in the entry above is not capitalized because it appears in lowercase letters in the original.

### 29. A Short Story, Play, or Poem in an Anthology

> Chopin, Kate. "The Storm." *Literature: Reading, Reacting,*
> *Writing*. Ed. Laurie G. Kirszner and Stephen R. Mandell.
> 8th ed. Boston: Wadsworth, 2013. 306-09. Print.

> Shakespeare, William. *Othello, the Moor of Venice. Shakespeare:*
> *Six Plays and the Sonnets*. Ed. Thomas Marc Parrott and
> Edward Hubler. New York: Scribner's, 1956. 145-91. Print.

### 30. An Essay in an Anthology or Edited Collection

> Crevel, René. "From *Babylon*." *Surrealist Painters and Poets:*
> *An Anthology*. Ed. Mary Ann Caws. Cambridge: MIT P,
> 2001. 175-77. Print.

*Note:* Supply inclusive page numbers for the entire essay, not just for the page or pages you cite in your paper.

### 31.  More Than One Essay from the Same Anthology

List each essay from the same anthology separately, followed by a cross-reference to the entire anthology. Also list complete publication information for the anthology itself.

Agar, Eileen. "Am I a Surrealist?" Caws 3-7.

Caws, Mary Ann, ed. *Surrealist Painters and Poets: An*
　　　*Anthology*. Cambridge: MIT P, 2001. Print.

Crevel, René. "From *Babylon*." Caws 175-77.

### 32.  A Scholarly Article Reprinted in a Collection

Booth, Wayne C. "Why Ethical Criticism Can Never Be Simple."
　　　*Style* 32.2 (1998): 351-64. Rpt. in *Mapping the Ethical*
　　　*Turn: A Reader in Ethics, Culture, and Literary Theory.*
　　　Ed. Todd F. Davis and Kenneth Womack. Charlottesville:
　　　UP of Virginia, 2001. 16-29. Print.

### 33.  An Article in a Reference Book (Signed/Unsigned)

For a **signed** article, begin with the author's name. For unfamiliar reference books, include full publication information.

Drabble, Margaret. "Expressionism." *The Oxford Companion*
　　　*to English Literature*. 6th ed. New York: Oxford UP,
　　　2000. Print.

If the article is **unsigned,** begin with the title. For familiar reference books, do not include full publication information.

"Cubism." *The Encyclopedia Americana*. 2012 ed. Print.

*Note:* Omit page numbers when the reference book lists entries alphabetically. If you are listing one definition among several from a dictionary, include the abbreviation **Def.** ("Definition") along with the letter and/or number that corresponds to the definition.

"Justice." Def. 2b. *The Concise Oxford Dictionary*. 11th ed.
　　　2008. Print.

*Dissertations, Pamphlets, Government Publications, and Legal Sources*

### 34. A Dissertation (Published)

Cite a published dissertation the same way you would cite a book, but add relevant dissertation information before the publication information.

> Rodriguez, Jason Anthony. *Bureaucracy and Altruism:*
>
> > *Managing the Contradictions of Teaching.* Diss. U of
> >
> > Texas at Arlington, 2003. Ann Arbor: UMI, 2004. Print.

*Note:* University Microfilms, which publishes most of the dissertations in the United States, is also available online by subscription. For the proper format for citing online databases, see entries 53–58.

### 35. A Dissertation (Unpublished)

Use quotation marks for the title of an unpublished dissertation.

> Bon Tempo, Carl Joseph. "Americans at the Gate: The Politics
>
> > of American Refugee Policy." Diss. U of Virginia, 2004.
> >
> > Print.

### 36. A Pamphlet

Cite a pamphlet as you would a book. If no author is listed, begin with the title (italicized).

> *The Darker Side of Tanning.* Schaumburg: The American
>
> > Academy of Dermatology, 2010. Print.

### 37. A Government Publication

If the publication has no listed author, begin with the name of the government, followed by the name of the agency. You may use an abbreviation if its meaning is clear: **United States. Cong. Senate.**

> United States. Office of Consumer Affairs. *2003 Consumer's*
>
> > *Resource Handbook.* Washington: GPO, 2003. Print.

When citing two or more publications by the same government, use three unspaced hyphens (followed by a period) in place of the name for the second and subsequent entries. When you cite more than one work from the same agency of that government, use an additional set of unspaced hyphens in place of the agency name.

United States. FAA. *Passenger Airline Safety in the Twenty-First Century*. Washington: GPO, 2003. Print.

---. ---. *Recycled Air in Passenger Airline Cabins*. Washington: GPO, 2002. Print.

### 38. A Historical or Legal Document

In general, you do not need a works-cited entry for familiar historical documents. Parenthetical references in the text are sufficient—for example, **(US Const., art. 3, sec. 2)**.

If you cite an act in the works-cited list, include the name of the act, its Public Law (Pub. L.) number, its Statutes at Large (Stat.) cataloging number, its enactment date, and its publication medium.

Children's Health Act. Pub. L. 106-310. 114 Stat. 1101. 17 Oct. 2000. Print.

In works-cited entries for **legal cases,** abbreviate names of cases, but spell out the first important word of each party's name. Include the volume number, abbreviated name (not italicized), and inclusive page numbers of the law report; the name of the deciding court; the decision year; and publication information for the source. Do not italicize the case name in the works-cited list.

Abbott v. Blades. 544 US 929. Supreme Court of the US. 2005. *United States Reports*. Washington: GPO, 2007. Print.

## MLA ENTRIES FOR MISCELLANEOUS PRINT AND NONPRINT SOURCES

### Lectures and Interviews

### 39. A Lecture

Grimm, Mary. "An Afternoon with Mary Grimm." Visiting Writers Program. Dept. of English, Wright State U, Dayton. 16 Apr. 2004. Lecture.

### 40. A Personal Interview

Tannen, Deborah. Telephone interview. 8 June 2012.

West, Cornel. Personal interview. 28 Dec. 2013.

### 41. A Published Interview

Huston, John. "The Outlook for Raising Money: An Investment Banker's Viewpoint." *NJBIZ* 30 Sept. 2002: 2-3. Print.

*Letters*

### 42. A Personal Letter

Include the abbreviation **TS** (for "typescript") after the date of a typed letter.

> Tan, Amy. Letter to the author. 7 Apr. 2012. TS.

### 43. A Published Letter

> Joyce, James. "Letter to Louis Gillet." 20 Aug. 1931. *James*
>
> > *Joyce.* By Richard Ellmann. New York: Oxford UP, 1965.
> >
> > 631. Print.

### 44. A Letter in a Library's Archives

Include the abbreviation **MS** (for "manuscript") after the date of a handwritten letter.

> Stieglitz, Alfred. Letter to Paul Rosenberg. 5 Sept. 1923. MS.
>
> > Stieglitz Archive. Yale U Arts Lib., New Haven.

*Films, Videotapes, Radio and Television Programs, and Recordings*

### 45. A Film

Include the title of the film (italicized), the distributor, and the date, along with other information that may be useful to readers, such as the names of the performers, the director, and the screenwriter. Conclude with the publication medium.

> *Citizen Kane.* Dir. Orson Welles. Perf. Welles, Joseph Cotten,
>
> > Dorothy Comingore, and Agnes Moorehead. RKO, 1941.
> >
> > Film.

If you are focusing on the contribution of a particular person, begin with that person's name.

> Welles, Orson, dir. *Citizen Kane.* Perf. Welles, Joseph Cotten,
>
> > Dorothy Comingore, and Agnes Moorehead. RKO, 1941.
> >
> > Film.

### 46. A Videotape, DVD, or Laser Disc

Cite a videotape, DVD, or laser disc as you would cite a film, but include the original release date (when available).

> *Bowling for Columbine.* Dir. Michael Moore. 2002. United
>
> > Artists and Alliance Atlantis, 2003. DVD.

### 47. A Radio or Television Program

"War Feels Like War." *P.O.V.* Dir. Esteban Uyarra. PBS. WPTD,

Dayton, 6 July 2004. Television.

### 48. A Recording

List the composer, conductor, or performer (whomever you are focusing on), followed by the title, publisher, year of issue, and publication medium (**CD-ROM**, **MP3 file**, and so on).

Boubill, Alain, and Claude-Michel Schönberg. *Miss Saigon.*

Perf. Lea Salonga, Claire Moore, and Jonathan Pryce.

Cond. Martin Koch. Geffen, 1989. CD-ROM.

Marley, Bob. "Crisis." *Kaya.* Kava Island, 1978. LP.

*Paintings, Photographs, Cartoons, and Advertisements*

### 49. A Painting

Hopper, Edward. *Railroad Sunset.* 1929. Oil on canvas.

Whitney Museum of American Art, New York.

### 50. A Photograph

Cite a photograph in a museum's collection in the same way you cite a painting.

Stieglitz, Alfred. *The Steerage.* 1907. Photograph. Los Angeles

County Museum of Art, Los Angeles.

For a personal photograph, include a descriptive title (without quotation marks or italics), the name of the photographer, and the date.

Rittenhouse Square in winter. Personal photograph by the

author. 8 Feb. 2012.

See entry 76 for how to cite a photograph available on the Web only.

### 51. A Cartoon or Comic Strip

Trudeau, Garry. "Doonesbury." Comic strip. *Philadelphia*

*Inquirer* 15 Sept. 2003, late ed.: E13. Print.

### 52. An Advertisement

Microsoft. Advertisement. *National Review* 8 June 2010:

17. Print.

| | Entries for Sources |
|---|---|
| **MLA** ELECTRONIC SOURCES | from Online |
| | Databases |

To cite information from an online database, supply the publication information (including page numbers, if available; if unavailable, use **n. pag.**) followed by the name of the database (italicized), the publication medium (**Web**), and the date of access. Figure 11.4 shows where you can find this information.

Author's   First      Title of short story      Title of periodical    Date of
last name   name       (in quotation marks)      (italicized)           publication

Keillor, Garrison. "Love Me: A Short Story." *Atlantic* July-Aug.

    2003: 115-22. *Academic Search Elite*. Web. 2 May 2011.

     Inclusive     Name of database    Publication    Date of
  page numbers    (italicized)        medium      access

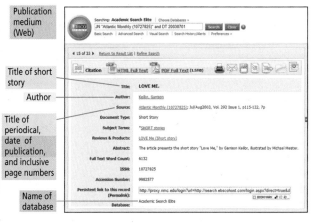

Publication medium (Web)

Title of short story

Author

Title of periodical, date of publication, and inclusive page numbers

Name of database

**FIGURE 11.4** Opening screen from an online database showing the location of the information needed for documentation. © EBSCO.

## Journal Articles, Magazine Articles, News Services, and Dissertations from Online Databases

### 53. A Scholarly Journal Article with a Print Version

Schaefer, Richard J. "Editing Strategies in Television News

    Documentaries." *Journal of Communication* 47.4 (1997):

    69-89. *InfoTrac OneFile Plus*. Web. 2 Oct. 2013.

#### 54. A Scholarly Journal Article with no Print Version

Maeseele, Thomas. "From Charity to Welfare Rights? A Study
 of Social Care Practices." *Social Work and Society: The
 International Online-Only Journal* 8.1 (2010): n. pag.
 *Academic Search Elite.* Web. 20 May 2012.

#### 55. A Monthly Magazine Article

Livermore, Beth. "Meteorites on Ice." *Astronomy* July 1993:
 54-58. *Expanded Academic ASAP Plus.* Web. 12 Nov. 2012.

Wright, Karen. "The Clot Thickens." *Discover* Dec. 1999:
 n. pag. *MasterFILE Premier.* Web. 10 Oct. 2013.

#### 56. A News Service

Ryan, Desmond. "Some Background on the Battle of
 Gettysburg." *Knight Ridder/Tribune News Service* 7 Oct.
 1993: n. pag. *InfoTrac OneFile Plus.* Web. 16 Nov. 2013.

#### 57. A Newspaper Article

Meyer, Greg. "Answering Questions about the West Nile
 Virus." *Dayton Daily News* 11 July 2002: Z3-7.
 *LexisNexis.* Web. 17 Feb. 2011.

#### 58. A Published Dissertation

Rodriguez, Jason Anthony. *Bureaucracy and Altruism:
 Managing the Contradictions of Teaching.* Diss. U of
 Texas at Arlington, 2003. *ProQuest.* Web. 4 Mar. 2012.

**MLA** ELECTRONIC SOURCES  Entries for Sources from Internet Sites

MLA style* recognizes that full source information for
Internet sources is not always available. Include in your
citation whatever information you can reasonably obtain:
the author or editor of the site (if available); the name of the
site (italicized); the version number of the source (if applicable); the name of any institution or sponsor (if unavailable, include the abbreviation **N.p.** for "no publisher"); the

*The documentation style for Internet sources presented here conforms to
the most recent guidelines published in the *MLA Handbook for Writers of
Research Papers* (7th ed.) and found online at <http://www.mlahandbook.org>.

date of electronic publication or update (if unavailable, include the abbreviation **n.d.** for "no date of publication"); the publication medium (**Web**); and the date you accessed the source. MLA recommends omitting the URL from the citation unless it is necessary to find the source (as in entry 62). Figure 11.5 shows where you can find this information.

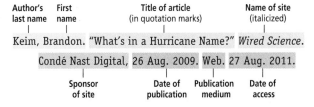

Author's last name | First name | Title of article (in quotation marks) | Name of site (italicized)

Keim, Brandon. "What's in a Hurricane Name?" *Wired Science.* Condé Nast Digital, 26 Aug. 2009. Web. 27 Aug. 2011.

Sponsor of site | Date of publication | Publication medium | Date of access

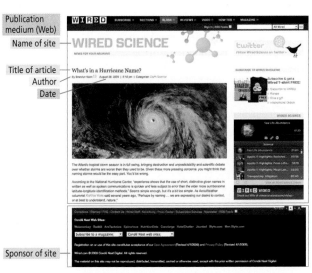

**FIGURE 11.5** Part of an online article showing the location of the information needed for documentation. Wired.com © 2009 Condé Nast Digital. All rights reserved. Image from NOAA.

### *Internet-Specific Sources*

**59. An Entire Web Site**

Nelson, Cary, ed. *Modern American Poetry*. Dept. of English, U of Illinois, Urbana-Champaign, 2002. Web. 26 May 2013.

**60. A Document within a Web Site**

"June 6, 1944: D-Day." *History.com*. History Channel, 1999. Web. 7 June 2012.

### 61. A Home Page for a Course

Walker, Janice R. "ENGL 1101-Composition I, Fall 2010."
Course home page. *Georgia Southern University*.
Dept. of Writing and Linguistics, Georgia Southern U,
6 Aug. 2010. Web. 8 Sept. 2012.

### 62. A Personal Home Page

Gainor, Charles. Home page. U of Toronto, 22 July 2012. Web.
10 Nov. 2013. <http://www.chass.utoronto.ca:9094/
~char>.

*Note:* If an electronic address (URL) is necessary, MLA requires that you enclose the URL within angle brackets to distinguish the address from the punctuation in the rest of the citation. If a URL will not fit on a line, the entire URL will be automatically carried over to the next line. If you prefer to divide the URL, divide it only after a slash. (Do not insert a hyphen.)

### 63. A Radio Program Accessed from an Internet Archive

"Teenage Skeptic Takes on Climate Scientists." Narr. David
Kestenbaum. *Morning Edition*. Natl. Public Radio.
WNYC, New York, 15 Apr. 2008. Transcript. *NPR*. Web.
30 Mar. 2010.

### 64. An E-mail

Mauk, Karen R. Message to the author. 28 June 2013. E-mail.

### 65. A Posting on an Online Forum or Blog

Schiller, Stephen. "Paper Cost and Publishing Costs."
*New York Times*. New York Times, 24 Apr. 2002. Web.
17 May 2002.

Merry. "The Way We Roll. . . ." *EnviroMom*. EnviroMom,
27 June 2008. Web. 3 July 2012.

*Articles, Books, Reviews, Letters, and Reference
Works on the Internet*

### 66. An Article in a Scholarly Journal

When you cite an article you accessed from an electronic source that also has a print version, include the publication information for the print source, the inclusive page numbers (if available), the publication medium (**Web**), and the date you accessed it.

> DeKoven, Marianne. "Utopias Limited: Post-Sixties and
>
> Postmodern American Fiction." *Modern Fiction Studies*
>
> 41.1 (1995): 75-97. Web. 20 Jan. 2010.

### 67. An Article in a Magazine

> Weiser, Jay. "The Tyranny of Informality." *Time*. Time,
>
> 26 Feb. 1996. Web. 1 Mar. 2011.

### 68. An Article in a Newspaper

> Bilton, Nick. "Three Reasons Why the iPad Will Kill Amazon's
>
> Kindle." *New York Times*. New York Times, 27 Jan. 2010.
>
> Web. 16 Feb. 2011.

### 69. An Article in a Newsletter

> Sullivan, Jennifer S., comp. "Documentation Preserved,
>
> New Collections." *AIP Center for History of Physics* 39.2
>
> (2007): 2-3. Web. 26 Feb. 2011.

### 70. A Book

> Douglass, Frederick. *My Bondage and My Freedom*. Boston,
>
> 1855. *Google Book Search*. Web. 8 June 2012.

### 71. A Review

> Ebert, Roger. Rev. of *Star Wars: Episode I—The Phantom*
>
> *Menace,* dir. George Lucas. *Chicago Sun-Times*. Digital
>
> Chicago, 8 June 2000. Web. 22 June 2013.

### 72. A Letter to the Editor

> Chen-Cheng, Henry H. Letter. *New York Times*. New York
>
> Times, 19 July 1999. Web. 1 Jan. 2011.

### 73. An Article in an Encyclopedia

Include the article's title, the title of the database (italicized), the version number (if available), the sponsor, the date of electronic publication, the publication medium (**Web**), and the date of access.

> "Hawthorne, Nathaniel." *Encyclopaedia Britannica Online*.
>
> Encyclopaedia Britannica, 2012. Web. 16 May 2012.

### 74. A Government Publication

Cite an online government publication as you would cite a print version; end with the information required for an electronic source.

United States. Dept. of Justice. Office of Justice Programs.
*Violence against Women: Estimates from the Redesigned National Crime Victimization Survey*. By Ronet Bachman and Linda E. Saltzman. Aug. 1995. *Bureau of Justice Statistics*. Web. 10 July 2010.

*Paintings, Photographs, Cartoons, and Maps on the Internet*

### 75. A Painting

Seurat, Georges-Pierre. *Evening, Honfleur*. 1886. Museum of Mod. Art, New York. *MoMA.org*. Web. 8 Jan. 2012.

### 76. A Photograph

Brady, Mathew. *Ulysses S. Grant 1822-1885*. 1864. *Mathew Brady's National Portrait Gallery*. Web. 2 Oct. 2013.

### 77. A Cartoon

Stossel, Sage. "Star Wars: The Next Generation." Cartoon. *Atlantic Unbound*. Atlantic Monthly Group, 2 Oct. 2002. Web. 14 Nov. 2011.

### 78. A Map

"Philadelphia, Pennsylvania." Map. *U.S. Gazetteer*. US Census Bureau, n.d. Web. 17 July 2012.

**MLA** OTHER ELECTRONIC SOURCES

*DVD-ROMs, CD-ROMs, and Computer Software*

### 79. A Nonperiodical Publication on DVD-ROM or CD-ROM

Cite a nonperiodical publication on DVD-ROM or CD-ROM the same way you would cite a book, but include the appropriate medium of publication.

"Windhover." *The Oxford English Dictionary*. 2nd ed. Oxford: Oxford UP, 2001. DVD-ROM.

"Whitman, Walt." *DiskLit: American Authors*. Boston: Hall, 2000. CD-ROM.

80. **A Periodical Publication on DVD-ROM or CD-ROM**

> Zurbach, Kate. "The Linguistic Roots of Three Terms."
>
> > *Linguistic Quarterly* 37 (1994): 12-47. CD-ROM. *InfoTrac:*
> >
> > *Magazine Index Plus.* Information Access. Jan. 2011.

81. **Computer Software or a Video Game**

> *The Sims 3 Deluxe.* Redwood City: Electronic Arts. 2010. DVD.

*Digital Files*

82. **A Word-Processing Document**

> Russell, Brad. "Work Trip Notes." File last modified on 22 Mar.
>
> > 2013. *Microsoft Word* file.

83. **An MP3 File**

> U2. "Beautiful Day." *All That You Can't Leave Behind.*
>
> > Universal-Island, 2000. MP3 file.

## Close-Up  HOW TO CITE SOURCES NOT LISTED IN THIS CHAPTER

The examples listed in this chapter represent the sources you will most likely encounter in your research. If you encounter a source that is not listed here, find the model that most closely matches it, and adapt the guidelines for your use.

For example, suppose you wanted to include **an obituary** from a print newspaper in your list of works cited. The models that most closely resemble this type of entry are *an editorial in a newspaper* (entry 8) and *a letter to the editor* (entry 9). If you used these models as your guide, your entry would look like this:

> Boucher, Geoff, and Elaine Woo. "Michael Jackson's
>
> > Life Was Infused with Fantasy and Tragedy."
> >
> > Obituary. *Los Angeles Times* 2 July 2009:
> >
> > 4. Print.

Follow the same procedure for an electronic source. Suppose you wanted to include a posting from a **social networking site,** such as *Facebook*. The models

*(continued)*

**HOW TO CITE SOURCES NOT LISTED IN THIS CHAPTER** *(continued)*

that most closely resemble this type of entry are a *personal home page* (entry 62) and a *blog posting* (entry 65). If you used these models as your guide, your entry would look like this:

> Branagh, Kenneth. Wall post. *Facebook.com*. 15 Mar.
>
> 2013. Web. 16 Mar. 2013.

### 3 Content Notes

**Content notes**—multiple bibliographic citations or other material that does not fit smoothly into your paper—are indicated by a **superscript** (raised numeral) in the text. Notes can appear either as footnotes at the bottom of the page or as endnotes on a separate sheet entitled **Notes**, placed after the last page of the paper and before the works-cited list. Content notes are double-spaced within and between entries. The first line is indented one-half inch, and subsequent lines are typed flush left.

*For Multiple Citations*

#### In the Paper

Many researchers emphasize the necessity of having dying patients share their experiences.[1]

#### In the Note

1. Kübler-Ross 27; Stinnette 43; Poston 70; Cohen and Cohen 31-34; Burke 1: 91-95.

*For Other Material*

#### In the Paper

The massacre during World War I is an event the survivors could not easily forget.[2]

#### In the Note

2. For a firsthand account of these events, see Bedoukian 178-81.

# 11b MLA-Style Manuscript Guidelines

Although MLA papers do not usually include abstracts or internal headings, this situation is changing. Be sure you know what your instructor expects.

The guidelines in the three checklists that follow are based on the latest version of the *MLA Handbook for Writers of Research Papers*.

---

**CHECKLIST**

## Typing Your Paper

When typing your paper, use the student paper in **11c** as your model.

❏ Leave a one-inch margin at the top and bottom and on both sides of the page. Double-space your paper throughout.

❏ Capitalize all important words in your title, but not prepositions, articles, coordinating conjunctions, or the *to* in infinitives (unless they begin or end the title or subtitle). Do not italicize your title or enclose it in quotation marks. Never put a period after the title, even if it is a sentence.

❏ Number all pages of your paper consecutively—including the first—in the upper right-hand corner, one-half inch from the top, flush right. Type your last name followed by a space before the page number on every page.

❏ Set off quotations of more than four lines of prose or more than three lines of poetry by indenting the whole quotation one inch. If you quote two or more paragraphs, indent the first line of each paragraph an additional quarter inch. (If the first sentence does not begin a paragraph, do not indent it. Indent the first line only in successive paragraphs.)

❏ Citations should follow MLA documentation style.

See 11a

---

**CHECKLIST**

## Using Visuals

❏ Insert visuals into the text as close as possible to where they are discussed.

See 40d

❏ For **tables**, follow these guidelines: *Above the table*, label each table with the word **Table** followed by an arabic numeral (for instance, **Table 1**). Double-space, and type a descriptive caption, with the first line flush with the left-hand margin; indent subsequent lines one-quarter inch. Capitalize the caption as if it were a title.

*continued*

## Using Visuals *(continued)*

*Below the table*, type the word **Source,** followed by a colon and all source information. Type the first line of the source information flush with the left-hand margin; indent subsequent lines one-quarter inch.

❏ Label other types of visual material—graphs, charts, photographs, drawings, and so on—**Fig.** (Figure) followed by an arabic numeral (for example, **Fig. 2**). Directly below the visual, type the label and a title or caption on the same line, followed by source information. Type all lines flush with the left-hand margin.

❏ Do not include the source of the visual in the works-cited list unless you use other material from that source elsewhere in the paper.

### CHECKLIST
## Preparing the MLA Works-Cited List

When typing your works-cited list, follow these guidelines:

❏ Begin the works-cited list on a new page after the last page of text or content notes, numbered as the next page of the paper.

See 11a3

❏ Center the title **Works Cited** one inch from the top of the page. Double-space between the title and the first entry.

❏ Each entry in the works-cited list has three divisions: author, title, and publication information. Separate divisions with a period and one space.

❏ List entries alphabetically, with last name first. Use the author's full name as it appears on the title page. If a source has no listed author, alphabetize it by the first word of the title (not counting the article).

❏ Type the first line of each entry flush with the left-hand margin; indent subsequent lines one-half inch.

❏ Double-space within and between entries.

## 11c  Model MLA-Style Research Paper

The following student paper, "The Great Debate: *Wikipedia* and College-Level Research," uses MLA documentation style. It includes MLA-style in-text citations, a line graph, a notes page, and a works-cited list.

## Title Pages

Although MLA does not require a separate title page, some instructors prefer that you include one. If so, follow this format:

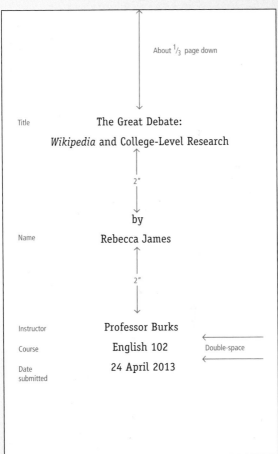

About ⅓ page down

Title        The Great Debate:

*Wikipedia* and College-Level Research

2"

by

Name       Rebecca James

2"

Instructor     Professor Burks

Course       English 102      Double-space

Date         24 April 2013
submitted

1"　　　　　　　　　　　　　　　¹/₂"

Rebecca James

Professor Burks

English 102

24 April 2013

Center title → The Great Debate: *Wikipedia*
and College-Level Research

Indent ¹/₂" → When confronted with a research assignment,
students and professionals alike often turn first to
*Wikipedia,* the popular free online encyclopedia.

Double-space With over 20,000,000 articles, *Wikipedia* is a valuable
resource for anyone seeking general information on
a topic. Recently, however, *Wikipedia* has become
a source of controversy. Many college instructors
say that students should not rely on *Wikipedia* as
an authoritative research source or cite it in their
bibliographies; they say that *Wikipedia* (like other
encyclopedias) should be used only as a starting point
for in-depth research. Some academics, troubled by
the site's lack of reliability, even discourage the use
of *Wikipedia* as a source of factual information. On the
other hand, some instructors (along with some college
librarians) believe that the issue is not so clear-cut.
They say that *Wikipedia* is here to stay and that if
the site has problems, it is their responsibility to help

Thesis statement improve it. All in all, the debate over *Wikipedia* has
been a positive development because it has led the
academic community to confront the challenges of
open, collaborative software on the Web.

　　　　*Wikipedia* is the most popular wiki, an open-
source Web site that allows users to edit as well
as contribute content. Derived from a Hawaiian

*Student's last name and page number on every page (including the first)*

*Outline point I: Definition of wiki and explanation* Wikipedia

James 2

word meaning "quick," the term *wiki* suggests the swiftness and ease with which users can access information on and contribute content to a site ("Wiki"). In accordance with the site's policies, users can edit existing articles and add new articles using *Wikipedia*'s editing tools, which do not require specialized programming knowledge or expertise. Since its creation in 2001 by Jimmy Wales, *Wikipedia* has grown into a huge database of articles on topics ranging from contemporary rock bands to obscure scientific and technical concepts. Because anyone can edit or add content to the site, however, many members of the academic community consider *Wikipedia* unreliable.

Without a professional editorial board to oversee its development, *Wikipedia* has several shortcomings that limit its trustworthiness. As *Wikipedia*'s own "Researching with *Wikipedia*" page concedes, "not everything in *Wikipedia* is accurate, comprehensive, or unbiased." "Reliability of *Wikipedia*," an article on *Wikipedia*, discusses the many problems that have been identified, presenting criticisms under categories such as "areas of reliability," "susceptibility to bias," and "false biographical information." Academics have similar objections. Villanova University communication department chair Maurice L. Hall has reservations about *Wikipedia*:

> As an open source that is not subjected to traditional forms of peer review, *Wikipedia* must be considered only as reliable as the credibility of the footnotes it uses. But

**Margin notes:**

Parenthetical documentation refers to material accessed from a Web site

Student's original conclusions; no documentation necessary

tline point ntroduction *Wikipedia*'s wbacks

Quotations from Internet source, introduced by author's name, are not followed by a paragraph or page number because this information was not provided in the electronic text

Quotation of more than four lines is typed as a block, indented 1", and double-spaced, with no quotation marks

James 3

I also tell students that the information can be skewed in directions of ideology or other forms of bias, and so that is why it cannot be taken as a final authority. (qtd. in Burnsed)

*Qtd. in* indicates that Hall's comments were quoted in Burnsed's article

In fact, in 2007, *Wikipedia*'s unreliability led Middlebury College's history department to prohibit students from citing *Wikipedia* as a research source—although it does not prohibit them from using the site for reference. Since then, however, many academics have qualified their criticisms of *Wikipedia*, arguing that although the site is not a reliable research source, it is a valuable stepping stone to more in-depth research. As retired reference librarian Joe Schallan explains, "*Wikipedia* can be useful, especially as a starting point for information on offbeat topics or niche interests that traditional encyclopedias omit." However, he believes that information from *Wikipedia* should be taken "with a very large grain of salt."

Because it is an open-source site, *Wikipedia* is not always reliable or accurate. Although many *Wikipedia* articles include citations, many others—especially those that are underdeveloped—do not. In addition, because anyone can create or edit them, *Wikipedia* articles can be inaccurate, biased, and even targets for vandalism. For example, some *Wikipedia* users tamper with the biographies of especially high-profile political or cultural figures.[1] According to the 2011 article "*Wikipedia* Vandalism Detection," 7% of *Wikipedia*'s articles are vandalized in some way (Adler et al. 277).

Outline point III: *Wikipedia*'s unreliability

Superscript number identifies content note

James 4

Although *Wikipedia* has an extensive protection policy that restricts the kinds of edits that can be made to its articles ("*Wikipedia*: Protection Policy"), there are limitations to *Wikipedia*'s control measures. As William Badke, an associate librarian at Trinity Western University, notes, *Wikipedia* can be "an environment for shallow thinking, debates over interpretation, and the settling of scores" (50).

Because they can be edited by anyone, *Wikipedia* articles are often poorly written. Emory University English professor Mark Bauerlein asserts that *Wikipedia* articles are written in a "flat, featureless, factual style" (153). Even though *Wikipedia* has instituted a coding system to label the shortcomings of its less-developed articles, a warning about an article's poor writing style is likely to go unnoticed by the typical user. Bauerlein argues that the poor writing of many *Wikipedia* articles reaffirms to students that sloppy writing and grammatical errors are acceptable in their own writing as well:

> Students relying on *Wikipedia* alone, year in and year out, absorb the prose as proper knowledge discourse, and knowledge itself seems blank and uninspiring. (153-54)

Thus, according to Bauerlein, *Wikipedia* articles have actually lowered the standards for what constitutes acceptable college-level writing.

Despite *Wikipedia*'s drawbacks, there is no denying the popularity of the site among both college students and professionals, who turn to it first for general factual information on a variety

line nt IV: kipedia's r writing

line nt V. A: ipedia's ularity benefits: report istic and e

James 5

of topics. According to a 2011 report by the Pew
Internet & American Life Project, 53% of American
adults use *Wikipedia,* with the majority of users
having or pursuing higher-education degrees
(Zickuhr and Rainie 2). Table 1 shows a breakdown of
the people who most commonly consult *Wikipedia.*

Table 1

*Wikipedia* User Profile

| | |
|---|---|
| **Total** | **53%** |
| Men | 56 |
| Women | 50 |
| **Age** | |
| 18-29 | 62 |
| 30-49 | 52 |
| 50-64 | 49 |
| 65+ | 33 |
| **Race/Ethnicity** | |
| White, non-Hispanic | 55 |
| Black, non-Hispanic (n=85) | 43 |
| Hispanic (n=61) | 40 |
| **Household Income** | |
| Less than $30,000 | 44 |
| $30,000-$49,999 | 49 |
| $50,000-$74,999 | 63 |
| $75,000+ | 61 |
| **Education level** | |
| Less than High School (n=46) | 30 |
| High School Diploma | 41 |
| Some College | 52 |
| College+ | 69 |
| **Home internet connection type** | |
| Dial-up (n=76) | 26 |
| Broadband | 59 |

Source: Pew Research Center's Internet & American Life Project,
April 29-May 30, 2010 Spring Change Assessment Survey. N=852
internet users age 18 and older.

Source: Kathryn Zickuhr and Lee Rainie; "*Wikipedia,*
   *Past and Present*"; *Pew Internet & American Life*
   *Project*; Pew Research Center, 13 Jan. 2011;
   Web; 7 Apr. 2013; 2.

There are good reasons why so many educated
adults use *Wikipedia.* Longer *Wikipedia* articles often
include comprehensive abstracts that summarize
their content. *Wikipedia* articles also often include

*Table summarizes relevant data. Source information is typed directly below the table.*

*Outline point V. B: Wikipedia' popularity and benef comprehen sive abstra links to ot' sources, a current an comprehen sive biblio phies*

links to other *Wikipedia* articles, allowing users to navigate quickly through related content. In addition, many *Wikipedia* articles link to other print and online sources, including reliable peer-reviewed sources. Another benefit, noted earlier by Villanova University's Maurice L. Hall, is the inclusion of current and comprehensive bibliographies in some *Wikipedia* articles. According to Alison J. Head and Michael B. Eisenberg, "*Wikipedia* plays an important role when students are formulating and defining a topic."[2] Assuming that *Wikipedia* users make the effort to connect an article's content with more reliable, traditional research sources, *Wikipedia* can be a valuable first step for serious researchers.

Superscript number identifies content note

*Wikipedia* has advantages over other online encyclopedias. Because users can update articles in real time from any location, *Wikipedia* offers up-to-the-minute coverage of political and cultural events as well as timely information on popular culture topics that receive little or no attention in other reference sources. In addition, because *Wikipedia* has such a broad user base, more topics are covered in *Wikipedia* than in other online resources. For example, a student researching the history of video gaming would find *Wikipedia*'s "Wii" article, with its numerous pages of information and hundreds of references, to be a valuable resource. In contrast, the "Nintendo Wii" article in the professionally edited *Encyclopaedia Britannica Online* consists of a few paragraphs and a handful of external resources. Even when there is little information

Outline point VI: *Wikipedia*'s advantages over other online encyclopedias

James 7

on a particular topic, *Wikipedia* allows users to create "stub" articles, which provide minimal information that users can expand over time. Thus, by offering immediate access to information on relatively obscure topics, *Wikipedia* can be a valuable first step in finding reliable research sources on such topics.

In their landmark 2008 study, Diomidis Spinellis and Panagiotis Louridas accurately predict that *Wikipedia* would become an even more comprehensive database of information that could eventually gain acceptance in the academic community. *Wikipedia*'s "About" page claims that the continual editing of articles "generally results in an upward trend of quality and a growing consensus over a neutral representation of information." In fact, *Wikipedia* has instituted control measures to help weed out inaccurate or biased information and to make its content more reliable. For example, evaluating articles on the basis of accuracy, neutrality, completeness, and style, *Wikipedia* ranks its best articles as "featured" and its second-best articles as "good."[3] Although no professional editorial board oversees the development of content within *Wikipedia,* experienced users may become editors, and this role allows them to monitor the process by which content is added and updated. Users may also use the "Talk" page to discuss an article's content and make suggestions for improvement. With such controls in place, some *Wikipedia* articles are comparable in scope and accuracy to articles in professionally edited online resources.

Outline point VII: *Wikipedia*'s ongoing improvement

Superscript number identifies content note

James 8

Although critics argue that the collaborative nature of the wiki format does not necessarily help improve content, Spinellis and Louridas's study seems to suggest the opposite. In examining trends of content development in *Wikipedia,* Spinellis and Louridas affirm that the coverage of various topics in *Wikipedia* tends to become more balanced over time:

> *Wikipedia*'s topic coverage has been criticized as too reflective of and limited to the interests of its young, tech-savvy contributors, covering technology and current affairs disproportionably more than, say, world history or the arts. We hypothesize that the addition of new *Wikipedia* articles is not a purely random process following the whims of its contributors but that references to nonexistent articles trigger the eventual creation of a corresponding article. Although it is difficult to claim that this process guarantees even and unbiased coverage of topics (adding links is also a subjective process), such a mechanism could eventually force some kind of balance in *Wikipedia* coverage. (71)

Spinellis and Louridas summarize their findings with a positive conclusion: "the apparently chaotic *Wikipedia* development process delivers growth at a sustainable rate" (71). Fig. 1 supports

James 9

this conclusion, illustrating how, in recent years, *Wikipedia* has achieved a relative balance between complete and incomplete (or stub) articles. In offering increasingly more consistent (as well as broader) coverage, *Wikipedia* is becoming a more reliable source of information than some of its critics might like to admit.

Graph summarizes relevant data. Source information is typed directly below the figure.

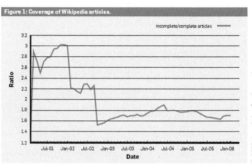

© 2008 Association for Computing Machinery, Inc. Reprinted by permission.

Fig. 1. Diomidis Spinellis and Panagiotis Louridas, "The Collaborative Organization of Knowledge"; *Communications of the ACM* 51.8 (2008): 71; *Academic Search Elite*; Web; 3 Apr. 2013.

Some argue that the academic community's reservations about *Wikipedia* have less to do with *Wikipedia*'s shortcomings and more to do with resistance to emergent digital research technologies. Harvard Law professor Jonathan L. Zittrain suggests that academia has, in effect, fallen behind, observing that "so many projects by universities and libraries are about knowledge and information online, . . . [but academics] just couldn't get *Wikipedia* going, or anything like it" (qtd. in Foster). A recent study suggested

Outline po IX: Academ community reservatior about *Wikipedia*

Ellipsis indicates that the student has omitted words from the quotation one reason for *Wikipedia*'s bad reputation among many college instructors: "the perceived detrimental effects of the use of Web 2.0 applications not included in the university suite" (Bayliss 36). Although Jimmy Wales, cofounder of *Wikipedia,* acknowledges that *Wikipedia* should serve only as a starting point for more in-depth research, he calls for the academic community to recognize *Wikipedia* as one of several new, important digital platforms that change the way people learn and disseminate knowledge. "Instead of fearing the power, complexity, and extraordinary potential of these new platforms," Wales says, "we should be asking how we can gain from their success" (qtd. in Goldstein). As William Badke, the Trinity Western University librarian, and others argue, members of the academic community are uniquely qualified to improve *Wikipedia* by expanding stub articles and by writing new articles about their areas of expertise. Badke suggests, "The most daring solution would be for academia to enter the world of *Wikipedia* directly" (50), asking how the academic community can improve this bank of information that students consult before any other research source.

In recent years, librarians across the country have committed their time and resources to enhancing *Wikipedia* articles that pertain to their own special collections and areas of expertise. Like William Badke, librarian Adam Bennington argues that the *Wikipedia* phenomenon presents

ine point brarians' ts to use improve *pedia*

a "teachable moment" that enables librarians and other members of the academic community to develop students' information literacy skills (47). Badke, Bennington, and other librarians believe that it is the responsibility of the academic community to bridge the divide between traditional research sources and the digital tools and technologies students are increasingly using to conduct college-level research.

Already, college instructors have found new uses and benefits of *Wikipedia* by incorporating it into their classrooms. In fact, *Wikipedia* has implemented a "classroom coordination project" to help instructors around the world build writing assignments based on *Wikipedia*. *Wikipedia*'s "School and University Projects" page offers guidelines and other resources as well as a list of numerous schools that incorporate *Wikipedia* into the classroom, noting that in such assignments "the student is dealing with a real world situation, which is not only more educational but also . . . more interesting." Jeff Byers, a professor of chemistry and biochemistry at Middlebury College (where one of the more famous *Wikipedia* "bans" was instituted not long ago), has students in his advanced organic chemistry course write and edit *Wikipedia* entries. Similarly, in her article "Writing for the World: *Wikipedia* as an Introduction to Academic Writing," Christine M. Tardy, an associate professor of writing, rhetoric, and discourse at DePaul University, encourages instructors to use

Outline p
XI: *Wikip*
in the
classroom

James 12

*Wikipedia* in the classroom and outlines some
sample writing assignments that can help students
"gain a real sense of audience and enjoy the
satisfaction of seeing their work published on
a high-traffic global website" (18). Instructors
like Byers and Tardy emphasize the collaborative
nature of *Wikipedia* writing assignments,
which offer students a unique opportunity to
experience the kinds of writing they are likely to
do after college. Additionally, *Wikipedia* writing
assignments encourage students to use critical
thinking skills, since they require students to
evaluate the articles they find on the site and to
use *Wikipedia* bibliographies as a starting place
to find more suitable research sources.

With emerging research on *Wikipedia* use
and with new efforts by colleges and universities
around the country to incorporate *Wikipedia* into
the classroom, the debate surrounding *Wikipedia*
seems to be shifting. Although instructors used to
seek ways to prevent students from using *Wikipedia*
as a research source, some in the academic
community are now acknowledging the importance
and usefulness of this online resource—at least
for general reference. Many former critics are
acknowledging that *Wikipedia* offers academics
an opportunity to participate in emergent digital
technologies that have changed the ways students
conduct research. In other words, instructors
acknowledge, they need to come to terms with
*Wikipedia* and develop guidelines for its use.

line point
Academics'
nging view
*Wikipedia*

James 13

More and more academics are realizing that improving *Wikipedia* actually benefits students, since the site is often the first place students go when starting a research project. To its credit, *Wikipedia* has taken steps to improve the site's reliability and accuracy. In her article "Boosting *Wikipedia* Quality," Robin Peek, an associate professor at Simmons College, describes two major initiatives *Wikipedia* has recently undertaken. The first is the "Rate This Page" feature, which allows users to evaluate articles on the basis of trustworthiness, objectivity, completeness, and writing quality. The second is the Public Policy Initiative, or PPI, which encourages instructors in public policy programs to develop *Wikipedia* writing assignments.

Conclusion restates the thesis and summarizes key points

Like any encyclopedia, *Wikipedia* is not a suitable source for college-level research. Beyond this fact, however, it may also not yet be as reliable as some other reference sources. Still, it is a valuable starting point for research. As academics and others continue to examine *Wikipedia*'s strengths and weaknesses, they may become more open to its use and more willing to work to improve it. In this sense, the debate over *Wikipedia* is likely to have a positive outcome. Meanwhile, however, students should exercise caution when evaluating general information they find on *Wikipedia* and refrain from citing it as a source.

James 14

Notes ← — Center title

↵ ½" → 1. In one well-known example, the
reputation of journalist John Seigenthaler was    ← Double-space
tarnished when a *Wikipedia* user edited his    ←
biography to claim inaccurately that Seigenthaler
was involved in the Kennedy assassination, a
lie that spread to other online sources.

2. Head and Eisenberg also note, however,
that "when students are in a deep research mode,
. . . it is library databases, such as *JSTOR* and
*PsycINFO*, for instance, that students use more
frequently than *Wikipedia*."

3. In addition, *Wikipedia*'s policies state that
the information in its articles must be verifiable
and must be based on documented, preexisting
research.

Center title ——————→

## Works Cited

Adler, B. Thomas, et al. "*Wikipedia* Vandalism
    Detection: Combining Natural Language,
    Metadata, and Reputation Features." *Lecture
    Notes in Computer Science* 6609 (2011):
    277-88. *Google Scholar*. Web. 3 Apr. 2013.

Badke, William. "What to Do with *Wikipedia*."
    *Online* Mar.-Apr. 2008: 48-50. *Academic
    Search Elite*. Web. 7 Apr. 2013.

Bauerlein, Mark. *The Dumbest Generation: How the
    Digital Age Stupefies Young Americans and
    Jeopardizes Our Future (or, Don't Trust Anyone
    Under 30)*. New York: Penguin, 2008. Print.

Bayliss, Gemma. "Exploring the Cautionary Attitude
    toward *Wikipedia* in Higher Education:
    Implications for Higher Education Institutions."
    *New Review of Academic Librarianship* 19.1 (2013):
    36-57. *Academic Search Elite*. Web. 3 Apr. 2013.

Bennington, Adam. "Dissecting the Web through
    *Wikipedia*." *American Libraries* Aug. 2008:
    46-48. Print.

Burnsed, Brian. "*Wikipedia* Gradually Accepted in
    College Classrooms." *USNews.com*. US News &
    World Rept., 20 June 2011. Web. 25 Mar. 2013.

Foster, Andrea L. "Professor Predicts Bleak Future
    for the Internet." *Chronicle of Higher Education*
    18 Apr. 2008: A29. *Academic Search Elite*. Web.
    3 Apr. 2013.

Goldstein, Evan R. "The Dumbing of America?"
    *Chronicle of Higher Education* 21 Mar. 2008:
    B4. *Academic Search Elite*. Web. 3 Apr. 2013.

Double-space

Newspaper article accessed from an online database

James 16

Head, Alison J., and Michael B. Eisenberg. "How *Journal*
Today's College Students Use *Wikipedia* *article*
*without*
for Course-Related Research." *First Monday* *pagination*
*accessed*
15.3 (2010): n. pag. *Google Scholar*. Web. *from Google*
*Scholar*
3 Apr. 2013.

Peek, Robin. "Boosting *Wikipedia* Quality." *Information*
*Today* Oct. 2011: 25. *Academic Search Elite*.
Web. 3 Apr. 2013.

"Reliability of *Wikipedia*." *Wikipedia*. Wikimedia
Foundation, 2013. Web. 25 Mar. 2013.

Schallan, Joe. "*Wikipedia* Woes." Letter. *American* *Signed letter*
*to the editor*
*Libraries* Apr. 2010: 9. Print. *in a montly*
*magazine*

Spinellis, Diomidis, and Panagiotis Louridas. "The
Collaborative Organization of Knowledge."
*Communications of the ACM* 51.8 (2008):
68-73. *Academic Search Elite*. Web.
3 Apr. 2013.

Tardy, Christine M. "Writing for the World:
*Wikipedia* as an Introduction to Academic
Writing." *English Teaching Forum* 48.1 (2010):
12+. *ERIC*. Web. 3 Apr. 2013.

"Wiki." *Encyclopaedia Britannica Online*. *Article in*
*an online*
Encyclopaedia Britannica, 2013. Web. *encyclopedia*
25 Mar. 2013.

"*Wikipedia*: About." *Wikipedia*. Wikimedia
Foundation, 2013. Web. 25 Mar. 2013.

"*Wikipedia:* Protection Policy." *Wikipedia*. Wikimedia *Unsigned*
*document*
Foundation, 2013. Web. 25 Mar. 2013. *within a Web*
*site*

"*Wikipedia*: Researching with *Wikipedia*."
*Wikipedia*. Wikimedia Foundation, 2013.
Web. 25 Mar. 2013.

James 17

"*Wikipedia:* School and University Projects."
     *Wikipedia*. Wikimedia Foundation, 2013. Web.
     25 Mar. 2013.

Zickuhr, Kathryn, and Lee Rainie. "*Wikipedia*, Past
     and Present." *Pew Internet & American Life
     Project*. Pew Research Center, 13 Jan. 2011.
     Web. 7 Apr. 2013.

# Directory of APA In-Text Citations

# Directory of APA Reference List Entries

## PRINT SOURCES: *Entries for Articles*

### Articles in Scholarly Journals

### Articles in Magazines and Newspapers

## PRINT SOURCES: *Entries for Books*

### Authors

### Editions, Multivolume Works, and Forewords

# CHAPTER 12

# APA Documentation Style

## 12a Using APA Style

**APA style*** is used extensively in the social sciences. APA documentation has three parts: *parenthetical references in the body of the paper*, a *reference list*, and optional *content footnotes*.

### 1 Parenthetical References

APA documentation uses short parenthetical references in the body of the paper keyed to an alphabetical list of references at the end of the paper. A typical parenthetical reference consists of the author's last name (followed by a comma) and the year of publication.

> Many people exhibit symptoms of depression after the death of a pet (Russo, 2009).

If the author's name appears in an introductory phrase, include the year of publication there as well.

> According to Russo (2009), many people exhibit symptoms of depression after the death of a pet.

When quoting directly, include the page number, preceded by **p.** in parentheses after the quotation.

> According to Weston (2006), children from one-parent homes read at "a significantly lower level than those from two-parent homes" (p. 58).

*Note:* A long quotation (forty words or more) is not set in quotation marks. It is set as a block, and the entire quotation is double-spaced and indented one-half inch from the left margin. Parenthetical documentation is placed one space after the final punctuation.

---

*APA documentation format follows the guidelines set in the *Publication Manual of the American Psychological Association,* 6th ed. Washington, DC: APA, 2010.

## Sample APA In-Text Citations

### 1. A Work by a Single Author

Many college students suffer from sleep deprivation (Anton, 2009).

### 2. A Work by Two Authors

There is growing concern over the use of psychological testing in elementary schools (Albright & Glennon, 2010).

### 3. A Work by Three to Five Authors

If a work has more than two but fewer than six authors, mention all names in the first reference; in subsequent references in the same paragraph, cite only the first author followed by **et al.** ("and others"). When the reference appears in later paragraphs, include the year.

*First Reference*

(Sparks, Wilson, & Hewitt, 2009)

*Subsequent References in the Same Paragraph*

(Sparks et al.)

*References in Later Paragraphs*

(Sparks et al., 2009)

### 4. A Work by Six or More Authors

When a work has six or more authors, cite the name of the first author followed by **et al.** and the year in all references.

(Miller et al., 2008)

---

**Close-Up**  CITING WORKS BY MULTIPLE AUTHORS

When referring to multiple authors in the text of your paper, join the last two names with **and.**

According to Rosen, Wolfe, and Ziff (2009). . . .

Parenthetical references (as well as reference list entries) require an **ampersand (&)**.

(Rosen, Wolfe, & Ziff, 2009)

### 5. Works by Authors with the Same Last Name

If your reference list includes works by two or more authors with the same last name, use each author's initials in all in-text citations.

> Both F. Bor (2010) and S. D. Bor (2009) concluded that no further study was needed.

### 6. A Work by a Corporate Author

If the name of a corporate author is long, abbreviate it after the first citation.

*First Reference*

> (National Institute of Mental Health [NIMH], 2010)

*Subsequent Reference*

> (NIMH, 2010)

### 7. A Work with No Listed Author

If a work has no listed author, cite the first two or three words of the title (followed by a comma) and the year. Use quotation marks around titles of periodical articles and chapters of books; use italics for titles of books, periodicals, brochures, reports, and the like.

> ("New Immigration," 2009)

### 8. A Personal Communication

Cite letters, memos, telephone conversations, personal interviews, emails, messages from electronic bulletin boards, and so on only in the text of your paper—*not* in the reference list.

> (R. Takaki, personal communication, October 17, 2009)

### 9. An Indirect Source

> Cogan and Howe offer very different interpretations of the problem (cited in Swenson, 2009).

### 10. A Specific Part of a Source

Use abbreviations for the words *page* (**p.**), and *pages* (**pp.**), but spell out *chapter* and *section*.

> These theories have an interesting history (Lee, 2010, chapter 2).

## 11. An Electronic Source

For an electronic source that does not show page numbers, use the paragraph number preceded by the abbreviation **para.**

> Conversation at the dinner table is an example of a family
>
> ritual (Kulp, 2010, para. 3).

In the case of an electronic source that has neither page nor paragraph numbers, cite both the heading in the source and the number of the paragraph following the heading in which the material is located.

> Healthy eating is a never-ending series of free choices
>
> (Shapiro, 2008, Introduction section, para. 2).

If the source has no headings, you may not be able to specify an exact location.

## 12. Two or More Works within the Same Parenthetical Reference

List works by different authors in alphabetical order, separated by semicolons.

> This theory is supported by several studies (Barson & Roth,
>
> 1995; Rose, 2001; Tedesco, 2010).

List two or more works by the same author or authors in order of date of publication (separated by commas), with the earliest date first.

> This theory is supported by several studies (Rhodes &
>
> Dollek, 2008, 2009, 2010).

For two or more works by the same author published in the same year, designate the work whose title comes first alphabetically *a*, the one whose title comes next *b*, and so on; repeat the year in each citation.

> This theory is supported by several studies (Shapiro, 2009a,
>
> 2009b).

## 13. A Table

If you use a table from a source, give credit to the author in a note at the bottom of the table. Do not include this information in the reference list.

> *Note.* From "Predictors of Employment and Earnings Among
>
> JOBS Participants," by P. A. Neenan and D. K. Orthner,
>
> 1996, *Social Work Research, 20*(4), p. 233.

## ❷ Reference List

The **reference list** gives the publication information for all the sources you cite. It should appear at the end of your paper on a new numbered page titled **References.** Entries in the reference list should be arranged alphabetically. Double-space within and between reference list entries. The first line of each entry should start at the left margin, with the second and subsequent lines indented one-half inch. (**See 12b** for full manuscript guidelines.)

### APA PRINT SOURCES Entries for Articles

Article citations include the author's name (last name first); the date of publication (in parentheses); the title of the article; the title of the periodical (italicized); the volume number (italicized); the issue number, if any (in parentheses); and the inclusive page numbers (including all digits). Figure 12.1 on page 166 shows where you can find this information.

Capitalize the first word of the article's title and subtitle as well as any proper nouns. Do not underline or italicize the title of the article or enclose it in quotation marks. Give the periodical title in full, and capitalize all words except articles, prepositions, and conjunctions of fewer than four letters. Use **p.** or **pp.** when referring to page numbers in newspapers, but omit this abbreviation when referring to page numbers in journals and popular magazines.

### *Articles in Scholarly Journals*

1. **An Article in a Scholarly Journal with Continuous Pagination throughout an Annual Volume**

   Miller, W. (1969). Violent crimes in city gangs. *Journal of Social Issues, 27,* 581–593.

2. **An Article in a Scholarly Journal with Separate Pagination in Each Issue**

   Williams, S., & Cohen, L. R. (2004). Child stress in early learning situations. *American Psychologist, 21*(10), 1–28.

*Note:* Do not leave a space between the volume and issue numbers.

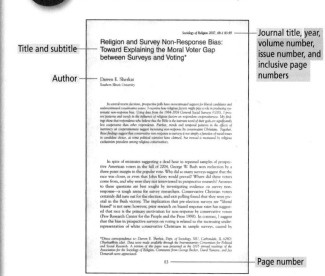

FIGURE 12.1 First page of an article showing the location of the information needed for documentation. © Association for the Sociology of Religion. Used by permission of Association for the Sociology of Religion, Inc.

| Author's last name | Initials | Year of publication (in parentheses) | | Title of article (only first word of title and subtitle capitalized) |

Sherkat, D. E. (2007). Religion and survey non-response bias: Toward explaining the moral voter gap between surveys and voting. *Sociology of Religion, 68*(1), 83–95.

Title of periodical (italicized; all major words captalized) — Volume number (italicized) — Issue number (in parentheses) — Inclusive page numbers (include all digits)

### 3. A Book Review in a Scholarly Journal (Unsigned)

A review with no author should be listed by title, followed by a description of the reviewed work in brackets.

Coming of age and joining the cult of thinness [Review of the book *The cult of thinness,* by Sharlene Nagy Hesse-Biber]. (2008, June). *Psychology of Women Quarterly, 32*(2), 221–222.

### *Articles in Magazines and Newspapers*

### 4. A Magazine Article

McCurdy, H. G. (2003, June). Brain mechanisms and intelligence. *Psychology Today, 46,* 61–63.

## 5. A Newspaper Article

If an article appears on nonconsecutive pages, give all page numbers, separated by commas (for example, **A1, A14**). If the article appears on consecutive pages, indicate the full range of pages (for example, **A7–A9**).

James, W. R. (1993, November 16). The uninsured and

health care. *Wall Street Journal,* pp. A1, A14.

## 6. A Newspaper Editorial (Unsigned)

An editorial with no author should be listed by title, followed by the label **Editorial** in brackets.

The plight of the underinsured [Editorial]. (2008, June 12).

*The New York Times,* p. A30.

## 7. A Letter to the Editor of a Newspaper

Williams, P. (2006, July 19). Self-fulfilling stereotypes [Letter

to the editor]. *Los Angeles Times,* p. A22.

## APA PRINT SOURCES Entries for Books

Book citations include the author's name (last name first); the year of publication (in parentheses); the book title (italicized); and publication information. Figures 12.2 and 12.3 on page 168 show where you can find this information.

Capitalize only the first word of the title and subtitle and any proper nouns. Include any additional necessary information—edition, report number, or volume number, for example—in parentheses after the title. In the publication information, write out in full the names of associations, corporations, and university presses. Include the words **Book** and **Press**, but do not include terms such as **Publishers**, **Co.,** or **Inc.**

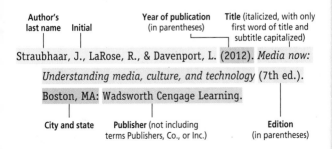

Author's last name | Initial      Year of publication (in parentheses)      Title (italicized, with only first word of title and subtitle capitalized)

Straubhaar, J., LaRose, R., & Davenport, L. (2012). *Media now:*

*Understanding media, culture, and technology* (7th ed.).

Boston, MA: Wadsworth Cengage Learning.

City and state      Publisher (not including terms Publishers, Co., or Inc.)      Edition (in parentheses)

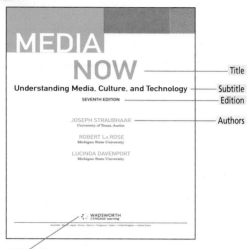

FIGURE 12.2 Title page from a book showing the location of the information needed for documentation.
© Cengage Learning, 2012; reprinted with permission.

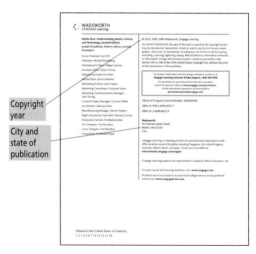

FIGURE 12.3 Copyright page from a book showing the location of the information needed for documentation.
© Cengage Learning, 2012; reprinted with permission.

## Authors

### 8. A Book with One Author

Maslow, A. H. (1974). *Toward a psychology of being.*

Princeton, NJ: Van Nostrand.

### 9. A Book with More Than One Author

List up to seven authors by last name and initials, using an ampersand (&) to connect the last two names. For more than seven authors, insert an ellipsis (three spaced periods) and add the last author's name.

Wolfinger, D., Knable, P., Richards, H. L., & Silberger, R. (2007). *The chronically unemployed*. New York, NY: Berman Press.

### 10. A Book with No Listed Author or Editor

*Teaching in a wired classroom*. (2012). Philadelphia, PA: Drexel Press.

### 11. A Book with a Corporate Author

When the author and the publisher are the same, include the word **Author** at the end of the citation instead of repeating the publisher's name.

League of Women Voters of the United States. (2008). *Local league handbook*. Washington, DC: Author.

### 12. An Edited Book

Lewin, K., Lippitt, R., & White, R. K. (Eds.). (1985). *Social learning and imitation*. New York, NY: Basic Books.

## *Editions, Multivolume Works, and Forewords*

### 13. A Work in Several Volumes

Jones, P. R., & Williams, T. C. (Eds.). (1990–1993). *Handbook of therapy* (Vols. 1–2). Princeton, NJ: Princeton University Press.

### 14. The Foreword, Preface, or Afterword of a Book

Taylor, T. (1979). Preface. In B. B. Ferencz, *Less than slaves* (pp. ii–ix). Cambridge, MA: Harvard University Press.

## *Parts of Books*

### 15. A Selection from an Anthology

Give inclusive page numbers preceded by **pp.** (in parentheses) after the title of the anthology. The title of the selection is not enclosed in quotation marks.

Lorde, A. (1984). Age, race, and class. In P. S. Rothenberg (Ed.), *Racism and sexism: An integrated study* (pp. 352–360). New York, NY: St. Martin's Press.

*Note:* If you cite two or more selections from the same anthology, give the full citation for the anthology in each entry.

### 16. An Article in a Reference Book

Edwards, P. (Ed.). (2006). Determinism. In *The encyclopedia of philosophy* (Vol. 2, pp. 359–373). New York, NY: Macmillan.

## Government and Technical Reports

### 17. A Government Report

U.S. Department of Health and Human Services, National Institutes of Health, National Institute of Mental Health. (2007). *Motion pictures and violence: A summary report of research* (DHHS Publication No. ADM 91-22187). Washington, DC: Government Printing Office.

### 18. A Technical Report

Attali, Y., & Powers, D. (2008). *Effect of immediate feedback and revision on psychometric properties of open-ended GRE® subject test items* (ETS GRE Board Research Report No. 04-05). Princeton, NJ: Educational Testing Service.

## APA ENTRIES FOR MISCELLANEOUS PRINT SOURCES

## Letters

### 19. A Personal Letter

References to unpublished personal letters, like references to all other personal communications, should be included only in the text of the paper, not in the reference list.

### 20. A Published Letter

Joyce, J. (1931). Letter to Louis Gillet. In Richard Ellmann, *James Joyce* (p. 631). New York, NY: Oxford University Press.

## APA ENTRIES FOR OTHER SOURCES

## Television Broadcasts, Films, CDs, Audiocassette Recordings, Interviews, and Computer Software

### 21. A Television Broadcast

Murphy, J. (Executive Producer). (2006, March 4). *The CBS evening news* [Television broadcast]. New York, NY: Columbia Broadcasting Service.

## 22. A Television Series

Sorkin, A., Schlamme, T., & Wells, J. (Executive Producers).
(2002). *The west wing* [Television series]. Los Angeles,
CA: Warner Bros. Television.

## 23. A Film

Spielberg, S. (Director). (1994). *Schindler's list* [Motion
picture]. United States: Universal.

## 24. A CD Recording

Marley, B. (1977). Waiting in vain. On *Exodus* [CD]. New York,
NY: Island Records.

## 25. An Audiocassette Recording

Skinner, B. F. (Speaker). (1972). *Skinner on Skinnerism*
[Cassette recording]. Hollywood, CA: Center for
Cassette Studies.

## 26. A Recorded Interview

Bartel, S. S. (1978, November 5). Interview by L. Clark
[Tape recording]. Billy Graham Center, Wheaton College.
BGC Archives, Wheaton, IL.

## 27. A Transcription of a Recorded Interview

Berry, D. W. (1986, February 14). *Interview with Donald
Wesley Berry—Collection 325*. Billy Graham Center,
Wheaton College. BGC Archives, Wheaton, IL.

## 28. Computer Software

Sharp, S. (2009). Career Selection Tests (Version 7.0)
[Software]. Chico, CA: Avocation Software.

**APA ELECTRONIC SOURCES** Entries for Sources
from Internet Sites

APA guidelines for documenting electronic sources focus
on Web sources, which often do not include all the bibliographic information that print sources do. For example,
Web sources may not include page numbers or a place of
publication. At a minimum, a Web citation should have a
title, a date (the date of publication, update, or retrieval),
and a Digital Object Identifier (DOI) (when available) or

an electronic address (URL). If possible, also include the author(s) of a source. Figure 12.4 shows where you can find this information.

When you need to divide a URL at the end of a line, break it after a double slash or before most other punctuation (do not add a hyphen). Do not add a period at the end of the URL.

Author's last name   Initials        Year of publication (in parentheses)   Title of article (only first word of title and subtitle as well as proper nouns capitalized)

Yip, T., Gee, G. C., & Takeuchi, D. T. (2008). Racial discrimination and psychological distress: The impact of ethnic identity and age among immigrant and United States-born Asian adults. *Developmental Psychology, 44*(3), 787–800. doi:10.1037 /0012-1649.44.3.787

Title of periodical (italicized)    Volume number (italicized)    Issue number (in parentheses)    Inclusive page numbers (include all digits)

DOI (without period at end)

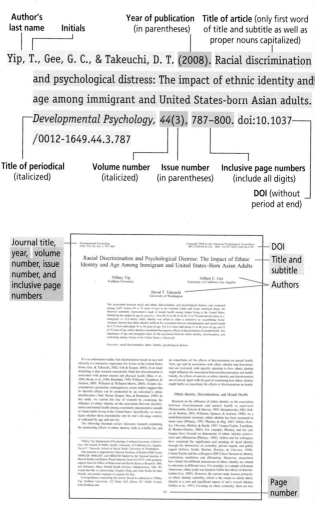

FIGURE 12.4 Part of an online article showing the location of the information needed for documentation. © 2008 by the American Psychological Association. Reproduced by permission. The use of this information does not imply endorsement by the publisher.

## Internet-Specific Sources

### 29. An Internet Article Based on a Print Source

If the article has a DOI, you do not need to include the retrieval date or the URL. Always include the volume number
(italicized) and the issue number (in parentheses, if available).

> Rutledge, P. C., Park, A., & Sher, K. J. (2008). 21st birthday
>
> drinking: Extremely extreme. *Journal of Consulting*
>
> *and Clinical Psychology, 76*(3), 511–516. doi:10.1037
>
> /0022-006X.76.3.511

### 30. An Article in an Internet-Only Journal

If the article does not have a DOI, include the URL. Always
include the URL (when available) for the archived version
of the article. If you accessed the article through an online
database, include the URL for the home page of the journal.
(If a single URL links to multiple articles, include the URL
for the journal's home page.) No retrieval date is needed
for content that is not likely to be changed or updated—for
example, a journal article or a book.

> Hill, S. A., & Laugharne, R. (2006). Patient choice survey in
>
> general adult psychiatry. *Psychiatry On-Line*. Retrieved
>
> from http://www.priory.co.uk/psych.htm

### 31. A Document from a University Web Site

> Beck, S. E. (2008, April 3). *The good, the bad & the ugly:*
>
> *Or, why it's a good idea to evaluate web sources.*
>
> Retrieved July 7, 2008, from New Mexico State
>
> University Library website: http://lib.nmsu.edu
>
> /instruction/evalcrit.html

### 32. A Web Document (No Author Identified, No Date)

A document with no author or date should be listed by
title, followed by the abbreviation **n.d.** (for "no date"), the
retrieval date, and the URL.

> *The stratocaster appreciation page.* (n.d.). Retrieved July 27,
>
> 2008, from http://members.tripod.com/~AFH

### 33. An Email

As with all other personal communications, citations for email
should be included only in the text of your paper, not in the
reference list.

### 34. A Posting to a Newsgroup

List the author's full name—or, if that is not available, the author's screen name. In brackets after the title, provide information that will help readers access the posting.

Silva, T. (2007, March 9). Severe stress can damage a

child's brain [Online forum comment]. Retrieved from

http://groups.google.com/group/sci.psychology

.psychotherapy.moderated

### 35. A Posting to a Blog

Jamie. (2010, June 26). Re: Trying to lose 50 million pounds

[Web log comment]. Retrieved from http://blogs.wsj

.com/numbersguy

### 36. A Searchable Database

Include the database name only if the material you are citing is obscure, out of print, or otherwise difficult to locate. No retrieval date is needed.

Murphy, M. E. (1940, December 15). When war comes. *Vital*

*Speeches of the Day, 7*(5), 139–144. Retrieved from

http://www.vsotd.com

## Abstracts and Newspaper Articles

### 37. An Abstract

Qiong, L. (2008, July). After the quake: Psychological

treatment following the disaster. *China Today, 57*(7),

18–21. Abstract retrieved from http://www.chinatoday

.com.cn/ctenglish/index.htm

### 38. An Article in a Daily Newspaper

Fountain, H. (2008, July 1). In sleep, we are birds of a

feather. *The New York Times.* Retrieved from http://

www.nytimes.com

## ③ Content Footnotes

APA format permits content notes, indicated by **superscripts** in the text. The notes are listed on a separate numbered page, titled **Footnotes,** after the reference list and before any appendices. Double-space all notes, indenting the first line of each note one-half inch and beginning subsequent lines flush left.

Number the notes with superscripts that correspond to the numbers in your text.

## 12b APA-Style Manuscript Guidelines

Social science papers label sections with headings. Sections may include an introduction (untitled), followed by headings like **Background, Method, Results,** and **Conclusion.** Each section of a social science paper is a complete unit with a beginning and an end so that it can be read separately and still make sense out of context. The body of the paper may include charts, graphs, maps, photographs, flowcharts, or tables.

---

**CHECKLIST**

### Typing Your Paper

When you type your paper, use the student paper in **12c** as your model.

❏ Leave one-inch margins at the top and bottom and on both sides. Double-space your paper throughout.

❏ Indent the first line of every paragraph and the first line of every content footnote one-half inch from the left-hand margin.

❏ Set off a **long quotation** (more than forty words) in a block format by indenting the entire quotation one-half inch from the left-hand margin. Do not indent the first line further.

❏ Number all pages consecutively. Each page should include a **page header** (an abbreviated title and a page number) typed one-half inch from the top of the page. Type the page header flush left and the page number flush right.

❏ Center major headings, and type them with uppercase and lowercase letters. Place minor headings flush left, typed with uppercase and lowercase letters. Use boldface for both major and minor headings. *See 40b*

❏ Format items in a series as a numbered list. *See 40c*

❏ Arrange the pages of the paper in the following order:

  ❏ **Title page** (page 1) with a running head (in all uppercase letters), page number, title, your name, and the name of your school. (Your instructor may require additional information.)

  ❏ **Abstract and keywords** (page 2)

  ❏ **Text of paper** (beginning on page 3)

  ❏ **Reference list** (new page)

  ❏ **Content footnotes** (new page)

  ❏ **Appendices** (start each appendix on a new page)

❏ Citations should follow APA documentation style. *See 12a*

**CHECKLIST**

## Using Visuals

APA style distinguishes between two types of visuals: **tables** and **figures** (charts, graphs, photographs, and diagrams). In manuscripts not intended for publication, tables and figures are included in the text. A short table or figure should appear on the page where it is discussed; a long table or figure should be placed on a separate page just after the page where it is discussed.

### Tables

Number all **tables** consecutively. Each table should have a *label* and a *title*.

❑ The **label** consists of the word **Table** (not in italics), along with an arabic numeral, typed flush left above the table.

❑ Double-space and type a brief explanatory **title** for each table (in italics) flush left below the label. Capitalize the first letters of principal words of the title.

Table 7

*Frequency of Negative Responses of Dorm Students to*

*Questions Concerning Alcohol Consumption*

### Figures

Number all **figures** consecutively. Each figure should have a *label* and a *caption*.

❑ The **label** consists of the word **Figure** (typed flush left below the figure) followed by the figure number (both in italics).

❑ The **caption** explains the figure and serves as a title. Double-space the caption, but do not italicize it. Capitalize only the first word and any proper nouns, and end the caption with a period. The caption follows the label (on the same line).

*Figure 1.* Duration of responses measured in seconds.

*Note:* If you use a table or figure from an outside source, include full source information in a note at the bottom of the table or figure. This information does not appear in your reference list.

**CHECKLIST**

## Preparing the APA Reference List

When typing your reference list, follow these guidelines:

❑ Begin the reference list on a new page after the last page of text, numbered as the next page of the paper.

❑ Center the title **References** at the top of the page.

❏ List the items in the reference list alphabetically (with author's last name first).

❏ Type the first line of each entry at the left margin. Indent subsequent lines one-half inch.

❏ Separate the major divisions of each entry with a period and one space.

❏ Double-space the reference list within and between entries.

## Close-Up   ARRANGING ENTRIES IN THE APA REFERENCE LIST

- Single-author entries precede multiple-author entries that begin with the same name.

   Field, S. (1987).

   Field, S., & Levitt, M. P. (1984).

- Entries by the same author or authors are arranged according to date of publication, starting with the earliest date.

   Ruthenberg, H., & Rubin, R. (1985).

   Ruthenberg, H., & Rubin, R. (1987).

- Entries with the same author or authors and date of publication are arranged alphabetically according to title. Lowercase letters (*a*, *b*, *c*, and so on) that indicate the order of publication are placed within parentheses.

   Wolk, E. M. (1996a). Analysis . . .

   Wolk, E. M. (1996b). Hormonal . . .

## 12c   Model APA-Style Research Paper

The following student paper, "Sleep Deprivation in College Students," uses APA documentation style. It includes a title page, an abstract, a reference list, a table, and a bar graph. The Web citations in this student paper do not have DOIs, so URLs have been provided instead.

$\uparrow_{1/2''}$

Running head: SLEEP DEPRIVATION                    1

Title

Sleep Deprivation in College Students

Your name

Andrew J. Neale

School

University of Texas

Course title

Psychology 215, Section 4

Instructor's
name

Dr. Reiss

Date

April 12, 2013

Center heading → Abstract

A survey was conducted of 50 first-year college students in an introductory biology class. The survey consisted of five questions regarding the causes and results of sleep deprivation and specifically addressed the students' study methods and the grades they received on the fall midterm. The study's hypothesis was that although students believe that forgoing sleep to study will yield better grades, sleep deprivation may actually cause a decrease in performance. The study concluded that while only 43% of the students who received either an A or a B on the fall midterm deprived themselves of sleep in order to cram for the test, 90% of those who received a C or a D were sleep deprived.

*Keywords:* sleep disorders, sleep deprivation, grade performance, grades and sleep, forgoing sleep

Abstract typed as a single paragraph in block format (not indented)

An optional list of keywords helps readers find your work in databases. Check with your instructor to see if this list is required.

SLEEP DEPRIVATION                    3

Sleep Deprivation in College Students

Indent ½" → For many college students, sleep is a luxury
they feel they cannot afford. Bombarded with
Double-space tests and assignments and limited by a 24-hour day,
students often attempt to make up time by doing
without sleep. Unfortunately, students may actually
hurt their academic performance by failing to get
Thesis statement enough sleep. According to several psychological
and medical studies, sleep deprivation can lead to
memory loss and health problems, both of which
can harm a student's academic performance.

**Background**

Sleep is often overlooked as an essential
part of a healthy lifestyle. Each day, millions of
Americans wake up without having gotten enough
sleep. This fact indicates that for many people,
sleep is viewed as a luxury rather than a necessity.
As National Sleep Foundation Executive Director
Richard L. Gelula observes, "Some of the problems
we face as a society—from road rage to obesity—
may be linked to lack of sleep or poor sleep"
(National Sleep Foundation, 2002, para. 3). In fact,
according to the National Sleep Foundation, sleep
deprivation causes "impairment in mood, attention
and memory, behavior control and quality of
life; lower academic performance and a decreased
motivation to learn; and health-related effects
including increased risk of weight-gain, lack of
exercise and use of stimulants" (2010, para. 5).

Sleep deprivation is particularly common
among college students, many of whom have

Full ti
(cente

Introdu

Heading
(centered and
boldfaced)

Literature
review
(paras. 2–7)
|
Quotation
requires its
own docu-
mentation
and a page
number (or
a paragraph
number for
Internet
sources)

1"

1"

1"

SLEEP DEPRIVATION                                    4

busy lives and are required to absorb a great deal of material before their exams. It is common for college students to take a quick nap between classes or fall asleep while studying in the library because they are sleep deprived. Approximately 44% of young adults experience daytime sleepiness at least a few days a month (National Sleep Foundation, 2002, para. 6). In particular, many students are sleep deprived on the day of an exam because they stayed up all night studying. These students believe that if they read and review immediately before taking a test—even though this usually means losing sleep—they will remember more information and thus get better grades. However, this is not the case.

A study conducted by professors Mary Carskadon at Brown University in Providence, Rhode Island, and Amy Wolfson at the College of the Holy Cross in Worcester, Massachusetts, showed that high school students who got adequate sleep were more likely to do well in their classes (Carpenter, 2001). According to this study, students who went to bed early on both weeknights and weekends earned mainly A's and B's. The students who received D's and F's averaged about 35 minutes less sleep per day than the high achievers (cited in Carpenter, 2001). The results of this study suggest that sleep is associated with high academic achievement.

Once students reach college, however, many believe that sleep is a luxury they can do without. For example, students believe that if they use the time they would normally sleep to study, they

Student uses past tense when discussing other researchers' studies

*Cited in* indicates an indirect source

SLEEP DEPRIVATION                    5

will do better on exams. A survey of 144 undergraduate students in introductory psychology classes disproved this assumption. According to this study, "long sleepers," those individuals who slept 9 or more hours out of a 24-hour day, had significantly higher grade point averages (GPAs) than "short sleepers," individuals who slept less than 7 hours out of a 24-hour day. Therefore, contrary to the belief of many college students, more sleep is often associated with a high GPA (Kelly, Kelly, & Clanton, 2001).

Many students believe that sleep deprivation is not the cause of their poor performance, but rather that a host of other factors are to blame. A study in the *Journal of American College Health* tested the effect that several factors have on a student's performance in school, as measured by students' GPAs. Some of the factors considered were exercise, sleep, nutritional habits, social support, time management techniques, stress management techniques, and spiritual health (Trockel, Barnes, & Egget, 2000). The most significant correlation discovered in the study was between GPA and the sleep habits of students. Sleep deprivation had a more negative impact on GPAs than any other factor (Trockel et al., 2000).

First reference includes all three authors; *et al.* replaces second and third authors in subsequent reference in same paragraph

Despite these findings, many students continue to believe that they will be able to remember more material if they do not sleep before an exam. They fear that sleeping will interfere with their ability to retain information.

SLEEP DEPRIVATION 6

Pilcher and Walters (1997), however, showed
that sleep deprivation actually impaired learning
skills. In this study, one group of students was
sleep deprived, while the other got 8 hours of
sleep before the exam. The students in each
group estimated how well they had performed on
the exam. The students who were sleep deprived
believed their performance on the test was better
than did those who were not sleep deprived, but
actually the performance of the sleep-deprived
students was significantly worse than that of
those who got 8 hours of sleep prior to the
test (Pilcher & Walters, 1997, cited in Bubolz,
Brown, & Soper, 2001). This study supports the
hypothesis that sleep deprivation harms cognitive
performance.

A survey of students in an introductory
biology class at the University of Texas, which
demonstrated the effects of sleep deprivation
on academic performance, also supported the
hypothesis that despite students' beliefs, forgoing
sleep does not lead to better test scores.

Student
uses past
tense when
discussing his
own research
study

### Method

To determine the causes and results of sleep
deprivation, a study of the relationship between
sleep and test performance was conducted. Fifty
first-year college students in an introductory
biology class were surveyed, and their performance
on the fall midterm was analyzed.

Each student was asked to complete a survey
consisting of the following five questions about

SLEEP DEPRIVATION                                    7

their sleep patterns and their performance on the fall midterm:

*Numbered list is indented 1/2" and set in block format*

1. Do you regularly deprive yourself of sleep when studying for an exam?

2. Did you deprive yourself of sleep when studying for the fall midterm?

3. What was your grade on the exam?

4. Do you feel your performance was helped or harmed by the amount of sleep you had?

5. Will you deprive yourself of sleep when you study for the final exam?

To maintain confidentiality, the students were asked not to put their names on the survey. Also, to determine whether the students answered question 3 truthfully, the group grade distribution from the surveys was compared to the number of A's, B's, C's, and D's shown in the instructor's record of the test results. The two frequency distributions were identical.

### Results

Analysis of the survey data indicated a significant difference between the grades of students who were sleep deprived and the grades of those who were not. The results of the survey

*Table 1 introduced*

are presented in Table 1.

The grades in the class were curved so that out of 50 students, 10 received A's, 20 received B's, 10 received C's, and 10 received D's. For the purposes of this survey, an A or B on the exam indicates that the student performed well.

A grade of C or D on the exam is considered a poor grade.

Table 1

*Results of Survey of Students in University of Texas Introduction to Biology Class Examining the Relationship between Sleep Deprivation and Academic Performance*

Table placed on page where it is discussed

| Grade totals | Sleep deprived | Not sleep deprived | Usually sleep deprived | Improved | Harmed | Continue sleep deprivation? |
|---|---|---|---|---|---|---|
| A = 10 | 4 | 6 | 1 | 4 | 0 | 4 |
| B = 20 | 9 | 11 | 8 | 8 | 1 | 8 |
| C = 10 | 10 | 0 | 6 | 5 | 4 | 7 |
| D = 10 | 8 | 2 | 2 | 1 | 3 | 2 |
| Total | 31 | 19 | 17 | 18 | 8 | 21 |

Table created by student; no documentation necessary

Of the 50 students in the class, 31 (or 62%) said they deprived themselves of sleep when studying for the fall midterm. Of these students, 17 (or 34% of the class) reported that they regularly deprive themselves of sleep before an exam.

Statistical findings in table discussed

Of the 31 students who said they deprived themselves of sleep when studying for the fall midterm, only 4 earned A's, and the majority of the A's in the class were received by those students who were not sleep deprived. Even more significant was the fact that of the 4 students who were sleep deprived and got A's, only one student claimed to usually be sleep deprived on the day of an exam. Thus, assuming the students who earn A's in a class do well in general, it is

SLEEP DEPRIVATION                                    9

possible that sleep deprivation did not help or harm these students' grades. Not surprisingly, of the 4 students who received A's and were sleep deprived, all said they would continue this behavior pattern.

The majority of those who deprived themselves of sleep received B's and C's on the exam. A total of 20 students earned a grade of B on the exam. Of those students, only 9, or 18% of the class, said they were deprived of sleep when they took the test.

Students who said they were sleep deprived when they took the exam received the majority of the poor grades. Ten students got C's on the midterm, and of these 10 students, 100% said they were sleep deprived when they took the test. Of the 10 students (20% of the class) who got D's, 8 said they were sleep deprived. Figure 1 shows the significant relationship that was found between poor grades on the exam and sleep deprivation.

Figure 1 introduced

### Conclusion

For many students, sleep is viewed as a luxury rather than as a necessity. Particularly during exam periods, students use the hours in which they would normally sleep to study. However, this behavior does not seem to be effective. The survey discussed here reveals a definite correlation between sleep deprivation and lower exam scores. In fact, the majority of students who performed well on the exam,

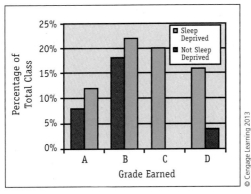

Figure placed
as close as
possible to
discussion in
paper

© Cengage Learning 2013

*Figure 1.* Results of a survey of students in a
University of Texas Introduction to Biology
class, examining the relationship between sleep
deprivation and academic performance.

Label and
caption

(No source
information
needed for
graph based
on student's
original data)

earning either A's or B's, were not deprived of
sleep. Therefore, students who choose studying
over sleep should consider that sleep deprivation
may actually lead to impaired academic
performance.

SLEEP DEPRIVATION 11

References

Bubolz, W., Brown, F., & Soper, B. (2001). Sleep habits and patterns of college students: A preliminary study. *Journal of American College Health, 50*, 131–135.

Carpenter, S. (2001). Sleep deprivation may be undermining teen health. *Monitor on Psychology, 32*(9). Retrieved from http://www.apa.org/monitor/oct01/sleepteen.html

Kelly, W. E., Kelly, K. E., & Clanton, R. C. (2001). The relationship between sleep length and grade-point average among college students. *College Student Journal, 35*(1), 84–90.

National Sleep Foundation. (2002, April 2). *Epidemic of daytime sleepiness linked to increased feelings of anger, stress and pessimism*. Retrieved from http://www.sleepfoundation.org

National Sleep Foundation. (2010, July 6). *Later school start times improved adolescent alertness*. Retrieved from http://www.sleepfoundation.org

Trockel, M., Barnes, M., & Egget, D. (2000). Health-related variables and academic performance among first-year college students: Implications for sleep and other behaviors. *Journal of American College Health, 49*, 125–131.

Center heading

Indent ½"

Double-space

Entries listed in alphabetical order

URL is provided for Web citation that does not have a DOI

# Directory of Chicago-Style Endnotes and Bibliography Entries

## PRINT SOURCES: *Entries for Articles*
### Articles in Scholarly Journals

### Articles in Magazines and Newspapers

## PRINT SOURCES: *Entries for Books*
### Authors and Editors

### Editions and Multivolume Works

### Parts of Books

### Religious Works

## ENTRIES FOR MISCELLANEOUS PRINT AND NONPRINT SOURCES

## ELECTRONIC SOURCES: *Entries for Sources from Online Publications*

## ELECTRONIC SOURCES: *Entries for Sources from an Online Database*

## ELECTRONIC SOURCES: *Entries for Sources from Internet Sites*

# CHAPTER 13

# Chicago Documentation Style

## 13a Using Chicago Humanities Style

*The Chicago Manual of Style* includes two citation methods, a notes-bibliography style used in history, in the humanities, and in some social science disciplines, and an author-date style used in the sciences and social sciences. **Chicago humanities style**\* has two parts: *notes at the end of the paper* (**endnotes**) and usually a *list of bibliographic citations* (**bibliography**). (Chicago style encourages the use of endnotes, but allows the use of footnotes at the bottom of the page.)

### 1 Endnotes and Footnotes

The notes format calls for a **superscript** (raised numeral) in the text after source material you have either quoted or referred to. This numeral, placed after all punctuation marks except dashes, corresponds to the numeral that precedes the endnote or footnote.

### Endnote and Footnote Format: Chicago Style

#### In the Text

By November of 1942, the Allies had proof that the Nazis were engaged in the systematic killing of Jews.[1]

#### In the Note

1. David S. Wyman, *The Abandonment of the Jews: America and the Holocaust 1941–1945* (New York: Pantheon Books, 1984), 65.

---

\* Chicago humanities style follows the guidelines set in *The Chicago Manual of Style*, 16th ed. Chicago: University of Chicago Press, 2010. The manuscript guidelines and sample research paper at the end of this chapter follow guidelines set in Kate L. Turabian's *A Manual for Writers of Research Papers, Theses, and Dissertations*, 7th ed. Chicago: University of Chicago Press, 2007. Turabian style, which is based on Chicago style, addresses formatting concerns specific to college writers.

## Close-Up SUBSEQUENT REFERENCES TO THE SAME WORK

In a paper with no bibliography, use the full citation in the first note for a work; in subsequent references to the same work, list only the author's last name, a comma, an abbreviated title, another comma, and a page number. In a paper with a bibliography, you may use the short form for all notes.

**First Note on Espinoza**

    1. J. M. Espinoza. *The First Expedition of Vargas in New Mexico, 1692* (Albuquerque: University of New Mexico Press, 1949), 10–12.

**Subsequent Note**

    5. Espinoza, *First Expedition,* 29.

*Note:* You may use the abbreviation *ibid.* ("in the same place") for subsequent references to the same work as long as there are no intervening references. *Ibid.* takes the place of the author's name, the work's title, and the page number if they are the same as those in the previous note. If the page number is different, cite *Ibid.* and the page number.

**First Note on Espinoza**

    1. J. M. Espinoza. *The First Expedition of Vargas in New Mexico, 1692* (Albuquerque: University of New Mexico Press, 1949), 10–12.

**Next Note**

    2. Ibid., 23.

### 2 Bibliography

The **bibliography** provides complete publication information for the works consulted. Bibliography entries are arranged alphabetically by the author's last name or the first major word of the title (if there is no author). Single-space within an entry; double-space between entries.

# Sample Chicago-Style Endnotes and Bibliography Entries

**CHICAGO** PRINT SOURCES Entries for Articles

Article citations generally include the name of the author (last name first); the title of the article (in quotation marks); the title of the periodical (in italics); the volume number, issue number, and date; and the page reference. Months are spelled out in full, not abbreviated.

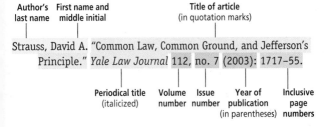

Author's last name | First name and middle initial | Title of article (in quotation marks)

Strauss, David A. "Common Law, Common Ground, and Jefferson's Principle." *Yale Law Journal* 112, no. 7 (2003): 1717–55.

Periodical title (italicized) | Volume number | Issue number | Year of publication (in parentheses) | Inclusive page numbers

## *Articles in Scholarly Journals*

1. **An Article in a Scholarly Journal with Continuous Pagination throughout an Annual Volume**

*Endnote*

> 1. John Huntington, "Science Fiction and the Future," *College English* 37 (Fall 1975): 341.

*Bibliography*

> Huntington, John. "Science Fiction and the Future." *College English* 37 (Fall 1975): 340–58.

2. **An Article in a Scholarly Journal with Separate Pagination in Each Issue**

*Endnote*

> 2. R. G. Sipes, "War, Sports, and Aggression: An Empirical Test of Two Rival Theories," *American Anthropologist* 4, no. 2 (1973): 80.

*Bibliography*

> Sipes, R. G. "War, Sports, and Aggression: An Empirical Test of Two Rival Theories." *American Anthropologist* 4, no. 2 (1973): 65–84.

*Articles in Magazines and Newspapers*

### 3. An Article in a Weekly Magazine (Signed/Unsigned)
*Endnote*

Signed

> 3. Pico Iyer, "A Mum for All Seasons," *Time,* April 8, 2002, 51.

Unsigned

> 3. "Burst Bubble," *New Scientist,* July 27, 2002, 24.

Although both endnotes above specify page numbers, the corresponding bibliography entries include page numbers only when the pages are consecutive (as in the second example that follows).

### *Bibliography*

Signed

> Iyer, Pico. "A Mum for All Seasons." *Time,* April 8, 2002.

Unsigned

> "Burst Bubble." *New Scientist,* July 27, 2002, 24–25.

### 4. An Article in a Monthly Magazine (Signed)
*Endnote*

> 4. Tad Suzuki, "Reflecting Light on Photo Realism," *American Artist*, March 2002, 47.

### *Bibliography*

> Suzuki, Tad. "Reflecting Light on Photo Realism." *American Artist,* March 2002, 46–51.

### 5. An Article in a Monthly Magazine (Unsigned)
*Endnote*

> 5. "Repowering the U.S. with Clean Energy Development," *BioCycle,* July 2002, 14.

### *Bibliography*

> "Repowering the U.S. with Clean Energy Development." *BioCycle,* July 2002, 14.

### 6. An Article in a Newspaper (Signed)
*Endnote*

Because the pagination of newspapers can change from edition to edition, Chicago style recommends not giving page numbers for newspaper articles.

6. Francis X. Clines, "Civil War Relics Draw Visitors, and Con Artists," *New York Times,* August 4, 2002, national edition.

### Bibliography

Clines, Francis X. "Civil War Relics Draw Visitors, and Con Artists." *New York Times,* August 4, 2002, national edition.

### 7. An Article in a Newspaper (Unsigned)
### Endnote

7. "Feds Lead Way in Long-Term Care," *Atlanta Journal-Constitution,* July 21, 2002, sec. E.

**Note:** Omit the initial article the from the newspaper's title, but include a city name in the title, even if it is not part of the actual title.

If you provide a note or mention the name of the newspaper and publication date in your text, you do not need to list unsigned articles or other newspaper items in your bibliography.

### 8. A Letter to the Editor of a Newspaper
### Endnote

8. Arnold Stieber, letter to the editor, *Seattle Times,* July 4, 2009.

### Bibliography

Stieber, Arnold. Letter to the editor. *Seattle Times,* July 4, 2009.

### 9. A Book Review in a Newspaper
### Endnote

9. Janet Maslin, "The Real Lincoln Bedroom: Love in a Time of Strife," review of *The Lincolns: Portrait of a Marriage,* by Daniel Mark Epstein, *New York Times*, July 3, 2008.

### Bibliography

Maslin, Janet. "The Real Lincoln Bedroom: Love in a Time of Strife." Review of *The Lincolns: Portrait of a Marriage,* by Daniel Mark Epstein. *New York Times*, July 3, 2008.

## CHICAGO PRINT SOURCES Entries for Books

Capitalize the first, last, and all major words of titles and subtitles. Chicago style italicizes book titles.

Author's last name    First name and middle Initial    Title (italicized, all major words capitalized)    City and state (to clarify unfamiliar or ambiguous city)

Wartenberg, Thomas E. *The Nature of Art*. Belmont, CA:
     Wadsworth, 2002.

Publisher's name     Year of publication

## Authors and Editors

### 10. A Book by One Author or Editor
*Endnote*

> 10. Robert Dallek, *An Unfinished Life: John F. Kennedy, 1917–1963* (New York: Little, Brown, 2003), 213.

*Bibliography*

> Dallek, Robert. *An Unfinished Life: John F. Kennedy, 1917–1963*. New York: Little, Brown, 2003.

If the book has an editor rather than an author, add a comma and **ed.** after the name: **John Fields, ed.** Follow with a comma in a note.

### 11. A Book by Two or Three Authors or Editors
*Endnote*
*Two Authors*

> 11. Jack Watson and Grant McKerney, *A Cultural History of the Theater* (New York: Longman, 1993), 137.

*Three Authors*

> 11. Nathan Caplan, John K. Whitmore, and Marcella H. Choy, *The Boat People and Achievement in America: A Study of Economic and Educational Success* (Ann Arbor: University of Michigan Press, 1990), 51.

*Bibliography*
*Two Authors*

> Watson, Jack, and Grant McKerney. *A Cultural History of the Theater*. New York: Longman, 1993.

*Three Authors*

> Caplan, Nathan, John K. Whitmore, and Marcella H. Choy. *The Boat People and Achievement in America: A Study of Economic and Educational Success*. Ann Arbor: University of Michigan Press, 1990.

## 12. A Book by More Than Three Authors or Editors
*Endnote*

Chicago style favors **et al.** rather than **and others** after the first name in endnotes. Add a comma and **eds.** after the names of the editors in both the endnotes and the bibliography.

> 12. Robert E. Spiller et al., eds., *Literary History of the United States* (New York: Macmillan, 1953), 24.

*Bibliography*

List all authors' or editors' names in the bibliography.

> Spiller, Robert E., Willard Thorp, Thomas H. Johnson, and Henry Seidel Canby, eds. *Literary History of the United States.* New York: Macmillan, 1953.

## 13. A Book with No Listed Author or Editor
*Endnote*

> 13. *Merriam-Webster's Guide to Punctuation and Style,* 4th ed. (Springfield, MA: Merriam-Webster, 2008), 22.

*Bibliography*

> *Merriam-Webster's Guide to Punctuation and Style.* 4th ed. Springfield, MA: Merriam-Webster, 2008.

## 14. A Book by a Corporate Author

If a publication issued by an organization does not identify a person as the author, the organization is listed as the author even if its name is repeated in the title, in the series title, or as the publisher.

*Endnote*

> 14. National Geographic Society, *National Parks of the United States,* 6th ed. (Washington, DC: National Geographic Society, 2009), 77.

*Bibliography*

> National Geographic Society. *National Parks of the United States.* 6th ed. Washington, DC: National Geographic Society, 2009.

## 15. A Book with an Author and an Editor
*Endnote*

> 15. William Bartram, *The Travels of William Bartram,* ed. Mark Van Doren (New York: Dover Press, 1955), 85.

*Bibliography*

> Bartram, William. *The Travels of William Bartram.* Edited by Mark Van Doren. New York: Dover Press, 1955.

## 16. A Book Quoted in a Secondary Source
*Endnote*

> 16. Henry Adams, *Mont Saint-Michel and Chartres* (New York: Penguin Books, 1986), 296, quoted in Karen Armstrong, *A History of God: The 4000-Year Quest of Judaism, Christianity and Islam* (New York: Ballantine Books, 1993), 203–4.

*Bibliography*

Adams, Henry. *Mont Saint-Michel and Chartres,* 296. New York: Penguin Books, 1986. Quoted in Armstrong, *A History of God,* 203–4.

Armstrong, Karen. *A History of God: The 4000-Year Quest of Judaism, Christianity, and Islam.* New York: Ballantine Books, 1993.

### Editions and Multivolume Works

## 17. A Subsequent Edition of a Book
*Endnote*

> 17. Laurie G. Kirszner and Stephen R. Mandell, *The Wadsworth Handbook,* 10th ed. (Boston: Wadsworth, 2014), 52.

*Bibliography*

Kirszner, Laurie G., and Stephen R. Mandell. *The Wadsworth Handbook.* 10th ed. Boston: Wadsworth, 2014.

## 18. A Multivolume Work
*Endnote*

> 18. Kathleen Raine, *Blake and Tradition* (Princeton, NJ: Princeton University Press, 1968), 1:143.

*Bibliography*

Raine, Kathleen. *Blake and Tradition.* Vol. 1. Princeton, NJ: Princeton University Press, 1968.

### Parts of Books

## 19. A Chapter in a Book
*Endnote*

> 19. Roy Porter, "Health, Disease, and Cure," in *Quacks: Fakers and Charlatans in Medicine* (Stroud, UK: Tempus Publishing, 2003), 188.

### *Bibliography*

Porter, Roy. "Health, Disease, and Cure." In *Quacks: Fakers and Charlatans in Medicine,* 182–205. Stroud, UK: Tempus Publishing, 2003.

## 20. An Essay in an Anthology
### *Endnote*

20. G. E. R. Lloyd, "Science and Mathematics," in *The Legacy of Greece,* ed. Moses Finley (New York: Oxford University Press, 1981), 270.

### *Bibliography*

Lloyd, G. E. R. "Science and Mathematics." In *The Legacy of Greece,* edited by Moses Finley, 256–300. New York: Oxford University Press, 1981.

## *Religious Works*
### 21. Sacred Texts

References to religious works (such as the Bible or Qur'an) are usually limited to the text or notes and not listed in the bibliography. In citing the Bible, include the book (abbreviated), the chapter (followed by a colon), and the verse numbers. Identify the version, but do not include a page number.

### *Endnote*

21. Phil. 1:9–11 (King James Version).

## CHICAGO ENTRIES FOR MISCELLANEOUS PRINT AND NONPRINT SOURCES

### *Interviews*
### 22. A Personal Interview
### *Endnote*

22. Cornel West, interview by author, tape recording, June 8, 2013.

Personal interviews are cited in the notes or text but are usually not listed in the bibliography.

### 23. A Published Interview
### *Endnote*

23. Gwendolyn Brooks, interview by George Stavros, *Contemporary Literature* 11, no. 1 (Winter 1970): 12.

*Bibliography*

Brooks, Gwendolyn. Interview by George Stavros. *Contemporary Literature* 11, no. 1 (Winter 1970): 1–20.

## Letters and Government Documents

### 24. A Personal Letter
*Endnote*

24. Julia Alvarez, letter to the author, April 10, 2013.

Personal letters are mentioned in the text or a note but are not listed in the bibliography.

### 25. A Government Document
*Endnote*

25. US Department of Transportation, *The Future of High-Speed Trains in the United States: Special Study, 2007* (Washington, DC: Government Printing Office, 2008), 203.

*Bibliography*

US Department of Transportation. *The Future of High-Speed Trains in the United States: Special Study, 2007*. Washington, DC: Government Printing Office, 2008.

## Videotapes, DVDs, and Recordings

### 26. A Videotape or DVD
*Endnote*

26. *Interview with Arthur Miller,* directed by William Schiff (Mequon, WI: Mosaic Group, 1987), videocassette (VHS), 17 min.

*Bibliography*

*Interview with Arthur Miller*. Directed by William Schiff. Mequon, WI: Mosaic Group, 1987. Videocassette (VHS), 17 min.

### 27. A Recording
*Endnote*

27. Bob Marley and the Wailers, "Crisis," *Kaya*, Kava Island Records 423 095-3, 1978, compact disc.

*Bibliography*

Marley, Bob, and the Wailers. "Crisis." *Kaya*. Kava Island Records 423 095-3, 1978, compact disc.

## CHICAGO ELECTRONIC SOURCES

### Entries for Sources from Online Publications

Citations of sources from online publications usually include the author's name; the title of the article; the title of the publication; the publication information and date; the page numbers (if applicable); and the DOI (digital object identifier), a permanent identifying number, or URL (followed by a period). If no publication date is available or if your instructor or discipline requires one, include an access date before the DOI or URL.

You may break a DOI or URL that continues to a second line after a colon or double slash; before a comma, a period, a hyphen, a question mark, a percent symbol, a number sign, a tilde, or an underscore; or before or after an ampersand or equals sign.

Author's First               **Title of article**
last name name           (in quotation marks)

Dekoven, Marianne. "Utopias Limited: Post-Sixties and
      Postmodern American Fiction." *Modern Fiction Studies*
      41, no. 1 (1995). doi:10.1353/mfs.1995.0002.

Volume  Issue  Year of publication    DOI         Title of periodical
number number (in parentheses)                (italicized)

### *Articles, Books, and Reference Works on the Internet*

#### 28. An Article in an Online Scholarly Journal
*Endnote*

      28. Richard J. Schaefer, "Editing Strategies in Television Documentaries," *Journal of Communication* 47, no. 4 (1997): 80, doi:10.1111/j1460-2446.1997.tb02726.x.

*Bibliography*

Schaefer, Richard J. "Editing Strategies in Television
    Documentaries." *Journal of Communication* 47,
    no. 4 (1997): 69–89. doi:10.1111/j1460-2446.1997
    .tb02726.x.

#### 29. An Article in an Online Magazine
*Endnote*

      29. Steven Levy, "I Was a Wi-Fi Freeloader," *Newsweek,* October 9, 2002, http://www.msnbc.com/news/816606.asp.

If there is no DOI for a source, cite the URL.

*Bibliography*

> Levy, Steven. "I Was a Wi-Fi Freeloader." *Newsweek,*
> October 9, 2002. http://www.msnbc.com
> /news/816606.asp.

### 30. An Article in an Online Newspaper
*Endnote*

> 30. William J. Broad, "Piece by Piece, the Civil War
> *Monitor* Is Pulled from the Atlantic's Depths," *New York
> Times on the Web,* July 18, 2002, http://query.nytimes.com.

*Bibliography*

> Broad, William J. "Piece by Piece, the Civil War *Monitor* Is
> Pulled from the Atlantic's Depths." *New York Times on
> the Web,* July 18, 2002. http://query.nytimes.com.

### 31. An Article in an Encyclopedia

If the reference book lists entries alphabetically, put the abbreviation **s.v.** (Latin for *sub verbo,* "under the word") before the entry name. If there is no publication or revision
date for the entry, give the date of access before the DOI
or URL.

*Endnote*

> 31. *Encyclopaedia Britannica Online,* s.v. "Adams,
> John," accessed July 5, 2010, http://www.britannica.com
> /EBchecked/topic/5132/John-Adams.

Dictionary and encyclopedia entries are not listed in the bibliography.

### 32. A Book
*Endnote*

> 32. Frederick Douglass, *My Bondage and My Freedom*
> (Boston, 1855), http://etext.virginia.edu/toc/modeng
> /public/DouMybo.html.

*Bibliography*

> Douglass, Frederick. *My Bondage and My Freedom.* Boston,
> 1855. http://etext.virginia.edu/toc/modeng/public
> /DouMybo.html.

Older works available online may not include all publication information. Give the DOI or URL as the last part of the
citation.

### 33. A Government Publication
*Endnote*

> 33. US Department of Transportation, Federal Motor Carrier Safety Administration, *Safety Belt Usage by Commercial Motor Vehicle Drivers (SBUCMVD) 2007 Survey, Final Report* (Washington, DC: Government Printing Office, 2008), http://www.fmcsa.dot.gov/safety-security/safety -belt/exec-summary-2007.htm.

*Bibliography*

> US Department of Transportation. Federal Motor Carrier Safety Administration. *Safety Belt Usage by Commercial Motor Vehicle Drivers (SBUCMVD) 2007 Survey, Final Report*. Washington, DC: Government Printing Office, 2008. http://www.fmcsa.dot.gov/safety-security /safety-belt/exec-summary-2007.htm.

**CHICAGO** ELECTRONIC SOURCES Entries for Sources from an Online Database

*Sources from an Online Database*

Many articles and other materials published in print and electronically are also archived and available online through free or subscription databases.

### 34. A Scholarly Journal Article
*Endnote*

> 34. Monroe Billington, "Freedom to Serve: The President's Committee on Equality of Treatment and Opportunity in the Armed Forces, 1949–1950," *Journal of Negro History* 51, no. 4 (1966): 264, http://www.jstor.org /stable/2716101.

Use a DOI, a number that applies to an article in all of the media in which it may be published, rather than a URL if one is available. If you use a URL, cite the shorter, more stable form that will take you to the article's location in a database.

*Bibliography*

> Billington, Monroe. "Freedom to Serve: The President's Committee on Equality of Treatment and Opportunity in the Armed Forces, 1949–1950," *Journal of Negro History* 51, no. 4 (1966): 262–74. http://www.jstor .org/stable/2716101.

If there is no stable URL, include the name of the database and put any identifying database number in parentheses: (**ERIC**). If the article or document does not have a date of publication or revision, include an access date.

## CHICAGO ELECTRONIC SOURCES Entries for Sources from Internet Sites

### *Internet-Specific Sources*

### 35. A Web Site or Home Page
*Endnote*

> 35. David Perdue, "Dickens's Journalistic Career," David Perdue's Charles Dickens Page, accessed October 25, 2010, http://www.fidnet.com/~dap1955/dickens.

Titles of Web sites are in regular type (roman). Titles of pages or sections on a site are in quotation marks. If there is no date of publication, give an access date. Web site content is not usually listed in a bibliography.

### 36. An Email
*Endnote*

> 36. Meg Halverson, "Scuba Report," email message to author, April 2, 2010.

Email messages can also be mentioned in the text; they are not listed in the bibliography.

### 37. A Listserv Posting
Include the name of the list, the date of the individual posting, and the URL for the archive.

*Endnote*

> 37. Dave Shirlaw to Underwater Archeology discussion list, September 6, 2010, http://lists.asu.edu/archives/sub-arch.html.

Listserv postings are not listed in the bibliography.

## 13b  Chicago Humanities Manuscript Guidelines

### CHECKLIST
### Typing Your Paper

When you type your paper, use the student paper in **13c** as your model.

❑ On the title page, type the full title of your paper. Also include your name, the course title, and the date.

❑ Double-space all text in your paper. Single-space block quotations, table titles, figure captions, footnotes, endnotes, and bibliography entries. Double-space between footnotes, endnotes, and bibliography entries.

❑ Leave a one-inch margin at the top, at the bottom, and on both sides of the page.

❑ Indent the first line of each paragraph one-half inch. Set off a long prose block quotation (five or more lines) from the text by indenting the quotation one-half inch from the left-hand margin. Do not use quotation marks. Double-space before and after the block quotation.

❑ Number all pages consecutively at the top of the page (centered or flush right) or centered at the bottom. Page numbers should appear at a consistent distance (at least three-fourths of an inch) from the top margin. Do not number the title page; the first full page of the paper is page 1.

❑ Use superscript numbers to indicate in-text citations. Type superscript numbers at the end of cited material (quotations, paraphrases, or summaries). Place the note number at the end of a sentence or clause (with no intervening space). The number follows any punctuation mark except a dash, which it precedes.

❑ Citations should follow Chicago humanities documentation style.

See 13a

### CHECKLIST
### Using Visuals

According to *The Chicago Manual of Style,* there are two types of visuals: **tables** and **figures** (or **illustrations**), including charts, graphs, photographs, maps, and diagrams.

### Tables

❑ Give each **table** a label and a consecutive arabic number (**Table 1, Table 2**) followed by a period.

*continued*

## Using Visuals *(continued)*

❏ Give each table a concise descriptive title in noun form without a period. Place the title after the table number.

❏ Place both the label and the title flush left above the table.

❏ Place source information flush left below the table, introduced by the word **Source** or **Sources**. Otherwise style the source as a complete footnote.

*Source:* David E. Fisher and Marshall Jon Fisher, *Tube: The Invention of Television* (Washington, DC: Counterpoint Press, 1996), 185.

If you do not cite this source elsewhere in your paper, do not list it in your bibliography.

### Figures

❏ Give each **figure** a label, a consecutive arabic number, and a caption.

❏ Place the label, the number, and a period flush left below the figure. Then, leave a space and add the caption.

❏ Place source information (credit line) at the end of the caption after a period.

Figure 1. Television and its influence on young children. Photograph from ABC Photos.

---

### CHECKLIST

## Preparing the Chicago-Style Endnotes Page

When typing your endnotes page, follow these guidelines:

❏ Begin the endnotes on a new page after the last page of the text of the paper and preceding the bibliography.

❏ Type the title **Notes** and center it one inch from the top of the page. Then double-space and type the first note.

❏ Number the page on which the endnotes appear as the next page of the paper.

❏ Type and number notes in the order in which they appear in the paper, beginning with number 1. Type the note number on (not above) the line, followed by a period and one space.

❏ Indent the first line of each note one-half inch; type subsequent lines flush with the left-hand margin.

❏ Single-space lines within a note. Double-space between notes.

❏ Break DOIs and URLs after a colon or double slashes, before punctuation marks (period, single slash, comma, hyphen, and so on), or before or after the symbols = and &.

**CHECKLIST**

## Preparing the Chicago-Style Bibliography

When typing your bibliography, follow these guidelines:

❑ Begin entries on a separate page after the endnotes.

❑ Type the title **Bibliography** and center it one inch from the top of the page. Then double-space and type the first entry.

❑ List entries alphabetically according to the author's last name.

❑ Type the first line of each entry flush with the left-hand margin. Indent subsequent lines one-half inch.

❑ Single-space within an entry; double-space between entries.

## 13c Model Chicago Humanities Research Paper (Excerpts)

The following pages are from a student paper, "The Flu of 1918 and the Potential for Future Pandemics," written for a history course. It uses Chicago humanities documentation and has a title page, notes page, and bibliography. The Web citations in this student paper do not have DOIs, so URLs have been provided instead.

Title page is
not numbered

Title boldfaced
and centered

**The Flu of 1918 and the Potential for**

**Future Pandemics**

Name

Rita Lin

Course title

American History 301

Date

May 3, 2013

1

### The Flu of 1918 and the Potential for
### Future Pandemics

Title if required by instructor (centered and boldfaced)

In November 2002, a mysterious new illness surfaced in China. By May 2003, what became known as SARS (Severe Acute Respiratory Syndrome) had been transported by air travelers to Europe, South America, South Africa, Australia, and North America, and the worldwide death toll had grown to 250.[1] By June 2003, there were more than 8,200 suspected cases of SARS in 30 countries and 750 deaths related to the outbreak, including 30 in Toronto. Just when SARS appeared to be waning in Asia, a second outbreak in Toronto, the hardest hit of all cities outside of Asia, reminded everyone that SARS remained a deadly threat.[2] As SARS continued to claim more victims and expand its reach, fears of a new pandemic spread throughout the world.

The belief that a pandemic could occur in the future is not a far-fetched idea. During the twentieth century, there were three, and the most deadly one, in 1918, had several significant similarities to the SARS outbreak. As David Brown points out, the 1918 influenza pandemic is in many ways a mirror reflecting the causes and symptoms, as well as the future potential, of SARS. Both are caused by a virus, lead to respiratory illness, and spread through casual contact and coughing. Outbreaks of both are often traced to one individual, quarantine is the major weapon against the spread of both, and both probably arose from mutated animal viruses. Moreover, as Brown observes, the greatest fear regarding SARS was that it would become so

2

widespread that transmission chains would be undetectable, and health officials would be helpless to restrain outbreaks. Such was the case with the 1918 influenza, which also began mysteriously in China and was transported around the globe (at that time by World War I military ships). By the time the flu lost its power in the spring of 1919, just one year later, it had killed more than 50 million people worldwide,[3] more than twice as many as those who died during the four and a half years of World War I. Thus, if SARS is a reflection of the potential for a future flu pandemic—and experts believe it is—the international community needs to acknowledge the danger, accelerate its research, and develop an extensive virus surveillance system.

Clearly, the 1918 flu was different from anything previously known to Americans. Among the peculiarities of the pandemic were its origin and cause. In the spring of 1918, the virus, in relatively mild form, mysteriously appeared on a Kansas military base. After apparently dying out, the flu returned to the United States in late August. At that point, the influenza was no ordinary flu; it "struck with incredible speed, often killing a victim within hours of contact[,] . . . so fast that such infections rarely had time to set in."[4] Unlike previous strains, the 1918 flu struck healthy young people.

Thesis statement

History of 1918 pandemic

Brackets indicate that comma was added by student writer

10

## Notes

center title (boldfaced) and double-space before first note

    1. Nancy Shute, "SARS Hits Home," *U.S. News & World Report*, May 5, 2003, 42.

indent ½"

    2. "Canada Waits for SARS News as Asia Under Control," *Sydney Morning Herald on the Web*, June 2, 2003, http://www.smh.com.au.

Single-space within a note; double-space between notes

    3. David Brown, "A Grim Reminder in SARS Fight: In 1918, Spanish Flu Swept the Globe, Killing Millions," MSNBC News Online, June 4, 2003, http://www.msnbc.com/news/921901.asp.

A long URL for an online newspaper article can be shortened after the first single slash

    4. Doug Rekenthaler, "The Flu Pandemic of 1918: Is a Repeat Performance Likely?—Part 1 of 2," Disaster Relief: New Stories, February 22, 1999, http://www.disasterrelief.org/Disasters/990219Flu.

Endnotes listed in order in which they appear in the paper

    5. Lynette Iezzoni, *Influenza 1918: The Worst Epidemic in American History* (New York: TV Books, 1999), 40.

    6. "1918 Influenza Timeline," *Influenza 1918,* 1999, http://www.pbs.org/wgbh/amex/influenza/timeline/index.html.

Subsequent references to the same source include author's last name, shortened title, and page number(s)

    7. Iezonni, *Influenza 1918,* 131–32.

    8. Brown, "Grim Reminder."

*Ibid.* is used for a subsequent reference to the same source when there are no intervening references

    9. Iezonni, *Influenza 1918,* 88–89.

    10. Ibid., 204.

13

# Bibliography

"1918 Influenza Timeline." *Influenza 1918,* 1999. http://www.pbs.org/wgbh/amex/influenza /timeline/index.html.

Billings, Molly. "The Influenza Pandemic of 1918." Human Virology at Stanford: Interesting Viral Web Pages, June 1997. http://www.stanford .edu/group/virus/uda/index.html.

Brown, David. "A Grim Reminder in SARS Fight: In 1918, Spanish Flu Swept the Globe, Killing Millions." MSNBC News Online, June 4, 2003. http://www.msnbc.com/news/921901.asp.

"Canada Waits for SARS News as Asia Under Control." *Sydney Morning Herald on the Web,* June 2, 2003. http://www.smh.com.au/text.

Cooke, Robert. "Drugs vs. the Bug of 1918: Virus' Deadly Code Is Unlocked to Test Strategies to Fight It." *Newsday,* October 1, 2002.

Crosby, Alfred W., Jr. *America's Forgotten Pandemic: The Influenza of 1918.* New York: Cambridge University Press, 1989.

Dandurant, Daren. "Virus Changes Can Make Flu a Slippery Foe to Combat." MSNBC News Online, January 17, 2003. http://www.msnbc.com /local/sco/m8052.asp.

Center title (boldfaced) and double-space before first entry

First line of each entry is flush with the left-hand margin; subsequent lines are indented $1/2$"

Single-space within entries; double-space between them

URLs are provided for Web citations that do not have DOIs

Entries are listed alphabetically according to the author's last name

# Directory of CSE Reference List Entries

PRINT SOURCES: *Entries for Articles*
### Articles in Scholarly Journals

### Articles in Magazines and Newspapers

PRINT SOURCES: *Entries for Books*
### Authors

### Parts of Books

### Professional and Technical Publications

# ENTRIES FOR MISCELLANEOUS PRINT AND NONPRINT SOURCES
### Films, Videotapes, Recordings, and Maps

ELECTRONIC SOURCES: *Entries for Sources from Internet Sites*
### Internet-Specific Sources

# CHAPTER 14

# CSE and Other Documentation Styles

## 14a Using CSE Style

**CSE style,**\* recommended by the Council of Science Editors (CSE), is used in biology, zoology, physiology, anatomy, and genetics. CSE style has two parts—*documentation in the text* and a *reference list.*

### 1 Documentation in the Text

**CSE style** permits either of two documentation formats: *citation-sequence format* or *name-year format.*

*Citation-Sequence Format* The **citation-sequence format** calls for either superscripts (raised numbers) in the text of the paper (the preferred form) or numbers inserted parenthetically in the text of the paper.

> One study[1] has demonstrated the effect of low dissolved
>
> oxygen.

These numbers refer to a list of references at the end of the paper. Entries are numbered in the order in which they appear in the text of the paper. For example, if **James** is mentioned first in the text, **James** will be number 1 in the reference list. When you refer to more than one source in a single note, the numbers are separated by a hyphen if they are in sequence and by a comma if they are not.

> Some studies[2-3] dispute this claim.

> Other studies[3,6] support these findings.

---

\*CSE style follows the guidelines set in the style manual of the Council of Science Editors: *Scientific Style and Format: The CSE Manual for Authors, Editors, and Publishers,* 7th ed. New York: Rockefeller UP, 2006.

*Note:* The **citation-name** format is a variation of the citation-sequence format. In the citation-name format, the names in the reference list are listed in alphabetical order. The numbers assigned to the references are used as in-text references, regardless of the order in which they appear in the paper.

*Name-Year Format* The **name-year format** calls for the author's name and the year of publication to be inserted parenthetically in the text. If the author's name is used to introduce the source material, only the date of publication is needed in the parenthetical citation.

> A great deal of heat is often generated during this process (McGinness 2010).

> According to McGinness (2010), a great deal of heat is often generated during this process.

When two or more works are cited in the same parentheses, the sources are arranged chronologically (from earliest to latest) and separated by semicolons.

> Epidemics can be avoided by taking tissue cultures (Domb 2010) and by intervention with antibiotics (Baldwin and Rigby 2005; Martin and others 2006; Cording 2010).

*Note:* The citation **Baldwin and Rigby 2005** refers to a work by two authors; the citation **Martin and others 2006** refers to a work by three or more authors.

## 2 Reference List

The format of the reference list depends on the documentation format you use. If you use the **name-year** documentation format, your reference list will resemble the reference list for an **APA** paper (**see Chapter 12**). If you use the **citation-sequence** documentation style (as in the paper in **14c**), your sources will be listed by number, in the order in which they appear in your paper, on a **References** page. In either case, double-space within and between entries; type each number flush left, followed by a period and one space; and align the second and subsequent lines with the first letter of the author's last name. (The following examples illustrate citation-sequence documentation style.)

## CSE PRINT SOURCES Entries for Articles

List the author or authors by last name; after one space, list the initial or initials (unspaced) of the first and middle names (followed by a period); the title of the article (not in quotation marks, and with only the first word capitalized); the abbreviated name of the journal (with all major words capitalized, but not italicized or underlined); the year (followed by a semicolon); the volume number, the issue number (in parentheses), followed by a colon; and inclusive page numbers. No spaces separate the year, the volume number, and the page numbers.

| Author's last name | Initial | Title of article (only first word capitalized) | Volume number |
|---|---|---|---|

2. Davies P. How to build a time machine: it wouldn't be easy, but it might be possible. Sci Am. (2003;287(3):50–55.

Number of entry — Title of periodical (abbreviated) — Year of publication / Semicolon — Issue number (in parentheses) — Inclusive page numbers

### Articles in Scholarly Journals

#### 1. An Article in a Journal Paginated by Issue

1. Sarmiento JL, Gruber N. Sinks for anthropogenic carbon. Phy Today. 2002;55(8):30-36.

#### 2. An Article in a Journal with Continuous Pagination

2. Brazil K, Krueger P. Patterns of family adaptation to childhood asthma. J Pediatr Nurs. 2002;17:167-173.

*Note:* Omit the month (and the day for weeklies) and issue number for journals with continuous pagination through an annual volume.

### Articles in Magazines and Newspapers

#### 3. A Magazine Article (Signed)

3. Nadis S. Using lasers to detect E.T. Astronomy. 2002 Sep:44-49.

*Note:* Month names longer than three letters are abbreviated by their first three letters.

#### 4. A Magazine Article (Unsigned)

4. Brown dwarf glows with radio waves. Astronomy. 2001 Jun:28.

## 5. A Newspaper Article (Signed)

5. Husted B. Don't wiggle out of untangling computer wires. Atlanta Journal-Constitution. 2002 Jul 21;Sect Q:1 (col 1).

## 6. A Newspaper Article (Unsigned)

6. Scientists find gene tied to cancer risk. New York Times (Late Ed.). 2002 Apr 22;Sect A:18 (col 6).

## CSE PRINT SOURCES Entries for Books

List the author or authors (last name first); the title (not underlined, and with only the first word capitalized); the place of publication; the full name of the publisher (followed by a semicolon); the year (followed by a period); and the total number of pages (including back matter, such as the index).

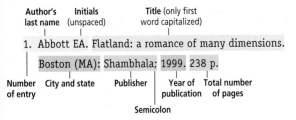

Author's last name | Initials (unspaced) | Title (only first word capitalized)

1. Abbott EA. Flatland: a romance of many dimensions. Boston (MA): Shambhala; 1999. 238 p.

Number of entry | City and state | Publisher | Year of publication | Total number of pages | Semicolon

### Authors

## 7. A Book with One Author

7. Hawking SW. A brief history of time: from the big bang to black holes. New York (NY): Bantam; 1995. 198 p.

*Note:* No comma follows the author's last name, and no period separates the unspaced initials of the first and middle names.

## 8. A Book with More Than One Author

8. Horner JR, Gorman J. Digging dinosaurs. New York (NY): Workman; 1988. 210 p.

## 9. An Edited Book

9. Goldfarb TD, editor. Taking sides: clashing views on controversial environmental issues. 2nd ed. Guilford (CT): Dushkin; 1987. 323 p.

*Note:* The publisher's state, province, or country can be added within parentheses to clarify the location. The two-letter postal service abbreviation can be used for the state or province.

**10. An Organization as Author**

> 10. National Institutes of Health (US). Human embryonic
>     stem-cell derived neurons treat stroke in rats. Bethesda
>     (MD): US Dept. of Health and Human Services; 2008. 92 p.

### Parts of Books

**11. A Chapter or Other Part of a Book with a Separate Title but with the Same Author**

> 11. Asimov I. Exploring the earth and cosmos: the
>     growth and future of human knowledge. New York
>     (NY): Crown; 1984. Part III, The horizons of matter;
>     p. 245-294.

**12. A Chapter or Other Part of a Book with a Different Author**

> 12. Gingerich O. Hints for beginning observers. In: Mallas
>     JH, Kreimer E, editors. The Messier album: an observer's
>     handbook. Cambridge (GB): Cambridge Univ Pr; 1978.
>     p. 194-195.

### Professional and Technical Publications

**13. Published Proceedings of a Conference**

> 13. Al-Sherbini A. New applications of lasers in photobiology
>     and photochemistry. Modern Trends of Physics Research,
>     1st International Conference; 2004 May 12-14; Cairo,
>     Egypt. Melville (NY): American Institute of Physics;
>     2005. 14 p.

**14. A Technical Report**

> 14. Forman, GL. Feature selection for text classification.
>     2007 Feb 12. Hewlett-Packard technical reports HPL-
>     2007-16R1. 24 p. Available from www.hpl.hp.com/
>     techreports/2007/HPL-2007-16R1.html

# CSE ENTRIES FOR MISCELLANEOUS PRINT AND NONPRINT SOURCES

## *Films, Videotapes, Recordings, and Maps*

### 15. An Audiocassette

15. Bronowski J. The ascent of man [audiocassette]. New
York: Jeffrey Norton Pub; 1974. 1 audiocassette: 2-track,
55 min.

### 16. A Film, Videotape, or DVD

16. Stoneberger B, Clark R, editors. Women in science
[videocassette]. American Society for Microbiology,
producer. Madison (WI): Hawkhill; 1998. 1 videocassette:
42 min., sound, color, 1/2 in. Accompanied by: 1 guide.

### 17. A Map
### *A Sheet Map*

17. Amazonia: a world resource at risk [ecological map].
Washington (DC): National Geographic Society; 2008.
1 sheet.

### *A Map in an Atlas*

17. Central Africa [political map]. In: Hammond citation
world atlas. Maplewood (NJ): Hammond; 2008. p. 114-
115. Color, scale 1:13,800,000.

# CSE ELECTRONIC SOURCES Entries for Sources from Internet Sites

With Internet sources, include a description of the medium,
the date of access, and the URL.

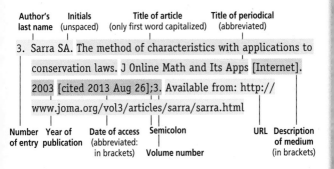

| Author's last name | Initials (unspaced) | Title of article (only first word capitalized) | Title of periodical (abbreviated) |

3. Sarra SA. The method of characteristics with applications to
conservation laws. J Online Math and Its Apps [Internet].
2003 [cited 2013 Aug 26];3. Available from: http://
www.joma.org/vol3/articles/sarra/sarra.html

Number of entry | Year of publication | Date of access (abbreviated; in brackets) | Semicolon | Volume number | URL | Description of medium (in brackets)

*Internet-Specific Sources*

### 18. An Online Journal

18. Lasko P. The *Drosophila melanogaster* genome: translation factors and RNA binding proteins. J Cell Biol [Internet]. 2000 [cited 2012 Aug 15]; 150(2):F51-56. Available from: http://www.jcb.org/search.dtl

### 19. An Online Book

19. Bohm D. Causality and chance in modern physics [Internet]. Philadelphia: Univ of Pennsylvania Pr; c1999 [cited 2011 Aug 17]. Available from: http://www .netlibrary.com/ebook_info.asp?product_id517169

## 14b CSE-Style Manuscript Guidelines

**CHECKLIST**

### Typing Your Paper

When you type your paper, use the student paper in **14c** as your model.

❑ Do not include a title page. Type your name, the course, and the date flush left one inch from the top of the first page.

❑ If required, include an **abstract** (a 250-word summary of the paper) on a separate numbered page.

❑ Double-space throughout.

❑ Insert tables and figures in the body of the paper. Number tables and figures in separate sequences (**Table 1, Table 2; Fig. 1, Fig. 2;** and so on).

❑ Number pages consecutively in the upper right-hand corner; include a shortened title before the number.

See 14a ❑ When you cite source material in your paper, follow CSE documentation style.

**CHECKLIST**

### Preparing the CSE Reference List

When typing your reference list, follow these guidelines:

❑ Begin the reference list on a new page after the last page of the paper, numbered as the next page.

- ❏ Center the title **References, Literature Cited,** or **References Cited** one inch from the top of the page.
- ❏ For citation-sequence format, list entries in the order in which they first appear in the paper—not alphabetically. For name-year format, list entries alphabetically.
- ❏ Number the entries consecutively; type the note numbers flush left on (not above) the line, followed by a period.
- ❏ Leave one space between the period and the first letter of the entry; align subsequent lines directly beneath the first letter of the author's last name.
- ❏ Double-space within and between entries.

## 14c Model CSE-Style Research Paper (Excerpts)

The following pages are from a student paper that explores the dangers of global warming for humans and wildlife. The paper, which cites seven sources and includes a line graph, illustrates CSE citation-sequence format.

Abbreviated title and page number

1"

½"

Sara Castillo

Ecology 4223.01

April 10, 2013

Center title →

Polar Ice Caps Could Melt by the

End of This Century

Indent ½" →

The Arctic and Antarctica are homes to the

earth's polar ice caps, and global warming appears

Double-space to be melting them. When polar temperatures

increase, parts of floating ice sheets and glaciers

Introduction break off and melt. This process could eventually

cause the ocean levels to rise and have disastrous

Thesis statement effects on plants, animals, and human beings.

There are ways to minimize this disaster, but

they will only be effective if governments act

immediately.

The polar ice caps are melting at a rapid

rate, and much of the scientific community

1"          1"

agrees that global warming is one of the causes.

The greenhouse effect, the mechanism that

causes global warming, occurs when molecules of

greenhouse gases in the atmosphere reflect the

rays of the sun back to the earth. This mechanism

enables our planet to maintain a temperature

adequate for life. However, as the concentration

of greenhouse gases in the atmosphere increases,

more heat from the sun is retained, and the

Superscript numbers temperature of the earth rises.[1]

correspond to sources Greenhouse gases include carbon dioxide

in the reference $(CO_2)$, methane, and nitrous oxide.[2] Since the

list beginning of the industrial revolution in the late

1800s, people have been burning fossil fuels

1"

Polar Ice Caps 2

that create $CO_2$.[3] This $CO_2$ has led to an increase in the greenhouse effect and has contributed to the global warming that is melting the polar ice caps. As Figure 1 shows, the surface temperature of the earth has increased by about 1 degree Celsius (1.8 degrees Fahrenheit) since the 1850s. Some scientists have predicted that temperatures will increase even further.

Figure 1 Introduced

Figure placed close to where it is discussed

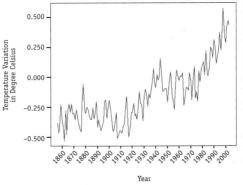

Reprinted by permission of Climatic Research Unit, School of Environmental Sciences, University of East Anglia.

Fig. 1. Global temperature variation from the average during the base period 1860-2000 (adapted from Climatic research unit: data: temperature 2003) [Internet]. [cited 2013 Mar 11]. Available from: http://www.cru.uea.ac.uk/cru/data/temperature.

Label, caption, and full source information

It is easy to see the effects of global warming. For example, the Pine Island Glacier in Antarctica was depleted at a rate of 1.6 meters per year between 1992 and 1999. This type of melting is very likely to increase the fresh water that

Polar Ice Caps 8

References

Book with one author
1. Edmonds A. A closer look at the greenhouse effect. Brookfield (CT): Copper Beach Books; 1997. 32 p.

Book with more than one author
2. Smith RL, Smith TM. Elements of ecology. 5th ed. San Francisco (CA): Benjamin Cummings; 2003. 534 p.

Entries listed in order in which they first appear in the paper
3. Pringle L. Global warming: the threat of earth's changing climate. New York (NY): Sea and Star Books; 2001. 48 p.

4. Perkins S. Antarctic glacier thins and speeds up. Sci News. 2001;159(5):70.

Online journal
5. Pearce F. Arctic to lose all summer ice by 2100. NewScientist [Internet]. 2002 [cited 2013 Mar 11]; 70(2):99-133. Available from: http://www .newscientist.com

Print journal
6. The pacific decadal oscillation. BioSci. 2000 Aug:32-39.

7. Woods M. Science on ice. Brookfield (CT): Millbrook Press; 1995. 96 p.

Double-space

## 14d Using Other Documentation Styles

The following style manuals describe documentation formats and manuscript guidelines used in various fields.

### CHEMISTRY

Coghill, Anne M., and Lorrin R. Garson, eds. *The ACS Style Guide: Effective Communication of Scientific Information.* 3rd ed. Washington: American Chemical Society, 2006. Print.

## GEOLOGY

Hansen, Wallace R., ed. *Suggestions to Authors of the Reports of the United States Geological Survey.* 7th ed. Washington: GPO, 1991. Print.

## GOVERNMENT DOCUMENTS

Cheney, Debora. *The Complete Guide to Citing Government Information Resources: A Manual for Social Science & Business Research.* 3rd ed. Bethesda: Congressional Information Service, 2002. Print.

United States Government Printing Office. *Style Manual.* Washington: GPO, 2009. Print.

## JOURNALISM

Christian, Darrell, Sally Jacobsen, and David Minthorn, eds. *The Associated Press Stylebook and Briefing on Media Law 2011.* 46th ed. New York: Basic, 2011. Print.

## LAW

*The Bluebook: A Uniform System of Citation.* Comp. Editors of Columbia Law Review et al. 18th ed. Cambridge: Harvard Law Review Association, 2008. Print.

## MATHEMATICS

American Mathematical Society. *AMS Author Handbook.* Providence: American Mathematical Society, 2012. Web.

## MEDICINE

Iverson, Cheryl. *AMA Manual of Style: A Guide for Authors and Editors.* 10th ed. Oxford: Oxford UP, 2007. Print.

## MUSIC

Holoman, D. Kern. *Writing about Music: A Style Sheet.* 2nd ed. Berkeley: U of California P, 2008. Print.

## PHYSICS

American Institute of Physics. *AIP Style Manual.* 5th ed. Melville: American Institute of Physics, 2000. Print.

## SCIENTIFIC AND TECHNICAL WRITING

Rubens, Philip, ed. *Science and Technical Writing: A Manual of Style.* 2nd ed. New York: Routledge, 2001. Print.

# Writing Grammatical Sentences

CHAPTER **15**

# Revising Run-Ons

## 15a Recognizing Comma Splices and Fused Sentences

<sub>See A2.3</sub> A **run-on** is an error that occurs when two <u>independent clauses</u> are joined incorrectly. There are two kinds of run-ons: *comma splices* and *fused sentences*.

A **comma splice** is a run-on that occurs when two independent clauses are joined with just a comma. **A fused sentence** is a run-on that occurs when two independent clauses are joined with no punctuation.

**Comma Splice:** Charles Dickens created the character of Mr. Micawber, he also created Uriah Heep.

**Fused Sentence:** Charles Dickens created the character of Mr. Micawber he also created Uriah Heep.

## 15b Correcting Comma Splices and Fused Sentences

To correct a comma splice or fused sentence, use one of the following four strategies:

1. Add a period between the clauses, creating two separate sentences.
2. Add a semicolon between the clauses, creating a compound sentence.
3. Add a coordinating conjunction between the clauses, creating a compound sentence.
4. Subordinate one clause to the other, creating a complex sentence.

### ① Add a Period

You can add a period between the independent clauses, creating two separate sentences. This is a good strategy to use when the clauses are long or when they are not closely related.

In 1894 Frenchman Alfred Dreyfus was falsely con-
victed of treason, his struggle for justice pitted the
army against the civil libertarians.

*[handwritten correction: . His replacing the comma]*

## 2 Add a Semicolon

You can add a **semicolon** between two closely related clauses that convey parallel or contrasting information. The result will be a **compound sentence**.

*See 29a*

*See 21a1*

Chippendale chairs have straight legs, however, Queen Anne chairs have curved legs.

*[handwritten correction: ; inserted before however]*

*Note:* When you use a **transitional word or phrase** (such as *however, therefore,* or *for example*) to connect two independent clauses, the transitional element must be preceded by a semicolon and followed by a comma. If you use a comma alone, you create a comma splice. If you omit punctuation entirely, you create a fused sentence.

*See 4b*

## 3 Add a Coordinating Conjunction

You can use a coordinating conjunction (*and, or, but, nor, for, so, yet*) to join two closely related clauses of equal importance into one **compound sentence**. The coordinating conjunction you choose indicates the relationship between the clauses: addition (*and*), contrast (*but, yet*), causality (*for, so*), or a choice of alternatives (*or, nor*). Be sure to add a comma before the coordinating conjunction.

*See 21a1*

Elias Howe invented the sewing machine, Julia Ward Howe was a poet and social reformer.

*[handwritten correction: and inserted]*

## 4 Create a Complex Sentence

When the ideas in two independent clauses are not of equal importance, you can use an appropriate subordinating conjunction or a relative pronoun to join the clauses into one **complex sentence**, placing the less important idea in the dependent clause.

*See 21a2*

Stravinsky's ballet *The Rite of Spring* shocked Parisians
in 1913/ *because* its rhythms seemed erotic.

Lady Mary Wortley Montagu , *who* had suffered from
smallpox herself, ~~she~~ helped spread the practice of
inoculation.

CHAPTER **16**

# Revising Fragments

## 16a  Recognizing Fragments

A **sentence fragment** is an incomplete sentence—a clause or
a phrase—that is punctuated as if it were a sentence. A sentence may be incomplete for any of the following reasons:

● **It has no subject.**

Many astrophysicists now believe that galaxies are
distributed in clusters. <u>And even form supercluster
complexes.</u>

● **It has no verb.**

Every generation has its defining moments. <u>Usually the
events with the most news coverage.</u>

● **It has neither a subject nor a verb.**

Researchers are engaged in a variety of studies.
<u>Suggesting a link between alcoholism and heredity.</u>
(*Suggesting* is a <u>**verbal**</u>, which cannot serve as a sentence's
main verb.)

See
A1.3

See
A2.3
● **It is a <u>dependent clause</u>.**

Bishop Desmond Tutu was awarded the 1984 Nobel
Peace Prize. <u>Because he struggled to end apartheid.</u>

The pH meter and the spectrophotometer are two scientific instruments. <u>That changed the chemistry laboratory
dramatically.</u>

*Note:* A sentence cannot consist of a single clause that begins with a subordinating conjunction (such as *because*) or a relative pronoun (such as *that*); moreover, unless it is a question, a sentence cannot consist of a single clause beginning with *when, where, who, which, what, why,* or *how.*

## 16b Correcting Fragments

If you identify a fragment in your writing, use one of the following three strategies to correct it.

### 1 Attach the Fragment to an Independent Clause

In most cases, the simplest way to correct a fragment is by attaching it to an adjacent independent clause that contains the missing words.

President Lyndon Johnson did not seek reelection/ ~~For~~ a number of reasons. (**prepositional phrase** fragment) [for]
> See A2.3

Students sometimes take a leave of absence/ ~~To~~ decide on definite career goals. (**verbal phrase** fragment) [to]
> See A2.3

The pilot changed course/ ~~Realizing~~ that the weather was worsening. (verbal phrase fragment) [, realizing]

Brian was the star forward of the Blue Devils/ ~~The~~ team with the best record. (**appositive** fragment) [, the]
> See 19b3

Fairy tales are full of damsels in distress/ ~~Such~~ as Rapunzel. (appositive fragment) [, such]

People with dyslexia have trouble reading/ ~~And~~ may also find it difficult to write. (part of compound predicate) [and]

They took only a compass and a canteen/ ~~And~~ some trail mix. (part of compound object) [and]

Property taxes rose sharply/ ~~Although~~ city services declined. (**dependent clause** fragment) [although]
> See A2.3

The battery is dead/ ~~Which~~ means the car won't start. (dependent clause fragment) [, which]

## Close-Up  LISTS

When a fragment takes the form of a list, add a colon to
connect the list to the independent clause that introduces it.

See
32a1

Tourists often outnumber residents in at least four

:

European cities⁄, Venice, Florence, Canterbury,

and Bath.

### 2  Delete the Subordinating Conjunction or Relative Pronoun

When a fragment consists of a dependent clause that is
punctuated as though it were a complete sentence, you can
correct it by attaching it to an adjacent independent clause,
as illustrated in **16b1**. Alternatively, you can simply delete
the subordinating conjunction or relative pronoun.

*City*
Property taxes rose sharply. ~~Although city~~ services
declined. (subordinating conjunction *although* deleted)

*This*
The battery is dead. ~~Which~~ means the car won't start.
(relative pronoun *which* replaced by *this,* a word that
can serve as the sentence's subject)

*Note:* Simply deleting the subordinating conjunction or relative pronoun, as in the two examples above, is usually the
least desirable way to revise a sentence fragment because it is
likely to create two choppy sentences and obscure the connection between them.

### 3  Supply the Missing Subject or Verb

Another way to correct a fragment is to add the missing
words (a subject or a verb or both) that are needed to make
the fragment a sentence.

*It was divided*
In 1948, India became independent. ~~Divided~~ into
the nations of India and Pakistan. (verbal phrase
fragment)

A familiar trademark can increase a product's sales.
*It reminds*
~~Reminding~~ shoppers that the product has a longstand-

ing reputation. (verbal phrase fragment)

## Close-Up    FRAGMENTS INTRODUCED BY TRANSITIONS

Some fragments are word groups that are introduced by
transitional words and phrases, such *as also, finally, in
addition,* and *now,* but are missing subjects and verbs.
To correct such a fragment, you need to add the missing
subject and verb.

See 4b

> *he found*
> Finally, a new home for the family.

> *we need*
> In addition, three new keyboards for the computer lab.

## 16c    Using Fragments Intentionally

Fragments are often used in speech and in personal emails
and other informal writing as well as in journalism, creative
writing, and advertising. In professional and academic writing, however, sentence fragments are generally not acceptable.

---

**CHECKLIST**

### Using Fragments Intentionally

In college writing, it is permissible to use fragments in the
following special situations:

❏ In lists

❏ In captions that accompany visuals

❏ In topic outlines

❏ In quoted dialogue

❏ In bulleted or numbered lists in *PowerPoint* presentations

❏ In titles and subtitles of papers and reports

# CHAPTER 17

# Understanding Agreement

**Agreement** is the correspondence between words in number, gender, or person. Subjects and verbs agree in **number** (singular or plural) and **person** (first, second, or third); pronouns and their antecedents agree in number, person, and gender.

See 23a4

## 17a Making Subjects and Verbs Agree

Singular subjects take singular verbs, and plural subjects take plural verbs.

See 18b1

**Present tense** verbs, except *be* and *have,* add *-s* or *-es* when the subject is third-person singular. (Third-person singular subjects include nouns; the personal pronouns *he, she, it,* and *one;* and many **indefinite pronouns**.)

See 17a4

> The <u>President</u> <u>has</u> the power to veto congressional legislation.
>
> <u>She</u> frequently <u>cites</u> statistics to support her points.
>
> In every group <u>somebody</u> <u>emerges</u> as a natural leader.

Present tense verbs do not add *-s* or *-es* when the subject is a plural noun, a first-person or second-person pronoun (*I, we, you*), or a third-person plural pronoun (*they*).

> <u>Experts</u> <u>recommend</u> that dieters avoid processed meat.
>
> At this stratum, <u>we</u> <u>see</u> rocks dating back ten million years.
>
> <u>They</u> <u>say</u> that some wealthy people have defaulted on their student loans.

In the following situations, making subjects and verbs agree can be challenging for writers.

### 1 When Words Come between Subject and Verb

If a modifying phrase comes between the subject and the verb, the verb should agree with the subject, not with a word in the modifying phrase.

The <u>sound</u> of the drumbeats <u>builds</u> in intensity in Eugene O'Neill's play *The Emperor Jones*.

The <u>games</u> won by the intramural team <u>are</u> few and far between.

This rule also applies to phrases introduced by *along with, as well as, in addition to, including,* and *together with.*

Heavy <u>rain</u>, along with high winds, <u>causes</u> hazardous driving conditions.

**2** **When Compound Subjects Are Joined by *And***

Compound subjects joined by *and* usually take plural verbs.

<u>Air bags and antilock brakes</u> <u>are</u> standard on all new models.

There are, however, two exceptions to this rule:

● Compound subjects joined by *and* that stand for a single idea or person are treated as a unit and take singular verbs.

<u>Rhythm and blues</u> <u>is</u> a forerunner of rock and roll.

● When *each* or *every* precedes a compound subject joined by *and,* the subject takes a singular verb.

<u>Every desk and file cabinet</u> <u>was</u> searched before the letter was found.

**3** **When Compound Subjects Are Joined by *Or***

Compound subjects joined by *or* (or by *either . . . or,* or *neither . . . nor*) may take either a singular or a plural verb.

If both subjects are singular, use a singular verb; if both are plural, use a plural verb. If one subject is singular and the other is plural, the verb agrees with the subject that is nearer to it.

<u>Either radiation treatments or chemotherapy</u> <u>is</u> combined with surgery for effective results.

<u>Either chemotherapy or radiation treatments</u> <u>are</u> combined with surgery for effective results.

**4** **With Indefinite Pronoun Subjects**

Most <u>indefinite pronouns</u>—*another, anyone, everyone, one, each, either, neither, anything, everything, something, nothing, nobody,* and *somebody*—are singular and take singular verbs. <sub>ESL 46c3</sub>

Anyone <u>is</u> welcome to apply for this grant.

Some indefinite pronouns—*both, many, few, several, others*—are plural and take plural verbs.

<u>Several</u> of the articles <u>are</u> useful.

A few indefinite pronouns—*some, all, any, more, most,* and *none*—can be singular or plural, depending on the noun they refer to.

> <u>Some</u> of this trouble <u>is</u> to be expected. (*Some* refers to *trouble.*)

> <u>Some</u> of the spectators <u>are</u> getting restless. (*Some* refers to *spectators.*)

### 5 With Collective Noun Subjects

A **collective noun** names a group of persons or things—for instance, *navy, union, association, band.* When a collective noun refers to the group as a unit (as it usually does), it takes a singular verb; when it refers to the individuals or items that make up the group, it takes a plural verb.

> To many people, the <u>royal family</u> <u>symbolizes</u> Great Britain. (The family, as a unit, is the symbol.)

> The <u>family</u> all <u>eat</u> at different times. (Each family member eats separately.)

Phrases that name fixed amounts—*three-quarters, twenty dollars, the majority*—are treated like collective nouns. When the amount denotes a unit, it takes a singular verb; when it denotes part of the whole, it takes a plural verb.

> <u>Three-quarters</u> of his usual salary <u>is</u> not enough to live on.

> <u>Three-quarters</u> of the patients <u>improve</u> dramatically after treatment.

*Note:* *The number* is always singular, and *a number* is always plural: *The number* of voters <u>has</u> declined; *A number* of students <u>have</u> missed the opportunity to preregister.

### 6 When Singular Subjects Have Plural Forms

A singular subject takes a singular verb even if the form of the subject is plural.

> <u>Statistics</u> <u>deals</u> with the collection and analysis of data.

When such a word has a plural meaning, however, use a plural verb.

> The statistics <u>prove</u> him wrong.

### 7 When Subject-Verb Order Is Inverted

Even when <u>word order</u> is inverted so that the verb comes <sup>ESL 46f</sup> before the subject (as it does in questions and in sentences beginning with *there is* or *there are*), the subject and verb must agree.

> <u>Is</u> <u>either</u> answer correct?
>
> There <u>are</u> currently thirteen circuit <u>courts</u> of appeals in the federal system.

### 8 With Linking Verbs

A <u>linking verb</u> should agree with its subject, not with the <sup>See 20a</sup> subject complement.

> The <u>problem</u> <u>was</u> termites.
>
> <u>Termites</u> <u>were</u> the problem.

### 9 With Relative Pronouns

When you use a <u>relative pronoun</u> (*who, which, that,* and so <sup>See A1.2</sup> on) to introduce a dependent clause, the verb in the dependent clause should agree in number with the pronoun's **antecedent,** the word to which the pronoun refers.

> The farmer is among the <u>ones</u> who <u>suffer</u> during a grain embargo.
>
> The farmer is the only <u>one</u> who <u>suffers</u> during a grain embargo.

## 17b Making Pronouns and Antecedents Agree

A pronoun must agree with its **antecedent**—the word or word group to which the pronoun refers.

Singular pronouns—such as *he, him, she, her, it, me, myself,* and *oneself*—should refer to singular antecedents. Plural pronouns—such as *we, us, they, them,* and *their*—should refer to plural antecedents.

### 1 With Compound Antecedents

In most cases, use a plural pronoun to refer to a **compound antecedent** (two or more words connected by *and*).

Mormonism and Christian Science were similar in their beginnings.

However, there are several exceptions to this general rule:

- Use a singular pronoun when a compound antecedent is preceded by *each* or *every*.

  Every programming language and software package has its limitations.

- Use a singular pronoun to refer to two or more singular antecedents linked by *or* or *nor*.

  Neither Thoreau nor Whitman lived to see his work read widely.

- When one part of a compound antecedent is singular and one part is plural, the pronoun agrees in person and number with the antecedent that is nearer to it.

  Neither the boy nor his parents had fastened their seat belts.

### 2 With Collective Noun Antecedents

If the meaning of a collective noun antecedent is singular (as it will be in most cases), use a singular pronoun. If the meaning is plural, use a plural pronoun.

The teachers' union announced its plan to strike. (The members acted as a unit.)

The team moved to their positions. (Each member acted individually.)

### 3 With Indefinite Pronoun Antecedents

See
17a4 Most **indefinite pronouns**—*each, either, neither, one, anyone,* and the like—are singular and take singular pronouns.

Neither of the men had his proposal ready by the deadline.

Each of these neighborhoods has its own traditions and values.

A few indefinite pronouns are plural; others can be singular or plural.

**Close-Up PRONOUN-ANTECEDENT AGREEMENT**

In speech and in informal writing, many people use the plural pronouns *they* or *their* with singular indefinite pronouns that refer to people, such as *someone, everyone,* and *nobody*.

Everyone can present their own viewpoint.

In college writing, however, avoid using a plural pronoun with a singular indefinite pronoun subject. Instead, you can use both the masculine and the feminine pronoun.

Everyone can present his or her own viewpoint.

Or, you can make the sentence's subject plural.

All participants can present their own viewpoints.

The use of *his* to refer to a singular indefinite pronoun is considered **sexist language**: *Everyone can present* his *own viewpoint*.

See 26c2

CHAPTER 18

# Using Verbs

## 18a Using Irregular Verbs

A **regular verb** forms both its past tense and its past participle by adding *-d* or *-ed* to the **base form** of the verb (the present tense form of the verb that is used with *I*).

## Principal Parts of Regular Verbs

| Base Form | Past Tense Form | Past Participle |
| --- | --- | --- |
| smile | smiled | smiled |
| talk | talked | talked |

**Irregular verbs** do not follow this pattern. The chart that follows lists the principal parts of the most frequently used irregular verbs.

## Frequently Used Irregular Verbs

| Base Form | Past Tense Form | Past Participle |
| --- | --- | --- |
| arise | arose | arisen |
| awake | awoke, awaked | awoke, awaked |
| be | was/were | been |
| beat | beat | beaten |
| begin | began | begun |
| bend | bent | bent |
| bet | bet, betted | bet |
| bite | bit | bitten |
| blow | blew | blown |
| break | broke | broken |
| bring | brought | brought |
| build | built | built |
| burst | burst | burst |
| buy | bought | bought |
| catch | caught | caught |
| choose | chose | chosen |
| cling | clung | clung |
| come | came | come |
| cost | cost | cost |
| deal | dealt | dealt |
| dig | dug | dug |
| dive | dived, dove | dived |
| do | did | done |
| drag | dragged | dragged |
| draw | drew | drawn |
| drink | drank | drunk |
| drive | drove | driven |
| eat | ate | eaten |

| Base Form | Past Tense Form | Past Participle |
|-----------|----------------|----------------|
| fall | fell | fallen |
| fight | fought | fought |
| find | found | found |
| fly | flew | flown |
| forget | forgot | forgotten, forgot |
| freeze | froze | frozen |
| get | got | gotten |
| give | gave | given |
| go | went | gone |
| grow | grew | grown |
| hang (suspend) | hung | hung |
| have | had | had |
| hear | heard | heard |
| keep | kept | kept |
| know | knew | known |
| lay (place/put) | laid | laid |
| lead | led | led |
| lend | lent | lent |
| let | let | let |
| lie (recline) | lay | lain |
| make | made | made |
| prove | proved | proved, proven |
| read | read | read |
| ride | rode | ridden |
| ring | rang | rung |
| rise | rose | risen |
| run | ran | run |
| say | said | said |
| see | saw | seen |
| set (place) | set | set |
| shake | shook | shaken |
| shrink | shrank, shrunk | shrunk, shrunken |
| sing | sang | sung |
| sink | sank | sunk |
| sit | sat | sat |
| speak | spoke | spoken |
| speed | sped, speeded | sped, speeded |
| spin | spun | spun |
| spring | sprang | sprung |
| stand | stood | stood |
| steal | stole | stolen |
| strike | struck | struck, stricken |
| swear | swore | sworn |
| swim | swam | swum |
| swing | swung | swung |
| take | took | taken |
| teach | taught | taught |

*continued*

### Frequently Used Irregular Verbs *(continued)*

| Base Form | Past Tense Form | Past Participle |
|-----------|-----------------|-----------------|
| throw | threw | thrown |
| wake | woke, waked | waked, woken |
| wear | wore | worn |
| wring | wrung | wrung |
| write | wrote | written |

## Close-Up  *LIE/LAY* AND *SIT/SET*

*Lie* means "to recline" and does not take an object ("He likes to *lie* on the floor"); *lay* means "to place" or "to put" and does take an object ("He wants to *lay* a rug on the floor").

| Base Form | Past Tense Form | Past Participle |
|-----------|-----------------|-----------------|
| lie | lay | lain |
| lay | laid | laid |

*Sit* means "to assume a seated position" and does not take an object ("She wants to *sit* on the table"); *set* means "to place" or "to put" and usually takes an object ("She wants to *set* a vase on the table").

| Base Form | Past Tense Form | Past Participle |
|-----------|-----------------|-----------------|
| sit | sat | sat |
| set | set | set |

## 18b  Understanding Tense

ESL
46a2

**Tense** is the form a verb takes to indicate when an action occurred or when a condition existed.

### 1 Using the Simple Tenses

The **simple tenses** include *present, past,* and *future:*

- The **present tense** usually indicates an action that is taking place at the time it is expressed or an action that occurs regularly.

  I <u>see</u> your point. (an action taking place when it is expressed)

We <u>wear</u> wool in the winter. (an action that occurs regularly)

**Close-Up** SPECIAL USES OF THE PRESENT TENSE

The present tense has four special uses.

**To Indicate Future Time:** The grades <u>arrive</u> next Thursday.

**To State a Generally Held Belief:** Studying <u>pays</u> off.

**To State a Scientific Truth:** An object at rest <u>tends</u> to stay at rest.

**To Discuss a Literary Work:** *Family Installments* <u>tells</u> the story of a Puerto Rican family.

- The **past tense** indicates that an action has already taken place.

    John Glenn <u>orbited</u> the earth three times on February 20, 1962. (an action completed in the past)

    As a young man, Mark Twain <u>traveled</u> through the Southwest. (an action that occurred once or many times in the past but did not extend into the present)

- The **future tense** indicates that an action will or is likely to take place.

    Halley's Comet <u>will reappear</u> in 2061. (a future action that will definitely occur)

    The decline of the housing market in Nevada <u>will</u> probably <u>continue</u>. (a future action that is likely to occur)

## 2 Using the Perfect Tenses

The **perfect tenses** indicate actions that were or will be completed before other actions or conditions. The perfect tenses are formed with the appropriate tense form of the auxiliary verb *have* plus the past participle:

- The **present perfect** tense can indicate either of two kinds of continuing action beginning in the past.

Dr. Kim <u>has finished</u> studying the effects of BHA on rats. (an action that began in the past and is finished at the present time)

My mother <u>has invested</u> her money wisely. (an action that began in the past and extends into the present)

- The **past perfect** tense indicates an action occurring before a certain time in the past.

  By 1946, engineers <u>had built</u> the first electronic digital computer.

- The **future perfect** tense indicates that an action will be finished by a certain future time.

  By Tuesday, the transit authority <u>will have run</u> out of money.

### 3 Using the Progressive Tenses

The **progressive tenses** indicate continuing action. They are formed with the appropriate tense of the verb *be* plus the present participle:

- The **present progressive** tense indicates that something is happening at the time it is expressed in speech or writing.

  The volcano <u>is erupting</u>, and lava <u>is flowing</u> toward the town.

- The **past progressive** tense can indicate either of two kinds of past action.

  Roderick Usher's actions <u>were becoming</u> increasingly bizarre. (a continuing action in the past)

  The French revolutionary Marat was stabbed to death while he <u>was bathing</u>. (an action occurring at the same time in the past as another action)

- The **future progressive** tense indicates a continuing action in the future.

  The treasury secretary <u>will be monitoring</u> the money supply very carefully.

- The **present perfect progressive** tense indicates action continuing from the past into the present and possibly into the future.

  Rescuers <u>have been working</u> around the clock.

- The **past perfect progressive** tense indicates that a past action went on until another one occurred.

    President Kennedy <u>had been working</u> on civil rights legislation before he was assassinated.

- The **future perfect progressive** tense indicates that an action will continue until a certain future time.

    By eleven o'clock, we <u>will have been driving</u> for seven hours.

## 18c Understanding Mood

**Mood** is the form a verb takes to indicate whether a writer is making a statement, asking a question, giving a command, or expressing a wish or a contrary-to-fact statement. There are three moods in English:

- The **indicative** mood states a fact, expresses an opinion, or asks a question: *Jackie Robinson <u>had</u> a great impact on professional baseball.*
- The **imperative** mood is used in commands and direct requests: *<u>Use</u> a dictionary.*
- The **subjunctive** mood is used to express wishes, contrary-to-fact conditions, and requests or recommendations.

The **present subjunctive** is used in *that* clauses after words such as *ask, demand, suggest, require,* and *recommend.* The present subjunctive uses the base form of the verb, regardless of the subject.

Captain Ahab demanded that his crew <u>hunt</u> the white whale.

The report recommended that doctors <u>be</u> more flexible.

The **past subjunctive** is used in **conditional statements** (statements beginning with *if, as if,* or *as though* that are contrary to fact and statements that express a wish). The past subjunctive has the same form as the past tense of the verb, except for the verb *be,* which uses *were,* even with singular subjects.

If John <u>went</u> home, he could see Marsha. (John is not home.)

The father acted as if he <u>were</u> having the baby. (The father couldn't be having the baby.)

I wish I <u>were</u> more organized. (expresses a wish)

*Note:* In many situations, the subjunctive mood can sound stiff or formal. To eliminate the need for a subjunctive construction, rephrase the sentence.

The group asked ~~that~~ the city council ^to^ ban smoking in public places.

## 18d Understanding Voice

**Voice** is the form a verb takes to indicate whether the subject of a sentence acts or is acted upon. When the subject of a verb does something—that is, acts—the verb is in the **active voice.** When something is done to the subject of a verb—that is, the subject is acted upon—the verb is in the **passive voice.**

**Active Voice:** Hart Crane <u>wrote</u> *The Bridge*.

**Passive Voice:** *The Bridge* <u>was written</u> by Hart Crane.

Because the active voice emphasizes the person or thing performing an action, it is usually clearer and stronger than the passive voice. Whenever possible, use active voice in your college writing.

^*The students chose investigative*^
~~Investigative~~ reporter Bob Woodward ~~was chosen by the students~~ as the graduation speaker.

Some situations, however, require the use of the passive voice—for example, when the actor is unknown or when the action itself is more important than the actor. This is often the case in scientific or technical writing.

Grits <u>are eaten</u> throughout the South. (Passive voice emphasizes the fact that grits are eaten; who eats them is not important.)

DDT <u>was found</u> in soil samples. (Passive voice emphasizes the discovery of DDT; who found it is not important.)

# CHAPTER 19

# Using Pronouns

## 19a Understanding Pronoun Case

Pronouns change **case** to indicate their function in a sentence. English has three cases: *subjective, objective,* and *possessive.*

### Pronoun Case Forms

**Subjective**

| I | he, she | it | we | you | they | who | whoever |
|---|---------|-----|-----|-----|------|-----|---------|

**Objective**

| me | him, her | it | us | you | them | whom | whomever |
|----|----------|-----|-----|-----|------|------|----------|

**Possessive**

| my | his, her | its | our | your | their | whose |
|------|----------|-----|------|-------|--------|-------|
| mine | hers | | ours | yours | theirs | |

### 1 Subjective Case

A pronoun takes the **subjective case** in these situations.

**Subject of a Verb:** I bought a new mountain bike.

**Subject Complement:** It was he for whom the men were looking.

### 2 Objective Case

A pronoun takes the **objective case** in these situations.

**Direct Object:** Our sociology teacher asked Adam and me to work on the project.

**Indirect Object:** The plumber's bill gave <u>them</u> quite a shock.

**Object of a Preposition:** Between <u>us</u> we own ten shares of stock.

---

## Close-Up  *I* AND *ME*

*I* is not necessarily more appropriate than *me*. In the following situation, *me* is correct.

Just between you and <u>me</u> [not *I*], I think the data are incomplete. (*Me* is the object of the preposition *between*.)

---

### 3 Possessive Case

A pronoun takes the **possessive case** when it indicates ownership (*our* car, *your* book). The possessive case is also used
See
A1.3 before a <u>gerund</u>.

Napoleon approved of <u>their</u> [not *them*] ruling Naples. (*Ruling* is a gerund.)

## 19b Determining Pronoun Case in Special Situations

### 1 In Comparisons with *Than* or *As*

When a comparison ends with a pronoun, the pronoun's function in the sentence determines your choice of pronoun case. If the pronoun functions as a subject, use the subjective case; if it functions as an object, use the objective case. You can determine the function of the pronoun by completing the comparison.

Darcy likes John more than <u>I</u>. (. . . more than *I* like John; *I* is the subject.)

Darcy likes John more than <u>me</u>. (. . . more than she likes *me*; *me* is the object.)

### 2 With *Who* and *Whom*

The case of the pronouns *who* and *whom* depends on their function *within their own clause*. When a pronoun serves as the subject of its clause, use *who* or *whoever;* when it functions as an object, use *whom* or *whomever.*

> The Salvation Army gives food and shelter to <u>whoever</u> is in need. (*Whoever* is the subject of the dependent clause.)
>
> I wonder <u>whom</u> jazz musician Miles Davis influenced. (*Whom* is the object of *influenced* in the dependent clause.)

---

## Close-Up   PRONOUN CASE IN QUESTIONS

To determine the case of *who* at the beginning of a question, use a personal pronoun to answer the question. The case of *who* should be the same as the case of the personal pronoun.

> <u>Who</u> wrote *The Age of Innocence*? <u>She</u> wrote it. (subject)
>
> <u>Whom</u> do you support for mayor? I support <u>her</u>. (object)

---

### 3  With Appositives

An **appositive** is a noun or noun phrase that identifies or renames an adjacent noun or pronoun. The case of a pronoun in an appositive depends on the function of the word the appositive identifies or renames.

> Two artists, <u>he</u> and Smokey Robinson, recorded for Motown Records. (*Artists* is the subject of the sentence, so the pronoun in the appositive *he and Smokey Robinson* takes the subjective case.)
>
> We heard two Motown recording artists, Smokey Robinson and <u>him</u>. (*Artists* is the object of the verb *heard*, so the pronoun in the appositive *Smokey Robinson and him* takes the objective case.)

### 4  With *We* and *Us* before a Noun

When a first-person plural pronoun directly precedes a noun, the case of the pronoun depends on the function of the noun in the sentence.

> <u>We</u> women must stick together. (*Women* is the subject of the sentence, so the pronoun *we* takes the subjective case.)

Good teachers make learning easy for <u>us</u> students.
(*Students* is the object of the preposition *for*, so the
pronoun *us* takes the objective case.)

## 19c Revising Pronoun Reference Errors

ESL
46c1

An <u>antecedent</u> is the word or word group to which a pronoun refers. The connection between a pronoun and its antecedent should be clear.

<u>Alicia</u> forgot <u>her</u> cell phone.

The <u>students</u> missed <u>their</u> train.

### 1 Ambiguous Antecedents

Sometimes it is not clear to which antecedent a pronoun—
for example, *this, that, which,* or *it*—refers. In such cases,
eliminate the ambiguity by substituting a noun for the pronoun.

The accountant took out his calculator and completed
*the calculator*
the tax return. Then, he put it into his briefcase. (The
pronoun *it* can refer either to *calculator* or to *tax
return.*)

Sometimes a pronoun—for example, *this*—does not seem
to refer to any specific antecedent. In such cases, supply a
noun to clarify the reference.

Some one-celled organisms contain chlorophyll yet
*paradox*
are considered animals. This illustrates the difficulty

of classifying single-celled organisms. (Exactly what
does *this* refer to?)

### 2 Remote Antecedents

The farther a pronoun is from its antecedent, the more difficult it is for readers to make a connection between them.
If a pronoun's antecedent is far away from it, replace the
pronoun with a noun.

During the mid-1800s, many Czechs began to immigrate

to America. By 1860, about 23,000 Czechs had left their

country. By 1900, 13,000 Czech immigrants were coming
                America's
to ͜its shores each year.

**3** Nonexistent Antecedents

Sometimes a pronoun refers to an antecedent that does not
appear in the sentence. In such cases, replace the pronoun
with a noun.

Our township has decided to build a computer lab in
                        Teachers
the elementary school. ͜T̶h̶e̶y̶ feel that fourth-graders

should begin using computers. (*They* refers to an
antecedent the writer has failed to mention.)

---

# Close-Up   WHO, WHICH, AND THAT

In general, *who* refers to people or to animals that have
names. *Which* and *that* refer to objects, events, or unnamed
animals. When referring to an antecedent, be sure to
choose the appropriate pronoun (*who, which,* or *that*).

David Henry Hwang, <u>who</u> wrote the Tony Award–winning
play *M. Butterfly,* also wrote *Yellow Face* and *Chinglish.*

The spotted owl, <u>which</u> lives in old-growth forests, is in
danger of extinction.

Houses <u>that</u> are built today are usually more energy
efficient than those built twenty years ago.

Never use *that* to refer to a person:
        who
The man ͜t̶h̶a̶t̶ won the trophy is my neighbor.

*Note:* *Which* introduces <u>nonrestrictive clauses</u>, which are
set off by commas. *That* introduces <u>restrictive clauses</u>,
which are not set off by commas. *Who* can introduce
either restrictive or nonrestrictive clauses.

See 28d1

# Using Adjectives and Adverbs

Adjectives and adverbs describe, limit, or qualify other words, phrases, or clauses. **Adjectives** modify nouns and pronouns. **Adverbs** modify verbs, adjectives, or other adverbs—or entire phrases, clauses, or sentences.

The function of a word in a sentence, not its form, determines whether it is an adjective or an adverb. Although many adverbs (such as *immediately* and *hopelessly*) end in *-ly*, others (such as *almost* and *very*) do not. Moreover, some words that end in *-ly* (such as *lively*) are adjectives.

For information on correct placement of adjectives and adverbs in a sentence, **see 46d1**. For information on correct order of adjectives in a series, **see 46d2**.

## 20a Using Adjectives

See
A1.3

Use an adjective, not an adverb, as a subject complement. A <u>subject complement</u> is a word that follows a linking verb and modifies the sentence's subject, not its verb. A **linking verb** does not show physical or emotional action. *Seem, appear, believe, become, grow, turn, remain, prove, look, sound, smell, taste, feel,* and the forms of the verb *be* are (or can be used as) linking verbs.

> Michelle seemed <u>brave</u>. (*Seemed* shows no action, so it is a linking verb. Because *brave* is a subject complement that modifies the noun *Michelle,* it takes the adjective form.)

> Michelle smiled <u>bravely</u>. (*Smiled* shows action, so it is not a linking verb. Because *bravely* modifies *smiled,* it takes the adverb form.)

*Note:* Sometimes the same verb can function as either a linking verb or an action verb.

> He looked <u>hungry</u>. (Here, *looked* is a linking verb; *hungry* modifies the subject.)

He looked <u>hungrily</u> at the sandwich. (Here, *looked* is an action verb; *hungrily* modifies the verb.)

## 20b Using Adverbs

Use an adverb, not an adjective, to modify verbs, adjectives, or other adverbs—or entire phrases, clauses, or sentences.

*very well*
Most students did ~~great~~ on the midterm.

*conservatively*
My parents dress a lot more ~~conservative~~ than my friends do.

### Close-Up  USING ADJECTIVES AND ADVERBS

In informal speech, adjective forms such as *good, bad, sure, real, slow, quick,* and *loud* are often used to modify verbs, adjectives, and adverbs. Avoid these informal modifiers in college writing.

*really well*
The program ran ~~real good~~ the first time we tried it, but
*badly*
the new system performed ~~bad.~~

## 20c Using Comparative and Superlative Forms

Most adjectives and adverbs have **comparative** and **superlative** forms.

### Comparative and Superlative Forms

| Form | Function | Example |
|------|----------|---------|
| Positive | Describes a quality; indicates no comparison | big, easily |
| Comparative | Indicates comparison between two qualities (greater or lesser) | bigger, more easily |
| Superlative | Indicates comparison among more than two qualities (greatest or least) | biggest, most easily |

## 1 Regular Comparative and Superlative Forms

To form the comparative and superlative, all one-syllable adjectives and many two-syllable adjectives (particularly those that end in *-y, -ly, -le, -er,* and *-ow*) add *-er* or *-est*: slow*er*, funni*er*; slow*est*, funni*est*. (Note that a final *y* becomes *i* before the *-er* or *-est* is added.)

Other two-syllable adjectives and all long adjectives form the comparative with *more* and the superlative with *most*: *more* famous, *more* incredible; *most* famous, *most* incredible.

Adverbs ending in *-ly* also form the comparative with *more* and the superlative with *most*: *more* slowly; *most* slowly. Other adverbs use the *-er* and *-est* endings: soon*er*; soon*est*.

All adjectives and adverbs form the comparative with *less* (*less* lovely; *less* slowly) and the superlative with *least* (*least* lovely; *least* slowly).

---

## Close-Up USING COMPARATIVES AND SUPERLATIVES

- Never use both *more* and *-er* to form the comparative, and never use both *most* and *-est* to form the superlative.

    Nothing could have been ~~more~~ easier.

    Jack is the ~~most~~ meanest person I know.

- Never use the superlative when comparing only two things.

    older
    Stacy is the ~~oldest~~ of the two sisters.

- Never use the comparative when comparing more than two things.

    earliest
    We chose the ~~earlier~~ of the four appointments.

---

## 2 Irregular Comparative and Superlative Forms

Some adjectives and adverbs have irregular comparative and superlative forms.

### Irregular Comparative and Superlative Forms

|  | Positive | Comparative | Superlative |
|---|---|---|---|
| **Adjectives:** | good | better | best |
|  | bad | worse | worst |
|  | a little | less | least |
|  | many, much, some | more | most |
| **Adverbs:** | well | better | best |
|  | badly | worse | worst |

## Close-Up ILLOGICAL COMPARATIVE AND SUPERLATIVE FORMS

Many adjectives—for example, *perfect, unique, excellent, impossible, parallel, empty,* and *dead*—are **absolutes**; therefore, they have no comparative or superlative forms.

> I saw ~~the most~~ <sup>a</sup> unique vase in the museum.

These adjectives can, however, be modified by words that suggest approaching the absolute state—*nearly* or *almost,* for example.

> He revised until his draft was <u>almost perfect</u>.

**Note:** Some adverbs, particularly those indicating time, place, and degree (*almost, very, here, immediately*), do not have comparative or superlative forms.

# Writing Effective Sentences

# CHAPTER 21

# Writing Varied Sentences

## 21a Using Compound and Complex Sentences

See A2.2 Paragraphs that mix <u>simple sentences</u> with compound and complex sentences are more varied—and therefore more interesting—than those that do not.

### 1 Compound Sentences

A **compound sentence** consists of two or more independent clauses joined with *coordinating conjunctions, transitional words and phrases, correlative conjunctions, semicolons,* or *colons.*

#### Coordinating Conjunctions

The pianist was nervous, <u>but</u> the concert was a success.

**Note:** Remember to use a comma before the coordinating conjunction—*and, or, nor, but, for, so,* and *yet*—that joins See A2.3 the two <u>independent clauses.</u>

See 4b *Transitional Words and Phrases* Frequently used <u>transitional words and phrases</u> include conjunctive adverbs such as *consequently, finally, still,* and *thus,* as well as expressions such as *for example, in fact,* and *for instance.*

The saxophone does not belong to the brass family; <u>in fact</u>, it is a member of the woodwind family.

**Note:** Use a semicolon—not a comma—before the transitional word or phrase that joins the two independent clauses.

#### Correlative Conjunctions

<u>Either</u> he left his coat in his locker, <u>or</u> he left it on the bus.

#### Semicolons

Alaska is the largest state; Rhode Island is the smallest.

*Colons*

He got his orders: he was to leave on Sunday.

## Close-Up   USING COMPOUND SENTENCES

Joining independent clauses into compound sentences helps to show readers the relationships between the clauses. Compound sentences can indicate the following relationships:

- Addition (*and, in addition, not only . . . but also*)
- Contrast (*but, however*)
- Causal relationships (*so, therefore, consequently*)
- Alternatives (*or, either . . . or*)

## 2 Complex Sentences

A **complex sentence** consists of one independent clause and at least one <u>dependent clause</u>. In a complex sentence, a **subordinating conjunction** or **relative pronoun** links the independent and dependent clauses and indicates the relationship between them.

See A2.3

   (dependent clause)       (independent clause)
[<u>After</u> the town was evacuated], [the hurricane began].

   (independent clause)       (dependent clause)
[Officials watched the storm] [<u>that</u> threatened to destroy the town].

             (dependent clause)
Town officials, [<u>who</u> were very concerned], watched the storm.

### Frequently Used Subordinating Conjunctions

| | | |
|---|---|---|
| after | before | until |
| although | if | when |
| as | once | whenever |
| as if | since | where |
| as though | that | wherever |
| because | unless | while |

**Relative Pronouns**

| that | whatever | who (whose, whom) |
| what | which | whoever (whomever) |

## Close-Up   USING COMPLEX SENTENCES

When you join clauses to create complex sentences, you help readers to see the relationships between your ideas. Complex sentences can indicate the following relationships:

- Time relationships (*before, after, until, when, since*)
- Contrast (*however, although*)
- Causal relationships (*therefore, because, so that*)
- Conditional relationships (*if, unless*)
- Location (*where, wherever*)
- Identity (*who, which, that*)

## 21b   Varying Sentence Length

Strings of short simple sentences can be tedious—and sometimes hard to follow, as the following paragraph illustrates.

> John Peter Zenger was a newspaper editor. He waged and won an important battle for freedom of the press in America. He criticized the policies of the British governor. He was charged with criminal libel as a result. Zenger's lawyers were disbarred by the governor. Andrew Hamilton defended him. Hamilton convinced the jury that Zenger's criticisms were true. Therefore, the statements were not libelous.

You can revise a series of choppy sentences like the ones in the paragraph above by using *coordination, subordination,* or *embedding* to combine sentences.

**Coordination** pairs similar elements—words, phrases, or clauses—giving equal weight to each.

> John Peter Zenger was a newspaper editor. He waged and won an important battle for freedom of the press in America.

He criticized the policies of the British governor and he was charged with criminal libel as a result. Zenger's lawyers were disbarred by the governor. Andrew Hamilton defended him. Hamilton convinced the jury that Zenger's criticisms were true. Therefore, the statements were not libelous.

*Two sentences linked with and, creating compound sentence*

**ESL TIP**

Some ESL students rely on simple sentences and coordination in their writing because they are afraid of making sentence structure errors. The result is a monotonous style. To add variety, try using **subordination** and **embedding** (as illustrated below) in your sentences.

**Subordination** places the more important idea in an independent clause and the less important idea in a dependent clause.

John Peter Zenger was a newspaper editor who waged and won an important battle for freedom of the press in America. He criticized the policies of the British governor, and he was charged with criminal libel as a result. When Zenger's lawyers were disbarred by the governor, Andrew Hamilton defended him. Hamilton convinced the jury that Zenger's criticisms were true. Therefore, the statements were not libelous.

*Simple sentences become dependent clauses, creating two complex sentences*

**Embedding** is the working of additional words and phrases into a sentence.

John Peter Zenger was a newspaper editor who waged and won an important battle for freedom of the press in America. He criticized the policies of the British governor, and he was charged with criminal libel as a result. When Zenger's lawyers were disbarred by the governor, Andrew Hamilton defended him, convincing the jury that Zenger's criticisms were true. Therefore, the statements were not libelous.

*The sentence Hamilton convinced the jury . . . becomes the phrase convincing the jury*

This final revision of the original string of choppy sentences is interesting and readable because it is now composed of varied and logically linked sentences. (The short simple sentence at the end has been retained for emphasis.)

## 21c Varying Sentence Openings

Rather than beginning every sentence with the subject (*I, He,* or *It,* for example), begin some sentences with modifying words, phrases, or clauses.

*Words*

> Proud and relieved, they watched their daughter receive her diploma.

> Hungrily, he devoured his lunch.

*Phrases*

> For better or for worse, credit cards are now widely available to college students.

> Located on the west coast of Great Britain, Wales is part of the United Kingdom.

> His interests widening, Picasso designed ballet sets and illustrated books.

*Clauses*

> After President Woodrow Wilson was incapacitated by a stroke, his wife unofficially performed many of his duties.

CHAPTER **22**

# Writing Concise Sentences

A sentence is not concise simply because it is short; a **concise** sentence contains only the words necessary to make its point.

## Close-Up TEXT MESSAGES

If you send texts, you already use certain strategies to make your writing concise: you omit articles and other nonessential words, and you use nonstandard spellings (*nite*) and shorthand (*ru home?*). However, this kind of language is not acceptable in college writing, where you need to use other strategies (such as those discussed in this chapter) to make your writing concise.

## 22a  Eliminating Wordiness

Whenever possible, delete nonessential words—*deadwood,*
*utility words,* and *circumlocution*—from your writing.

### 1  Eliminating Deadwood

The term **deadwood** refers to unnecessary phrases that take
up space and add nothing to meaning.

*Many*
~~There were many~~ factors ~~that~~ influenced his decision to
become a priest.

The two plots are ~~both~~ similar in ~~the way~~ that they trace
the characters' increasing rage.

*is*
The only truly tragic character in *Hamlet* ~~would have to~~
~~be~~ Ophelia.

*This*
~~In this~~ article ~~it~~ discusses lead poisoning.

Deadwood also includes unnecessary statements of opinion, such as *I feel, it seems to me, I believe,* and *in my opinion.*

*The*
~~In my opinion, I believe the~~ characters seem undeveloped.

*This*
~~As far as I'm concerned, this~~ course should not be
required.

### 2  Eliminating Utility Words

**Utility words** function as filler and have no real meaning
in a sentence. Utility words include nouns with imprecise
meanings (*factor, situation, type, aspect,* and so on); adjectives so general that they are almost meaningless (*good, bad,*
*important*); and common adverbs denoting degree (*basically,*
*actually, quite, very, definitely*).

Often, you can just delete a utility word; if you cannot,
replace it with a more precise word.

*Registration*
~~The registration situation~~ was disorganized.

It was ~~basically~~ a worthwhile book, but I didn't ~~actually~~
finish it.

### 3 Avoiding Circumlocution

**Circumlocution** is taking a roundabout way to say something (using ten words when five will do). Instead of complicated constructions, use concise, specific words and phrases that come right to the point.

> The
> ~~It is not unlikely that the~~ trend toward lower consumer
> probably
> spending will continue.

> while
> Joe was in the army ~~during the same time that~~ I was in college.

---

## Close-Up  REVISING WORDY PHRASES

If you cannot edit a wordy construction, substitute a more concise, more direct term.

| Wordy | Concise |
|---|---|
| at the present time | now |
| due to the fact that | because |
| in the vicinity of | near |
| have the ability to | be able to |

---

### 22b Eliminating Unnecessary Repetition

Although intentional repetition can add emphasis to your writing, **redundant** word groups (repeated words or phrases that say the same thing, such as *true facts* or *armed gunman*) and other kinds of unnecessary repetition can annoy readers and obscure your meaning. Correct unnecessary repetition by using one of the following strategies.

### 1 Deleting Redundancy

People's clothing ~~attire~~ can reveal a good deal about their personalities.

The two candidates share several positions ~~in common~~.

### 2 Substituting a Pronoun

Fictional detective Miss Marple has solved many

her
crimes. *The Murder at the Vicarage* was one of ~~Miss~~

~~Marple's~~ most challenging cases.

### 3 Creating an Appositive

Red Barber , was a sportscaster, He was known for his colorful expressions.

### 4 Creating a Compound

John F. Kennedy was the youngest man ever elected
*and*
president, He was the first Catholic to hold this office.

### 5 Creating a Complex Sentence

, which
Americans value freedom of speech, Freedom of speech
is guaranteed by the First Amendment.

## 22c Tightening Rambling Sentences

The combination of nonessential words, unnecessary repetition, and complicated syntax creates **rambling sentences.** Revising such sentences frequently requires extensive editing.

### 1 Eliminating Excessive Coordination

When you string a series of clauses together with coordinating conjunctions, you create a rambling, unfocused **compound sentence**. To revise such sentences, first identify the main idea, and state it in an independent clause; then, add the supporting details.

See 21a1

**Wordy:** Puerto Rico is a large Caribbean island, and it is very mountainous, and it has steep slopes, and they fall to gentle plains along the coast.

**Concise:** A large Caribbean island, Puerto Rico is very mountainous, with steep slopes falling to gentle plains along the coast. (Puerto Rico's mountainous terrain is the sentence's main idea.)

### 2 Eliminating Adjective Clauses

A series of **adjective clauses** is also likely to produce a rambling sentence. To revise, substitute concise modifying words or phrases for the adjective clauses.

See A2.3

**Wordy:** *Moby-Dick*, which is a novel about a white whale, was written by Herman Melville, who was friendly with Nathaniel Hawthorne, who urged him to revise the first draft.

**Concise:** *Moby-Dick*, a novel about a white whale, was written by Herman Melville, who revised the first draft at the urging of his friend Nathaniel Hawthorne.

### 3 Eliminating Passive Constructions

See 18d

Unnecessary use of the <u>passive voice</u> can also create a rambling sentence. Correct this problem by changing passive voice to active voice.

~~Water rights are being fought for in court by~~ Indian

tribes like the Papago in Arizona and the Pyramid
*are fighting in court for water rights.*
Lake Paiute in Nevada/

### 4 Eliminating Wordy Prepositional Phrases

When you revise, substitute adjectives or adverbs for wordy <u>prepositional phrases</u>.

See A2.3

       *dangerous*                 *exciting.*
The trip was ~~one of danger~~ but also ~~one of excitement.~~

      *confidently*               *authoritatively.*
He spoke ~~in a confident manner~~ and ~~with a lot of authority.~~

### 5 Eliminating Wordy Noun Constructions

See A2.3

Substitute strong verbs for wordy <u>noun phrases</u>.

    *decided*
We have ~~made the decision~~ to postpone the meeting
                          *appear*
until ~~the appearance of~~ all the board members.

CHAPTER 23

# Revising Awkward or Confusing Sentences

The most common causes of awkward or confusing sentences are *unnecessary shifts, mixed constructions, faulty predication,* and *illogical comparisons.*

## 23a  Revising Unnecessary Shifts

### 1  Shifts in Tense

Verb **tense** in a sentence or in a related group of sentences should shift only for a good reason—to indicate a change of time, for example. Unnecessary shifts in tense can be confusing.

See 18b

ESL 46a2

I registered for the advanced philosophy seminar

because I wanted a challenge. However, by the first week

*started*

I start having trouble understanding the reading.
(unnecessary shift from past to present)

### 2  Shifts in Voice

Unnecessary shifts from active to passive **voice** (or from passive to active) can be confusing.

See 18d

ESL 46a6

*he*

F. Scott Fitzgerald wrote *This Side of Paradise*, and

*wrote*

later *The Great Gatsby* was written. (unnecessary shift from active to passive)

### 3  Shifts in Mood

Unnecessary shifts in **mood** can also create awkward sentences.

See 18c

*be*

Next, heat the mixture in a test tube, and you should make sure it does not boil. (unnecessary shift from imperative to indicative)

### 4  Shifts in Person and Number

**Person** indicates who is speaking (first person—*I, we*), who is spoken to (second person—*you*), and who is spoken about (third person—*he, she, it,* and *they*). Most often, unnecessary shifts between the second and the third person are responsible for awkward sentences.

ESL 46a1

*you*

When one looks for a car loan, you compare the interest rates of several banks. (unnecessary shift from third to second person)

**Number** indicates one (singular—*novel, it*) or more than one (plural—*novels, they, them*). Singular pronouns should refer to singular **antecedents** and plural pronouns to plural antecedents.

See 19c

ESL 46c1

*he or she*

If a person does not study regularly, ~~they~~ will have a difficult time passing Spanish. (unnecessary shift from singular to plural)

## 23b    Revising Mixed Constructions

A **mixed construction** occurs when an introductory dependent clause, prepositional phrase, or independent clause is incorrectly used as the subject of a sentence.

Because she studies every day, ~~explains why~~ she gets good grades. (dependent clause incorrectly used as subject)

*, you can*

By calling for information, ~~is the way to~~ learn more about the benefits of ROTC. (prepositional phrase incorrectly used as subject)

*Being*

He was late ~~was what~~ made him miss the first act. (independent clause incorrectly used as subject)

## 23c    Revising Faulty Predication

**Faulty predication** occurs when a sentence's subject and predicate do not logically go together. Faulty predication often occurs in sentences that contain a linking verb—a form of the verb *be*, for example—and a subject complement.

*caused*

Mounting costs and decreasing revenues ~~were~~ the downfall of the hospital.

Faulty predication also occurs when a one-sentence definition contains the construction *is where* or *is when*. (In a definition, *is* must be preceded and followed by a noun or noun phrase.)

*the construction of*

Taxidermy is ~~where you construct~~ a lifelike representation of an animal from its preserved skin.

Finally, faulty predication occurs when the phrase *the reason is* precedes *because*. In this situation, *because* (which means "for the reason that") is redundant and should be deleted.

*that*

The reason we drive is ~~because~~ we are afraid to fly.

# CHAPTER 24

# Using Parallelism

**Parallelism**—the use of matching words, phrases, or clauses to express equivalent ideas—adds unity, balance, and coherence to your writing. Effective parallelism makes sentences easier to follow and emphasizes relationships among equivalent ideas, but <u>faulty parallelism</u> can create awkward sentences that obscure your meaning and confuse readers.

See 24b

## 24a Using Parallelism Effectively

### 1 With Items in a Series

Items in a series should be presented in parallel terms.

<u>Eat</u>, <u>drink</u>, and <u>be</u> merry.

<u>Baby food consumption</u>, <u>toy production</u>, and <u>school construction</u> are likely to decline as the U.S. population ages.

### 2 With Paired Items

Paired words, phrases, or clauses should be presented in parallel terms.

The thank-you note was <u>short</u> but <u>sweet</u>.

<u>Ask not what your country can do for you</u>; <u>ask what you can do for your country</u>. (John F. Kennedy)

Paired items linked by **correlative conjunctions** (such as *not only . . . but also* and *either . . . or*) should always be parallel.

The design team paid attention not only <u>to color</u> but also <u>to texture</u>.

Either <u>repeat physics</u> or <u>take calculus</u>.

Parallelism is also used with paired elements linked by *than* or *as*.

Richard Wright and James Baldwin chose <u>to live in Paris</u> rather than <u>to remain in the United States</u>.

Success is as much <u>a matter of hard work</u> as <u>a matter of luck</u>.

*Note:* Elements in **outlines** and **lists** should also be parallel.

See
6h1,
40c

## **24b** Revising Faulty Parallelism

**Faulty parallelism** occurs when elements in a sentence that express equivalent ideas are not presented in parallel terms.

Many residents of developing countries lack adequate
housing, sufficient food, and ~~their~~ *adequate* health-care

facilities ~~are also inadequate.~~

To correct faulty parallelism, match nouns with nouns, verbs with verbs, and phrases or clauses with similarly constructed phrases or clauses.

Popular exercises for men and women include spinning,
~~weights~~ *weight training*, and running.

I look forward to hearing from you and to ~~have~~ *having* an opportunity to tell you more about myself.

---

## Close-Up REPEATING KEY WORDS

Although the use of similar grammatical structures may be enough to convey parallelism, sometimes sentences are even clearer if certain key words (for example, articles, prepositions, and the *to* in infinitives) are also repeated in each element of a pair or series. In the following sentence, repeating the preposition *by* makes it clear that *not* applies only to the first phrase.

Computerization has helped industry by not allowing
labor costs to skyrocket, *by* increasing the speed of
production, and *by* improving efficiency.

# CHAPTER 25

# Placing Modifiers Carefully

A **modifier** is a word, phrase, or clause that describes, limits, or qualifies another word in the sentence. A modifier should be placed close to the word it modifies.

Wendy watched the storm, <u>fierce and threatening</u>. (*fierce and threatening* modifies *storm*)

**Faulty modification** is the awkward or confusing placement of modifiers or the modification of nonexistent words.

## 25a Revising Misplaced Modifiers

A **misplaced modifier** is a word or word group whose placement suggests that it modifies one word when it is intended to modify another.

**Confusing:** <u>With an IQ of just 52,</u> the lawyer argued that his client should not get the death penalty. (Does the lawyer have an IQ of 52?)

**Revised:** The lawyer argued that his client, <u>with an IQ of just 52,</u> should not get the death penalty.

### 1 Placing Limiting Modifiers

**Limiting modifiers**—such as *almost, only, even, hardly, just, merely, nearly, exactly, scarcely,* and *simply*—should immediately precede the words they modify. Different placements change the meaning of the sentence.

Nick *just* set up camp at the edge of town. (He did it just now.)

*Just* Nick set up camp at the edge of town. (He did it alone.)

Nick set up camp *just* at the edge of town. (His camp was precisely at the edge.)

When a limiting modifier is placed so that it is not clear whether it modifies a word before it or a word after it, it is called a **squinting modifier.**

⑦

The life that everyone thought would fulfill her totally bored her.

⑦

To correct a squinting modifier, place the modifier so that it is clear which word it modifies.

The life that everyone thought would <u>totally</u> fulfill her bored her. (She was expected to be totally fulfilled.)

The life that everyone thought would fulfill her bored her <u>totally</u>. (She was totally bored.)

## ❷ Relocating Misplaced Phrases

To avoid ambiguity, place phrases as close as possible to the words they modify:

● Place verbal phrases directly before or directly after the words they modify.

*Roller-skating along the shore,*
ᵥJane watched the boats˄~~roller skating along the shore.~~

● Place prepositional phrases immediately after the words they modify.

*with no arms*
*Venus de Milo* is a statue˄created by a famous artist˄~~with no arms.~~

## ❸ Relocating Misplaced Dependent Clauses

A dependent clause that serves as a modifier must be clearly related to the word it modifies.

● An **adjective clause** appears immediately *after* the word it modifies.

*, which will benefit everyone,*
This diet program˄will limit the consumption of

possible carcinogens˄~~which will benefit everyone.~~

● An **adverb clause** may appear in various positions, as long as its relationship to the word it modifies is clear.

<u>When Lincoln was president</u>, the Civil War raged.

The Civil War raged when Lincoln was president.

## 25b Revising Intrusive Modifiers

An **intrusive modifier** awkwardly interrupts a sentence, making the sentence difficult to understand.

● Revise when a long modifying phrase comes between an auxiliary verb and the main verb.

> *Without*
> ^She had, without giving it a second thought or consid-
> *she had*
> ering the consequences, ^planned to reenlist.

● Revise when a modifier creates an awkward **split infinitive**—that is, when the modifier comes between ("splits") the word *to* and the base form of the verb.

> *defeat his opponent*
> He hoped to ^quickly and easily ^defeat his opponent.

*Note:* A split infinitive is acceptable when the intervening modifier is short, especially if the alternative would be awkward or ambiguous: *She expected to almost beat her previous record.*

## 25c Revising Dangling Modifiers

A **dangling modifier** is a word or phrase that cannot logically modify any word in the sentence.

> Using this drug, many undesirable side effects are experienced. (Who is using this drug?)

● One way to correct this dangling modifier is to **create a new subject** by adding a word that the modifier (*using this drug*) can logically modify.

> Using this drug, patients experience many undesirable side effects.

● Another way to correct the dangling modifier is to **create a dependent clause.**

> Many undesirable side effects are experienced when this drug is used.

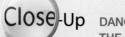

Close-Up DANGLING MODIFIERS AND
THE PASSIVE VOICE

See
18d

ESL
46a6

Many sentences that include dangling modifiers are in the passive voice. Changing the passive voice to the active voice corrects the dangling modifier by changing the subject of the sentence's main clause (*side effects*) to a word that the dangling modifier can logically modify (*patients*).

CHAPTER **26**

# Choosing Words

## 26a Choosing the Right Word

### 1 Denotation and Connotation

A word's **denotation** is its basic dictionary meaning—what it stands for without any emotional associations. A word's **connotations** are the emotional, social, and political associations it has in addition to its denotative meaning.

| Word | Denotation | Connotation |
|------|-----------|-------------|
| politician | someone who holds a political office | opportunist; wheeler-dealer |

If you use terms without considering their connotations, you risk confusing and possibly alienating your readers.

Close-Up USING A THESAURUS

A **thesaurus** lists **synonyms** (words that have the same meaning—for example, *well* and *healthy*) and **antonyms** (words that have opposite meanings—for example, *courage* and *cowardice*). Most online dictionaries, as well as *Microsoft Word*, enable you to access a thesaurus. When you consult a thesaurus, remember that no two words have exactly the same meaning.

## 2 Euphemisms

A **euphemism** is a mild or polite term used in place of a blunt term to describe something that is unpleasant or embarrassing. College writing is no place for euphemisms. Say what you mean—*pregnant,* not *expecting; died,* not *passed away;* and *strike,* not *work stoppage.*

## 3 Specific and General Words

**Specific** words refer to particular persons, items, or events; **general** words denote entire classes or groups. *Queen Elizabeth II,* for example, is more specific than *ruler; jeans* is more specific than *clothing;* and *hybrid car* is more specific than *vehicle.* You can use general words to describe entire classes of items, but you should use specific words to clarify such generalizations.

### Close-Up   USING SPECIFIC WORDS

Avoid general words such as *nice, great,* and *terrific* that say nothing and could be used in almost any sentence. These utility words convey only enthusiasm, not precise meanings. Replace them with more specific words.

See 22a2

## 4 Abstract and Concrete Words

**Abstract** words—*beauty, truth, justice,* and so on—refer to ideas, qualities, or conditions that cannot be perceived by the senses. **Concrete** words name things that readers can see, hear, taste, smell, or touch. The more concrete your words and phrases, the more vivid the images you evoke in your readers' minds.

## 5 Commonly Confused Words (Homophones)

Some words, such as *accept* and *except,* are pronounced alike but spelled differently. Because they are often confused, you should be careful when you use them.

| | |
|---|---|
| accept | to receive |
| except | other than |
| affect | to have an influence on (*verb*) |
| effect | result (*noun*); to cause (*verb*) |
| its | possessive of *it* |
| it's | contraction of *it is* |

For a full list of these and other homophones, along with their meanings and sentences illustrating their use, **see Appendix B.**

## 26b Avoiding Inappropriate Language

When you write, avoid language that is inappropriate for your audience and purpose.

### 1 Jargon

**Jargon,** the specialized or technical vocabulary of a trade, profession, or academic discipline, is useful for communicating in the field for which it was developed, but outside that field it is often confusing.

> *a heart attack.*
> The patient had ~~an acute myocardial infarction.~~

### 2 Pretentious Diction

Good writing is clear writing, and pompous or flowery language is no substitute for clarity. Revise to eliminate **pretentious diction,** inappropriately elevated and wordy language.

> *asleep*          *thought*                    *hiking*
> As I fell ~~into slumber,~~ I ~~cogitated~~ about my day ~~ambling~~ through ~~the splendor of~~ the Appalachian Mountains.

### 3 Clichés

**Clichés** are tired expressions that have lost their impact because they have been so overused. Familiar sayings like "The bottom line," "it is what it is," and "what goes around comes around," for example, do little to enhance your writing. Avoid the temptation to use clichés in your college writing.

## 26c Avoiding Offensive Language

### 1 Stereotypes

When referring to a racial, ethnic, or religious group, use words with neutral connotations or words that the group itself uses in *formal* speech or writing. Also avoid potentially offensive labels related to age, social class, occupation, physical or mental ability, or sexual orientation.

### 2 Sexist Language

Avoid **sexist language,** language that reinforces and promotes gender stereotypes. Sexist language entails much more than the use of derogatory words. For example, assuming that some professions are exclusive to one gender—for instance, that *nurse* denotes only women or that *engineer* denotes only men—is sexist. So is the use of job titles such as *mailman* for *letter carrier* and *stewardess* for *flight attendant*.

Sexist language also occurs when a writer fails to apply the same terminology to both men and women. For example, you should refer to two scientists with PhDs not as Dr. Sagan and Mrs. Yallow, but as Dr. Sagan and Dr. Yallow.

In your writing, always use *women*—not *girls* or *ladies*—when referring to adult females. Also avoid using the generic *he* or *him* when your subject could be either male or female. Instead, use the third-person plural or the phrase *he or she* (not *he/she*).

**Sexist:** Before boarding, each <u>passenger</u> should make certain that <u>he</u> has <u>his</u> ticket.

**Revised:** Before boarding, <u>passengers</u> should make certain that <u>they</u> have <u>their</u> tickets.

**Revised:** Before boarding, each <u>passenger</u> should make certain that <u>he</u> or <u>she</u> has a ticket.

*Note:* Be careful not to use *they* or *their* to refer to a singular antecedent.

Drivers
~~Any driver~~ caught speeding should have their driving privileges suspended.

## Close-Up ELIMINATING SEXIST LANGUAGE

For most sexist usages, there are nonsexist alternatives.

| Sexist Usage | Possible Revisions |
|---|---|
| 1. Mankind<br>Man's accomplishments<br>Man-made | People, human beings<br>Human accomplishments<br>Synthetic |
| 2. Female engineer (lawyer, accountant, etc.), male model | Engineer (lawyer, accountant, etc.), model |
| 3. Policeman/woman<br>Salesman/woman/girl<br><br>Businessman/woman | Police officer<br>Salesperson/sales representative<br>Businessperson, executive |
| 4. <u>Everyone</u> should complete <u>his</u> application by Tuesday. | Everyone should complete <u>his or her</u> application by Tuesday.<br><u>All students</u> should complete <u>their</u> applications by Tuesday. |

# Understanding Punctuation

(Further explanations and examples are located in the sections listed in parentheses after each example.)

### SEPARATING INDEPENDENT CLAUSES

**With a Comma and a Coordinating Conjunction**

The House approved the bill, but the Senate rejected it. (**28a**)

**With a Semicolon**

Paul Revere's *The Boston Massacre* is traditional American protest art; Edward Hicks's paintings are socially conscious art with a religious strain. (**29a**)

**With a Semicolon and a Transitional Word or Phrase**

Thomas Jefferson brought two hundred vanilla beans and a recipe for vanilla ice cream back from France; thus, he gave America its all-time favorite ice-cream flavor. (**29a**)

**With a Colon**

The survey presents an interesting finding: Americans do not trust the news media. (**32a2**)

### SEPARATING ITEMS IN A SERIES

**With Commas**

*Chipmunk, raccoon,* and *Mugwump* are Native American words. (**28b**)

**With Semicolons**

Laramie, Wyoming; Wyoming, Delaware; and Delaware, Ohio were three of the places they visited. (**29b**)

### SETTING OFF EXAMPLES, EXPLANATIONS, OR SUMMARIES

**With a Colon**

She had one dream: to play professional basketball. (**32a2**)

**With a Dash**

"Study hard," "Respect your elders," "Don't talk with your mouth full"—Sharon had often heard her parents say these things. (**32b2**)

### SETTING OFF NONESSENTIAL MATERIAL

**With a Single Comma**

In fact, Outward Bound has an excellent reputation. (**28d2**)

**With a Pair of Commas**

Mark McGwire, not Sammy Sosa, was the first to break Roger Maris's home run record. (**28d3**)

**With Dashes**

Neither of the boys—both nine-year-olds—had any history of violence. (**32b1**)

**With Parentheses**

In some European countries (notably Sweden and Denmark), high-quality day care is offered at little or no cost to parents. (**32c1**)

# CHAPTER 27

# Using End Punctuation

## 27a Using Periods

Use a period to signal the end of most sentences, including indirect questions.

Something is rotten in Denmark.

They wondered whether the water was safe to drink.

Also use periods in most abbreviations.

| | | |
|---|---|---|
| Mr. Spock | Aug. | Dr. Livingstone |
| 9 p.m. | etc. | 1600 Pennsylvania Ave. |

If an abbreviation ends the sentence, do not add another period.

He promised to be there at 6 a.m./

However, do add a question mark if the sentence is a question.

Did he arrive at 6 p.m.?

If the abbreviation falls *within* a sentence, use normal punctuation after the period.

He promised to be there at 6 p.m., but he forgot.

---

## Close-Up ABBREVIATIONS WITHOUT PERIODS

Abbreviations composed of all capital letters do not usually require periods unless they stand for initials of people's names (E. B. White).

MD    RN    BC

*(continued)*

---

> **ABBREVIATIONS WITHOUT PERIODS** (continued)
>
> Familiar abbreviations of names of corporations or government agencies and abbreviations of scientific and technical terms do not require periods.
>
> CD-ROM   NYU   DNA   CIA   WCAU-FM   FAQ
>
> **Acronyms**—new words formed from the initial letters or first few letters of a series of words—do not include periods.
>
> hazmat   Nascar   NATO   modem
>
> **Clipped forms** (commonly accepted shortened forms of words, such as *gym, dorm, math,* and *fax*) do not use periods.
>
> **Postal abbreviations** do not include periods.
>
> TX   CA   MS   PA   FL   NY

Use periods to mark divisions in dramatic, poetic, and biblical references.

*Hamlet* 2.2.1–5 (act, scene, lines)

*Paradise Lost* 7.163–167 (book, lines)

Judges 4.14 (chapter, verse)

See 11a1 **Note:** In **MLA parenthetical references**, titles of classic literary works and books of the Bible are often abbreviated. **(*Ham.* 2.2.1-5); (Judg. 4.14).**

**Note:** When you type an electronic address (URL), do not end it with a period, and do not add spaces after periods within the address.

## 27b Using Question Marks

Use a question mark to signal the end of a direct question.

Who was at the door?

Use a question mark in parentheses to indicate uncertainty about a date or number.

Aristophanes, the Greek playwright, was born in 448 (?) BC and died in 380 (?) BC.

## Close-Up EDITING MISUSED QUESTION MARKS

- Use a period, not a question mark, with an indirect question.

  The personnel officer asked whether he knew how to type?

- Do not use a question mark to convey sarcasm. Instead, suggest your attitude through your choice of words.

  *not very*
  I refused his generous (?) offer.

## 27c Using Exclamation Points

An exclamation point is used to signal the end of an emotional or emphatic statement, an emphatic interjection, or a forceful command.

Remember the Maine!

"No! Don't leave!" he cried.

*Note:* Except for recording dialogue, do not use exclamation points in college writing. Even in informal writing, use exclamation points sparingly—and never use two or more in a row.

CHAPTER **28**

# Using Commas

## 28a Setting Off Independent Clauses

Use a comma when you form a compound sentence by linking two independent clauses with a **coordinating conjunction** (*and, but, or, nor, for, yet, so*) or with a pair of **correlative conjunctions**. <sub>See A1.7</sub>

The House approved the bill , but the Senate rejected it.

Either the hard drive is full , or the modem is too slow.

*Note:* You may omit the comma if two clauses connected by a coordinating conjunction are very short: *Love it  or leave it.*

## 28b   Setting Off Items in a Series

Use commas between items in a series of three or more **coordinate elements** (words, phrases, or clauses joined by a coordinating conjunction).

*Chipmunk , raccoon ,* and *Mugwump* are Native American words.

You may pay by check , with a credit card , or in cash.

Brazilians speak Portuguese , Colombians speak Spanish , and Haitians speak French and Creole.

To avoid ambiguity, always use a comma before the *and* (or other coordinating conjunction) that separates the last two items in a series: *He was inspired by his parents, the Dalai Lama , and Mother Teresa.*

Use a comma between items in a series of two or more **coordinate adjectives**—adjectives that modify the same word or word group—unless they are joined by a conjunction.

She brushed her long , shining hair.

The baby was tired and cranky and wet. (no commas required)

---

**CHECKLIST**

### Punctuating Adjectives in a Series

❑ If you can reverse the order of the adjectives or insert *and* between the adjectives without changing the meaning, the adjectives are coordinate, and you should use a comma.

She brushed her long, shining hair.
She brushed her shining, long hair.
She brushed her long [and] shining hair.

❑ If you cannot reverse the order, the adjectives are not coordinate, and you should not use a comma.

Ten red balloons fell from the ceiling.
Red ten balloons fell from the ceiling.
Ten [and] red balloons fell from the ceiling.

*Note:* Numbers—such as *ten*—are not coordinate with other adjectives.

**ESL TIP**

For information on the order of adjectives in a series,
**see 46d2.**

## 28c Setting Off Introductory Elements

An introductory dependent clause, verbal phrase, or prepositional phrase is generally set off from the rest of the sentence by a comma.

When war came to Baghdad , many victims were children.
(dependent clause)

If an introductory *dependent clause* is short and designates time, you may omit the comma—provided the sentence will be clear without it: *When I exercise  I drink plenty of water.*

Pushing onward , Scott struggled toward the South Pole.
(verbal phrase)

During the Depression , movie attendance rose. (prepositional phrase)

If an introductory *prepositional phrase* is short and no ambiguity is possible, you may omit the comma: *After lunch  I took a four-hour nap.*

## Close-Up TRANSITIONAL WORDS AND PHRASES

When a transitional word or phrase begins a sentence, it is usually set off with a comma.

See
4b

However , any plan that is enacted must be fair.

In other words , we cannot act hastily.

## 28d Setting Off Nonessential Material

Use commas to set off nonessential material whether it appears at the beginning, in the middle, or at the end of a sentence.

**1** Nonrestrictive Modifiers

Use commas to set off **nonrestrictive modifiers,** which supply information that is not essential to the meaning of the words they modify. (*Do not* use commas to set off **restrictive modifiers,** which supply information that is essential to the meaning of the words they modify.)

> **Nonrestrictive** (commas required):  Actors, who have inflated egos, are often insecure. (*All* actors—not just those with inflated egos—are insecure.)

> **Restrictive** (no commas):  Actors who have inflated egos are often insecure. (Only those actors with inflated egos—not all actors—are insecure.)

In the following examples, commas set off only nonrestrictive modifiers—those that supply nonessential information. Commas do not set off restrictive modifiers, which supply essential information.

### Adjective Clauses

> **Restrictive:**  Speaking in public is something that most people fear.

> **Nonrestrictive:**  He ran for the bus, which was late as usual.

### Prepositional Phrases

> **Restrictive:**  The man with the gun demanded their money.

> **Nonrestrictive:**  The clerk, with a nod, dismissed me.

### Verbal Phrases

> **Restrictive:**  The candidates running for mayor have agreed to a debate.

> **Nonrestrictive:**  The marathoner, running his fastest, beat his previous record.

### Appositives

> **Restrictive:**  The film *Citizen Kane* made Orson Welles famous.

> **Nonrestrictive:**  *Citizen Kane*, Orson Welles's first film, made him famous.

**CHECKLIST**

## Restrictive and Nonrestrictive Modifiers

To determine whether a modifier is restrictive or nonrestrictive, answer these questions:

❏ Is the modifier essential to the meaning of the word it modifies (*The man with the gun*, not just any man)? If so, it is restrictive and does not take commas.

❏ Is the modifier introduced by *that* (*something that most people fear*)? If so, it is restrictive. *That* cannot introduce a nonrestrictive clause.

❏ Can you delete the relative pronoun without causing ambiguity or confusion (*something [that] most people fear*)? If so, the clause is restrictive.

❏ Is the appositive more specific than the noun that precedes it (*the film Citizen Kane*)? If so, it is restrictive.

## Close-Up  USING COMMAS WITH *THAT* AND *WHICH*

- *That* introduces only restrictive clauses, which are not set off by commas.

  I bought a used car <u>that</u> cost $2,000.

- *Which* introduces only nonrestrictive clauses, which are set off by commas.

  The used car I bought , <u>which</u> cost $2,000 , broke down after a week.

### 2 Transitional Words and Phrases

<u>Transitional words and phrases</u> qualify, clarify, and make connections. Because they are not essential to the sentence's meaning, however, they are always set off by commas when they interrupt a clause or when they begin or end a sentence. See 4b

The Outward Bound program , <u>for example</u> , is considered safe.

<u>In fact</u> , Outward Bound has an excellent reputation.

Other programs are not so safe , <u>however</u>.

*Note:* When a transitional word or phrase joins two independent clauses, it must be preceded by a semicolon and followed by a comma; *Laughter is the best medicine; of course, penicillin also comes in handy sometimes.*

### 3 Contradictory Phrases

A phrase that expresses a contradiction is usually set off from the rest of the sentence by one or more commas.

This medicine is taken after meals, never on an empty stomach.

Peyton Manning, not Eli Manning, plays for the Denver Broncos.

### 4 Miscellaneous Nonessential Elements

Other nonessential elements usually set off by commas include tag questions, names in direct address, mild interjections, and *yes* and *no.*

This is your first day on the job, isn't it?

I wonder, Mr. Honeywell, whether Mr. Albright deserves a raise.

Well, it's about time.

Yes, that's what I thought.

## 28e Using Commas in Other Conventional Contexts

### 1 With Direct Quotations

In most cases, use commas to set off a direct quotation from the **identifying tag** (*he said, she answered,* and so on).

Emerson said, "I greet you at the beginning of a great career."

"I greet you at the beginning of a great career," Emerson said.

"I greet you," Emerson said, "at the beginning of a great career."

When the identifying tag comes between two complete sentences, however, the tag is introduced by a comma but followed by a period.

"Winning isn't everything," Coach Vince Lombardi once said. "It's the only thing."

## 2 With Titles or Degrees Following a Name

Michael Crichton, MD, wrote *Jurassic Park*.

Hamlet, Prince of Denmark, is Shakespeare's most famous character.

## 3 In Dates and Addresses

On August 30, 1983, the space shuttle *Challenger* exploded.

Her address is 600 West End Avenue, New York, NY 10024.

*Note:* When only the month and year are given, do not use a comma to separate the month from the year: *May 1968*. Do not use a comma to separate the street number from the street or the state name from the zip code.

# 28f Using Commas to Prevent Misreading

In some cases, a comma is used to avoid ambiguity. For example, consider the following sentence.

Those who can, sprint the final lap.

Without the comma, *can* appears to be an auxiliary verb ("Those who can sprint. . . ."), and the sentence seems incomplete. The comma tells readers to pause and thus prevents confusion.

Also use a comma to acknowledge the omission of a repeated word, usually a verb, and to separate words repeated consecutively.

Pam carried the box; Tim, the suitcase.

Everything bad that could have happened, happened.

# 28g Editing Misused Commas

Do not use commas in the following situations.

## 1 To Set Off Restrictive Modifiers

The film, *Avatar*, was directed by James Cameron.

They planned a picnic, in the park.

## 2 Between a Subject and Its Predicate

A woman with dark red hair, opened the door.

### 3 Before or After a Series

Three important criteria are⁄ fat content, salt content, and taste.

The provinces Quebec, Ontario, and Alberta⁄ are in Canada.

### 4 Between a Verb and an Indirect Quotation or Indirect Question

General Douglas MacArthur vowed⁄ that he would return.

The landlord asked⁄ if we would sign a two-year lease.

### 5 In Compounds That Are Not Composed of Independent Clauses

During the 1400s plagues⁄ and pestilence were common. (compound subject)

Many women thirty-five and older are returning to college⁄ and tend to be good students. (compound predicate)

### 6 Before a Dependent Clause at the End of a Sentence

Jane Addams founded Hull House⁄ because she wanted to help Chicago's poor.

CHAPTER 29

# Using Semicolons

The **semicolon** is used only between items of equal grammatical rank: two independent clauses, two phrases, and so on.

## 29a Separating Independent Clauses

Use a semicolon between closely related independent clauses that convey parallel or contrasting information but are not joined by a coordinating conjunction.

Paul Revere's *The Boston Massacre* is an early example of American protest art; Edward Hicks's later "primitive" paintings are socially conscious art with a religious strain.

*Note:* Using only a comma or no punctuation at all between independent clauses creates a **run-on**.

See Ch. 15

Also use a semicolon between two independent clauses when the second clause is introduced by a transitional word or phrase (the transitional element is followed by a comma).

Thomas Jefferson brought two hundred vanilla beans and a recipe for vanilla ice cream back from France; thus, he gave America its all-time favorite ice cream flavor.

## 29b Separating Items in a Series

Use semicolons between items in a series when one or more of the items already include commas.

Three papers are posted on the bulletin board outside the building: a description of the exams; a list of appeal procedures for students who fail; and an employment ad from an automobile factory, addressed specifically to candidates whose appeals are turned down. (Andrea Lee, *Russian Journal*)

Laramie, Wyoming; Wyoming, Delaware; and Delaware, Ohio, were three of the places they visited.

## 29c Editing Misused Semicolons

Do not use semicolons in the following situations.

### 1 Between a Dependent and an Independent Clause

Because drugs can now suppress the body's immune reaction, fewer organ transplants are rejected.

### 2 To Introduce a List

Millions of people maintain a profile on one of three popular social networking sites: *Facebook*, *Twitter*, or *LinkedIn*.

# CHAPTER 30

# Using Apostrophes

Use an apostrophe to form the possessive case, to indicate omissions in contractions, and to form certain plurals.

## 30a Forming the Possessive Case

The possessive case indicates ownership. In English, the possessive case of nouns and indefinite pronouns is indicated either with a phrase that includes the word *of* (the hands *of* the clock) or with an apostrophe and, in most cases, an *s* (the clock's hands).

### 1 Singular Nouns and Indefinite Pronouns

To form the possessive case of **singular nouns** and **indefinite pronouns,** add -*'s*.

"The Monk's Tale" is one of Chaucer's *Canterbury Tales*.

When we would arrive was anyone's guess.

### 2 Singular Nouns Ending in -*s*

To form the possessive case of **singular nouns that end in -*s*,** add -*'s* in most cases.

Chris's goal was to become a surgeon.

Reading Henry James's *The Ambassadors* was not Maris's idea of fun.

The class's time was changed to 8 a.m.

*Note:* With some singular nouns that end in -*s*, pronouncing the possessive ending as a separate syllable can sound awkward. In such cases, it is acceptable to use just an apostrophe: *Crispus Attucks' death, Achilles' left heel, Aristophanes' Lysistrata.*

### 3 Regular Plural Nouns

To form the possessive case of **regular plural nouns** (those that end in -*s* or -*es*), add only an apostrophe.

Laid-off employees received two weeks' severance pay and three months' medical benefits.

The Lopezes' three children are triplets.

### 4 Irregular Plural Nouns

To form the possessive case of **nouns that have irregular plurals,** add -'s.

*The Children's Hour* is a play by Lillian Hellman.

### 5 Compound Nouns or Groups of Words

To form the possessive case of **compound words or groups of words,** add -'s to the last word.

The President accepted the Secretary of Defense's resignation.

This is someone else's responsibility.

### 6 Two or More Items

To indicate **individual ownership** of two or more items, add -'s to each item.

Ernest Hemingway's and Gertrude Stein's writing styles have some similarities.

To indicate **joint ownership,** add -'s only to the last item.

Lewis and Clark's expedition has been the subject of many books.

## 30b Indicating Omissions in Contractions

Apostrophes replace omitted letters in contractions that combine a pronoun and a verb (*he + will = he'll*) or the elements of a verb phrase (*do + not = don't*).

### Frequently Used Contractions

it's (it is, it has)          let's (let us)
he's (he is, he has)          we've (we have)
she's (she is, she has)       they're (they are)

*continued*

**Frequently Used Contractions** *(continued)*

who's (who is, who has)
isn't (is not)
wouldn't (would not)
couldn't (could not)
don't (do not)
won't (will not)

we'll (we will)
I'm (I am)
we're (we are)
you'd (you would)
we'd (we would)
they'd (they had)

*Note:* Contractions are very informal. Do not use contractions in college writing unless you are quoting a source that uses them.

## Close-Up  USING APOSTROPHES

Be careful not to confuse contractions (which always include apostrophes) with the possessive forms of personal pronouns (which never include apostrophes).

**Contractions**
Who's on first?
They're playing our song.
It's raining.
You're a real pal.

**Possessive Forms**
Whose book is this?
Their team is winning.
Its paws were muddy.
Your résumé is very
　impressive.

*Note:* In informal writing, an apostrophe may also be used to represent the century in a year: *class of '12, the '60s.* In college writing, however, write out the year in full: *class of 2012, the sixties.*

## 30c  Forming Plurals

In a few special situations, add -'s to form plurals.

● **Plurals of Letters**

The Italian language has no *j*'s, *k*'s, or *w*'s.

● **Plurals of Words Referred to as Words**

The supervisor would accept no *if*'s, *and*'s, or *but*'s.

See 35c *Note:* Elements spoken of as themselves (letters, numerals, or words) are set in italic type; the plural ending, however, is not.

## 30d Editing Misused Apostrophes

Do not use apostrophes in the following situations.

### 1 With Plural Nouns That Are Not Possessive

The Thompson's are not at home.

Down vest's are very warm.

The Philadelphia 76er's have had good years and bad.

### 2 To Form the Possessive Case of Personal Pronouns

This ticket must be your's or her's.

The next turn is their's.

Her doll had lost it's right eye.

The next great moment in history is our's.

CHAPTER **31**

# Using Quotation Marks

Use quotation marks to set off brief passages of quoted speech or writing, to set off titles, and to set off words used in special ways. Do not use quotation marks when quoting long passages of prose or poetry.

## 31a Setting Off Quoted Speech or Writing

When you quote a word, phrase, or brief passage of someone's speech or writing, enclose the quoted material in a pair of quotation marks.

Gloria Steinem said, "We are becoming the men we once hoped to marry."

Galsworthy writes that Aunt Juley is "prostrated by the blow" (329). (Note that in this example from a student paper, the end punctuation follows the parenthetical documentation.)

## Close-Up  USING QUOTATION MARKS WITH DIALOGUE

When you record **dialogue** (conversation between two or more people), enclose the quoted words in quotation marks. Begin a new paragraph each time a new speaker is introduced.

When you are quoting several paragraphs of dialogue by one speaker, begin each new paragraph with quotation marks. However, use closing quotation marks only at the end of the *entire quoted passage* (not at the end of each paragraph).

Special rules govern the punctuation of a quotation when it is used with an **identifying tag**—a phrase (such as *he said*) that identifies the speaker or writer.

### 1 Identifying Tag in the Middle of a Quoted Passage

Use a pair of commas to set off an identifying tag that interrupts a quoted passage.

"In the future," pop artist Andy Warhol once said, "everyone will be world famous for fifteen minutes."

If the identifying tag follows a complete sentence but the quoted passage continues, use a period after the tag. Begin the new sentence with a capital letter, and enclose it in quotation marks.

"Be careful," Erin warned. "Reptiles can be tricky."

### 2 Identifying Tag at the Beginning of a Quoted Passage

Use a comma after an identifying tag that introduces quoted speech or writing.

The Raven repeated, "Nevermore."

Use a <u>colon</u> instead of a comma before a quotation if the identifying tag is a complete sentence. <sub>See 32a</sub>

She gave her final answer: "No."

### 3 Identifying Tag at the End of a Quoted Passage

Use a comma to set off a quotation from an identifying tag that follows it.

"Be careful out there," the sergeant warned.

If the quotation ends with a question mark or an exclamation point, use that punctuation mark instead of the comma. In this situation, the identifying tag begins with a lowercase letter even though it follows end punctuation.

"Is Ankara the capital of Turkey?" she asked.

"Oh boy!" he cried.

*Note:* Commas and periods are always placed *before* quotation marks. For information on placement of other punctuation marks with quotation marks, **see 31d**.

## Close-Up   QUOTING LONG PROSE PASSAGES

Do *not* enclose a **long prose passage** (more than four lines) in quotation marks. Instead, set it off by indenting the entire passage one inch from the left-hand margin. Double-space above and below the quoted passage, and double-space between lines within it. Introduce the passage with a colon, and place parenthetical documentation one space after the end punctuation.

> The following portrait of Aunt Juley illustrates several of the devices Galsworthy uses throughout *The Forsyte Saga*, such as a journalistic detachment, a sense of the grotesque, and an ironic stance:
>
>> Aunt Juley stayed in her room, prostrated by the blow. Her face, discoloured by tears, was divided into compartments by the little ridges of pouting flesh which had swollen

*(continued)*

**QUOTING LONG PROSE PASSAGES** *(continued)*

> with emotion. . . . Her warm heart could
> not bear the thought that Ann was lying
> there so cold. (329)

Many similar portraits of characters appear throughout the novel.

When you quote a long prose passage that is a single paragraph, do not indent the first line. When quoting two or more paragraphs, however, indent the first line of each paragraph (including the first) an additional one-quarter inch. If the first sentence of the quoted passage does not begin a paragraph in the source, do not indent it—but do indent the first line of each subsequent paragraph. If the passage you are quoting includes material set in quotation marks, keep those quotation marks.

## Close-Up　QUOTING POETRY

See 32e

Treat one line of poetry like a short prose passage: enclose it in quotation marks and run it into the text. If you quote two or three lines of poetry, separate the lines with slashes, and run the quotation into the text. (Leave one space before and one space after the slash.)

If you quote more than three lines of poetry, set them off like a long prose passage. (For special emphasis, you may set off fewer lines in this way.) Do not use quotation marks, and be sure to reproduce *exactly* the spelling, capitalization, and indentation of the quoted lines.

Wilfred Owen, a poet who was killed in action in World War I, expressed the horrors of war with vivid imagery:

> Bent double, like old beggars under sacks.
> Knock-kneed, coughing like hags, we cursed
> 　　through sludge.
> Till on the haunting flares we turned our backs
> And towards our distant rest began to
> 　　trudge. (lines 1-4)

## 31b Setting Off Titles

Titles of short works and titles of parts of long works are enclosed in quotation marks. Other titles are <u>italicized</u>.

See 35a

### Titles Requiring Quotation Marks

**Articles in Magazines, Newspapers, and Professional Journals**
"Why Johnny Can't Write"

**Essays, Short Stories, Short Poems, and Songs**
"Fenimore Cooper's Literary Offenses"
"Flying Home"
"The Road Not Taken"
"The Star-Spangled Banner"

**Chapters or Sections of Books**
"Miss Sharp Begins to Make Friends" (Chapter 10 of *Vanity Fair*)

**Episodes of Radio or Television Series**
"Lucy Goes to the Hospital" (*I Love Lucy*)

**See 35a** for a list of titles that require italics.

## 31c Setting Off Words Used in Special Ways

Enclose a word used in a special or unusual way in quotation marks. (If you use *so-called* before the word, do not use quotation marks as well.)

It was clear that adults approved of children who were "readers," but it was not at all clear why this was so. (Annie Dillard)

Also enclose a **coinage**—an invented word—in quotation marks.

After the twins were born, the minivan became a "babymobile."

## 31d Using Quotation Marks with Other Punctuation

At the end of a quotation, punctuation is sometimes placed before the quotation marks and sometimes placed after the quotation marks:

- At the end of a quotation, place the comma or period *before* the quotation marks.

  Many, like poet Robert Frost, think about "the road not taken," but not many have taken "the one less traveled by."

- At the end of a quotation, place a semicolon or colon *after* the quotation marks.

  Students who do not pass the test receive "certificates of completion"; those who pass are awarded diplomas.

  Taxpayers were pleased with the first of the candidate's promised "sweeping new reforms": a balanced budget.

- If a question mark, exclamation point, or dash is part of the quotation, place the punctuation mark *before* the quotation marks.

  "Who's there?" she demanded.

  "Stop!" he cried.

  "Should we leave now, or —" Vicki paused, unable to continue.

- If a question mark, exclamation point, or dash is not part of the quotation, place the punctuation mark *after* the quotation marks.

  Did you finish reading "The Black Cat"?

  Whatever you do, don't yell "Uncle"!

  The first story—Updike's "*A & P*"— provoked discussion.

## Close-Up  QUOTATIONS WITHIN QUOTATIONS

Use *single* quotation marks to enclose a quotation within a quotation.

Claire noted, "Liberace always said, 'I cried all the way to the bank.'"

Also use single quotation marks within a quotation to set off a title that would normally be enclosed in double quotation marks.

I think what she said was, "Play it, Sam. Play 'As Time Goes By.'"

Use *double* quotation marks around quotations or titles within a <u>long prose passage</u>.

See 31a

## **31e** Editing Misused Quotation Marks

Do not use quotation marks in the following situations.

### **1** To Set Off Indirect Quotations

Do not use quotation marks to set off **indirect quotations** (someone else's written or spoken words that are not quoted exactly).

Freud wondered ⁁"what women wanted."⁁

### **2** To Set Off Slang or Technical Terms

Dawn is ⁁"into"⁁ running.

⁁"Biofeedback"⁁ is sometimes used to treat migraines.

*Note:* Do not use quotation marks (or italics) to set off titles of your own papers.

CHAPTER **32**

# **Using Other Punctuation Marks**

## **32a** Using Colons

The **colon** is a strong punctuation mark that points readers ahead to the rest of the sentence. When a colon introduces a list or series, explanatory material, or a quotation, it must be preceded by a complete sentence.

### **1** Introducing Lists or Series

Use colons to set off lists or series, including those introduced by phrases like *the following* or *as follows.*

Waiting tables requires three skills : memory, speed, and balance.

**2** Introducing Explanatory Material

Use colons to introduce material that explains, exemplifies, or summarizes.

> She had one dream: to play professional basketball.

Sometimes a colon separates two independent clauses, the second illustrating or clarifying the first.

> The survey presents an interesting finding: Americans do not trust the news media.

*Note:* When a complete sentence follows a colon, the sentence may begin with either a capital or a lowercase letter. However, if the sentence is a quotation, the first word is always capitalized (unless it is not capitalized in the source).

**3** Introducing Quotations

See 31a When you quote a <u>long prose passage</u>, always introduce it with a colon. Also use a colon before a short quotation when it is introduced by a complete sentence.

> With dignity, Bartleby repeated the words again: "I prefer not to."

---

### Other Conventional Uses of Colons

**To Separate a Title from a Subtitle**

> *Family Installments: Memories of Growing Up Hispanic*

**To Separate Minutes from Hours**

> 6:15 a.m.

See 42a **After the Salutation in a Business** <u>letter</u>

> Dear Dr. Evans:

**To Separate Place of Publication from Name of Publisher** See 11a2 in a <u>works-cited list</u>

> Boston: Wadsworth, 2015.

---

**4** Editing Misused Colons

Do not use colons in the following situations.

● After expressions such as *namely, for example, such as,* or *that is.*

The Eye Institute treats patients with a wide variety of conditions, such as⁄ myopia, glaucoma, and cataracts.

● Between verbs and their objects or complements or between prepositions and their objects.

James Michener wrote⁄ *Hawaii, Centennial, Space,* and *Poland.*

Hitler's armies marched through⁄ the Netherlands, Belgium, and France.

## 32b  Using Dashes

### 1 Setting Off Nonessential Material

Like commas, dashes can set off <u>nonessential material</u>, but unlike commas, dashes call attention to the material they set off. Indicate a dash with two unspaced hyphens (which your word-processing program will automatically convert to a dash).  <sub>See 28d</sub>

For emphasis, you may use dashes to set off explanations, qualifications, examples, definitions, and appositives.

Neither of the boys — both nine-year-olds — had any history of violence.

Too many parents learn the dangers of swimming pools the hard way — after their toddlers have drowned.

### 2 Introducing a Summary

Use a dash to introduce a statement that summarizes a list or series that appears before it.

"Study hard," "Respect your elders," "Don't talk with your mouth full" — Sharon had often heard her parents say these things.

### 3 Indicating an Interruption

In dialogue, a dash may indicate a hesitation or an unfinished thought.

"I think — no, I know — this is the worst day of my life," Julie sighed.

*Note:* Because a series of dashes can make a passage seem disorganized and out of control, you should be careful not to overuse them.

## 32c Using Parentheses

### 1 Setting Off Nonessential Material

Use **parentheses** to enclose material that expands, clarifies, illustrates, or supplements. (Note that unlike dashes, parentheses tend to de-emphasize the words they enclose.)

> In some European countries (notably Sweden and France), superb day care is offered at little or no cost to parents.

Also use parentheses to set off digressions and afterthoughts.

> Last Sunday we went to the new stadium (it was only half-filled) to see the game.

When a complete sentence set off by parentheses falls within another sentence, it should not begin with a capital letter or end with a period.

> Because the area is so cold (temperatures average in the low twenties), it is virtually uninhabitable.

When the parenthetical sentence does *not* fall within another sentence, however, it must begin with a capital letter and end with appropriate punctuation.

> The region is very cold. (Temperatures average in the low twenties.)

## Close-Up USING PARENTHESES WITH COMMAS

Never use a comma before parentheses. (A comma may follow the closing parenthesis, however.)

> George Orwell's *1984*, (1949), which focuses on the dangers of a totalitarian society, should be required reading.

### 2 Using Parentheses in Other Situations

Use parentheses around letters and numbers that identify points on a list, dates, cross-references, and documentation.

All reports must include the following components: (1) an opening summary, (2) a background statement, and (3) a list of conclusions.

Russia defeated Sweden in the Great Northern War (1700–1721).

Other scholars also make this point (see p. 54).

One critic has called the novel "puerile" (Arvin 72).

## 32d Using Brackets

When one set of parentheses falls within another, use **brackets** in place of the inner set.

In her classic study of American education between 1945 and 1960 (*The Troubled Crusade* [New York: Basic, 1963]), Diane Ravitch addresses issues like progressive education, race, educational reforms, and campus unrest.

Also use brackets within quotations to indicate to readers that the bracketed words are yours and not those of your source. You can bracket an explanation, a clarification, a correction, or an opinion.

"Even at Princeton he [F. Scott Fitzgerald] felt like an outsider."

If a quotation contains an error, indicate that the error is not yours by following it with the Latin word *sic* ("thus") in brackets.

As the Web site notes, "The octopuss [sic] is a cephalopod mollusk with eight arms."

 **Use brackets to indicate changes you make in order to fit a quotation smoothly into your sentence.**

See 9a

## 32e Using Slashes

### 1 Separating One Option from Another

The either/or fallacy is a common error in logic.

Writer/director M. Night Shyamalan spoke at the film festival.

In this situation, do not leave a space before or after the slash.

**2** Separating Lines of Poetry Run into the Text

The poet James Schevill writes, "I study my defects / And learn how to perfect them."

In this situation, leave one space before and one space after the slash.

## 32f  Using Ellipses

Use ellipses in the following situations.

**1** Indicating an Omission in Quoted Prose

Use an **ellipsis**—three *spaced* periods—to indicate that you have omitted words from a prose quotation. (Note that an ellipsis in the middle of a quoted passage can indicate the omission of a word, a sentence or two, even a whole paragraph or more.) When deleting material from a quotation, be very careful not to change the meaning of the original passage.

> **Original:**  "When I was a young man, being anxious to distinguish myself, I was perpetually starting new propositions." (Samuel Johnson)
>
> **With Omission:**  "When I was a young man, . . . I was perpetually starting new propositions."

Note that when you delete words immediately after an internal punctuation mark (such as the comma in the above example), you retain the punctuation mark before the ellipsis.

When you delete material at the end of a sentence, place the ellipsis *after* the sentence's period or other end punctuation.

> According to humorist Dave Barry, "from outer space Europe appears to be shaped like a large ketchup stain. . . ." (period followed by ellipsis)

*Note:* Never begin a quoted passage with an ellipsis.

When you delete material between sentences, place the ellipsis *after* any punctuation that appears in the original passage.

> **Deletion from Middle of One Sentence to End of Another:**  According to Donald Hall, "Everywhere one meets the idea that reading is an activity desirable in

itself. ⋅ ⋅ ⋅ People surround the idea of reading with piety
and do not take into account the purpose of reading."
(period followed by ellipsis)

**Deletion from Middle of One Sentence to Middle of
Another:** "When I was a young man, ⋅ ⋅ ⋅ I found that
generally what was new was false." (Samuel Johnson)
(comma followed by ellipsis)

**Note:** If a quoted passage already contains an ellipsis, MLA
recommends that you enclose your own ellipses in brackets
to distinguish them from those that appear in the original
quotation.

## Close-Up  USING ELLIPSES

If a quotation ending with an ellipsis is followed by parenthetical documentation, the final punctuation comes *after*
the documentation.

As Jarman argues, "Compromise was impossible . . ."
(161).

### 2 Indicating an Omission in Quoted Poetry

Use an ellipsis when you omit a word or phrase from a line
of poetry. When you omit one or more lines of poetry, use
a line of spaced periods. (The length may be equal either to
the line above it or to the missing line—but it should not be
longer than the longest line of the poem.)

**Original:**

> Stitch! Stitch! Stitch!
> In poverty, hunger, and dirt,
> And still with a voice of dolorous pitch,
> Would that its tone could reach the Rich,
> She sang this "Song of the Shirt"!
>
> (Thomas Hood)

**With Omission:**

> Stitch! Stitch! Stitch!
> In poverty, hunger, and dirt,
>
> ⋅ ⋅ ⋅ ⋅ ⋅ ⋅ ⋅ ⋅ ⋅ ⋅ ⋅ ⋅ ⋅ ⋅ ⋅ ⋅ ⋅ ⋅ ⋅ ⋅ ⋅ ⋅ ⋅ ⋅ ⋅
> She sang this "Song of the Shirt"!

PART 7

# Understanding Spelling and Mechanics

# CHAPTER 33

# Becoming a Better Speller

Like most students, you probably use a spell checker when you write. A spell checker, however, does not eliminate your need to know how to spell. For one thing, a spell checker will only check words that are listed in its dictionary. In addition, a spell checker will not tell you that you have confused two homophones, such as *principle* and *principal*. Finally, a spell checker will not catch typos that create a word, such as *form* for *from*. For this reason, you still need to proofread your papers.

Memorizing just a few simple rules (and their exceptions) can help you identify and correct words that you have misspelled.

## 33a The *ie/ei* Combinations

Use *i* before *e* (*belief, chief*) except after *c* (*ceiling, receive*) or when pronounced *ay*, as in *neighbor* or *weigh*. **Exceptions:** *either, neither, foreign, leisure, weird,* and *seize.* In addition, if the *ie* combination is not pronounced as a unit, the rule does not apply: *atheist, science.*

## 33b Doubling Final Consonants

The only words that double their consonants before a suffix that begins with a vowel (*-ed* or *-ing*) are those that pass the following three tests:

1. They have one syllable or are stressed on the last syllable.
2. They have only one vowel in the last syllable.
3. They end in a single consonant.

The word *tap* satisfies all three conditions: it has only one syllable, it has only one vowel (*a*), and it ends in a single consonant (*p*). Therefore, the final consonant doubles before a suffix beginning with a vowel (*tapped, tapping*).

## 33c Silent e before a Suffix

When a suffix that begins with a consonant is added to a word ending in a silent *e*, the *e* is usually kept: *hope/hopeful*. **Exceptions:** *argument, truly, ninth, judgment,* and *abridgment*.

When a suffix that begins with a vowel is added to a word ending in a silent *e*, the *e* is usually dropped: *hope/hoping*. **Exceptions:** *changeable, noticeable,* and *courageous*.

## 33d y before a Suffix

When a word ends in a consonant plus *y*, the *y* usually changes to an *i* when a suffix is added (*beauty + ful = beautiful*). The *y* is kept, however, when the suffix *-ing* is added (*tally + ing = tallying*) and in some one-syllable words (*dry + ness = dryness*).

When a word ends in a vowel plus *y*, the *y* is kept (*joy + ful = joyful*). **Exception:** *day + ly = daily*.

## 33e seed Endings

Endings with the sound *seed* are nearly always spelled *cede*, as in *precede*. **Exceptions:** *supersede, exceed, proceed,* and *succeed*.

## 33f -able, -ible

If the root of a word is itself a word, the suffix *-able* is most commonly used (*comfortable, agreeable*). If the root of a word is not a word, the suffix *-ible* is most often used (*compatible, incredible*).

## 33g Plurals

Most nouns form plurals by adding *-s*: *tortilla/tortillas, boat/boats*. There are, however, a number of exceptions:

● **Words Ending in -f or -fe** Some words ending in *-f* or *-fe* form plurals by changing the *f* to *v* and adding *-es* or -s: *life/lives, self/selves*. Others add just -s: *belief/beliefs, safe/safes*.

- **Words Ending in -y** Most words that end in a consonant followed by *y* form plurals by changing the *y* to *i* and adding -*es*: *baby/babies*. **Exceptions:** proper nouns such as *Kennedy* (plural *Kennedys*).

- **Words Ending in -o** Most words that end in a consonant followed by *o* add -*es* to form the plural: *tomato/tomatoes, hero/heroes*. **Exceptions:** *silo/silos, piano/pianos, memo/memos, soprano/sopranos*.

- **Words Ending in -s, -ss, -sh, -ch, -x, and -z** Words ending in -s, -ss, -sh, -ch, -x, and -z form plurals by adding -*es*: *Jones/Joneses, kiss/kisses, rash/rashes, lunch/lunches, box/boxes, buzz/buzzes*. **Exceptions:** Some one-syllable words that end in -s or -z double their final consonants when forming plurals: *quiz/quizzes*.

- **Compound Nouns** Hyphenated compound nouns whose first element is more important than the others form the plural with the first element: *sister-in-law/sisters-in-law, editor-in-chief/editors-in-chief*.

- **Foreign Plurals** Some words, especially those borrowed from Latin or Greek, keep their foreign plurals.

| **Singular** | **Plural** |
|---|---|
| basis | bases |
| criterion | criteria |
| datum | data |
| memorandum | memoranda |
| stimulus | stimuli |

# CHAPTER 34

# Knowing When to Capitalize

In addition to capitalizing the first word of a sentence (including a quoted sentence) and the pronoun *I*, always capitalize *proper nouns* and *important words in titles*.

**Close-Up** REVISING CAPITALIZATION ERRORS

In *Microsoft Word,* the AutoCorrect tool will automatically capitalize certain words—such as the first word of a sentence or the days of the week. Be sure to proofread your work, though, since the AutoCorrect tool will sometimes introduce capitalization errors into your writing.

## 34a Capitalizing Proper Nouns

**Proper nouns**—the names of specific persons, places, or things—are capitalized, and so are adjectives formed from proper nouns.

### 1 Specific People's Names

Always capitalize people's names: <u>S</u>usan <u>C</u>ollins, <u>B</u>arack <u>O</u>bama.

Capitalize a title when it precedes a person's name (<u>S</u>enator Susan Collins) or is used instead of the name (<u>D</u>ad). Do not capitalize titles that *follow* names (Susan Collins, the senator from Maine) or those that refer to the general position, not the particular person who holds it (a stay-at-home <u>d</u>ad).

You may, however, capitalize titles that indicate very high-ranking positions even when they are used alone or when they follow a name: the <u>P</u>ope; Barack Obama, <u>P</u>resident of the United States. Never capitalize a title denoting a family relationship when it follows an article or a possessive pronoun (an <u>u</u>ncle, his <u>m</u>om).

Capitalize titles that represent academic degrees or abbreviations of those degrees even when they follow a name: <u>D</u>r. Sanjay Gupta; Sanjay Gupta, <u>MD</u>.

### 2 Names of Particular Structures, Special Events, Monuments, and So On

the Brooklyn Bridge the Taj Mahal
the Eiffel Tower Mount Rushmore
the World Series the *Titanic*

 *Note:* Capitalize a common noun, such as *bridge, river, lake,* or *county,* when it is part of a proper noun (<u>L</u>ake Erie, Kings <u>C</u>ounty).

### 3 Places and Geographical Regions

Saturn                    the Straits of Magellan
Budapest                  the Western Hemisphere

Capitalize *north*, *south*, *east*, and *west* when they denote particular geographical regions but not when they designate directions.

There are more tornadoes in Kansas than in the East. (*East* refers to a specific region.)

Turn west at Broad Street and continue north to Market. (*West* and *north* refer to directions, not specific regions.)

### 4 Days of the Week, Months, and Holidays

Saturday                  Cinco de Mayo
January                   Diwali

### 5 Historical Periods, Events, Documents, and Names of Legal Cases

the Industrial Revolution     the Treaty of Versailles
the Battle of Gettysburg      *Brown v. Board of Education*

*Note:* Names of court cases are italicized in the text of your papers, but not in works-cited entries.

### 6 Philosophic, Literary, and Artistic Movements

Naturalism                Dadaism
Neoclassicism             Expressionism

### 7 Races, Ethnic Groups, Nationalities, and Languages

African American          Korean
Latino/Latina             Farsi

*Note:* When the words *black* and *white* denote races, they have traditionally not been capitalized. Current usage is divided on whether or not to capitalize *black*.

### 8 Religions and Their Followers; Sacred Books and Figures

Islam              the Qur'an        Buddha
the Talmud         Jews              God

*Note:* It is not necessary to capitalize pronouns referring to God (although some people do so).

**9** Specific Groups and Organizations

the Democratic Party
the International Brotherhood of Electrical Workers
the New York Yankees
the American Civil Liberties Union
the National Council of Teachers of English
the Rolling Stones

*Note:* When the name of a group or organization is abbreviated, the <u>abbreviation</u> uses capital letters in place of the capitalized words.

See 37b

IBEW ACLU NCTE

**10** Businesses, Government Agencies, and Other Institutions

General Electric        Lincoln High School
the Environmental       the University of Maryland
   Protection Agency

**11** Brand Names and Words Formed from Them

Velcro    Coke    Post-it    Rollerblades    AstroTurf

*Note:* Brand names that over long use have become synonymous with the product—for example, *nylon* and *aspirin*—are no longer capitalized. (Consult a dictionary to determine whether or not to capitalize a familiar brand name.)

**34b** Capitalizing Important Words in Titles

In general, capitalize all words in titles with the exception of articles (*a, an,* and *the*), prepositions, coordinating conjunctions, and the *to* in infinitives. If an article, preposition, or coordinating conjunction is the *first* or *last* word in the title, however, do capitalize it.

The Declaration of Independence
*Across the River and into the Trees*
*Madame Curie: A Biography*
"What Friends Are For"

## 34c Editing Misused Capitals

Do not capitalize the following:

- Seasons (summer, fall, winter, spring)
- Names of centuries (the twenty-first century)
- Names of general historical periods (the automobile age)
- Diseases and other medical terms (unless a proper noun is part of the name) or unless the disease is an **acronym**: smallpox, polio, Reyes syndrome, AIDS, SIDS

See 27a

**ESL TIP**

Do not capitalize a word simply because you want to emphasize its importance. If you are not sure whether a word should be capitalized, look it up in a dictionary.

CHAPTER **35**

# Using Italics

## 35a Setting Off Titles and Names

Use italics for the titles and names in the box that follows. All other titles are set off with **quotation marks**.

See 31b

### Titles and Names Set in Italics

**Books:** *Twilight, Harry Potter and the Deathly Hallows*

**Newspapers:** the *Washington Post*, the *Philadelphia Inquirer* (In MLA style, the word *the* is not italicized in titles of newspapers.)

**Magazines and Journals:** *Rolling Stone, Scientific American*

**Online Magazines and Journals:** *salon.com, theonion.com*

**Web Sites or Home Pages:** *urbanlegends.com, movie-mistakes.com*
**Pamphlets:** *Common Sense*
**Films:** *The Matrix, Citizen Kane*
**Television Programs:** *60 Minutes, The Bachelorette, American Idol*
**Radio Programs:** *All Things Considered, A Prairie Home Companion*
**Long Poems:** *John Brown's Body, The Faerie Queen*
**Plays:** *Macbeth, A Raisin in the Sun*
**Long Musical Works:** *Rigoletto, Eroica*
**Software Programs:** *Microsoft Word, PowerPoint*
**Search Engines and Web Browsers:** *Google, Safari, Internet Explorer*
**Databases:** *Academic Search Premier, Expanded Academic ASAP Plus*
**Paintings and Sculpture:** *Guernica, Pietà*
**Video Games:** *Halo: Combat Evolved, Grand Theft Auto V*
**Ships:** *Lusitania*, U.S.S. *Saratoga* (S.S. and U.S.S. are not italicized.)
**Trains:** *City of New Orleans, The Orient Express*
**Aircraft:** *The Hindenburg, Enola Gay* (Only particular aircraft, not makes or types such as Piper Cub or Airbus, are italicized.)
**Spacecraft:** *Challenger, Enterprise*

**Note:** Names of sacred books, such as the Bible and the Qur'an, and well-known documents, such as the Constitution and the Declaration of Independence, are neither italicized nor placed within quotation marks.

## 35b Setting Off Foreign Words and Phrases

Use italics to set off foreign words and phrases that have not become part of the English language.

> *"C'est la vie,"* Madeleine said when she saw the long line for basketball tickets.

> *Spirochaeta plicatilis* is a corkscrew-like bacterium.

If you are not sure whether a foreign word has been assimilated into English, consult a dictionary.

## 35c Setting Off Elements Spoken of as Themselves and Terms Being Defined

Use italics to set off letters, numerals, and words that refer to the letters, numerals, and words themselves.

Is that a *p* or a *g*?

I forget the exact address, but I know it has a *3* in it.

Does *through* rhyme with *cough*?

Also use italics to set off words and phrases that you go on to define.

A *closet drama* is a play meant to be read, not performed.

*Note:* When you quote a dictionary definition, put the word you are defining in italics and the definition itself in quotation marks.

To *infer* means "to draw a conclusion"; to *imply* means "to suggest."

## 35d  Using Italics for Emphasis

Italics may occasionally be used for emphasis.

Initially, poetry might be defined as a kind of language that says *more* and says it *more intensely* than does ordinary language. (Lawrence Perrine, *Sound and Sense*)

However, overuse of italics is distracting. Instead of italicizing, indicate emphasis with word choice and sentence structure.

CHAPTER **36**

# Using Hyphens

**Hyphens** have two conventional uses: to break a word at the end of a line and to link words in certain compounds.

## 36a  Breaking a Word at the End of a Line

A computer never hyphenates a word at the end of a line; if the full word will not fit, it is brought down to the next line. Sometimes, however, you may want to break a word with a hyphen—for example, to fill in excessive space at the end of a line when you want to increase a document's visual appeal.

When you break a word at the end of a line, divide it only between syllables, consulting a dictionary if necessary. Never divide a word at the end of a page, and never hyphenate a one-syllable word. In addition, never leave a single letter at the end of a line or carry only one or two letters to the next line.

If you divide a <u>compound word</u> at the end of a line, put See 36b the hyphen between the elements of the compound (*snow-mobile,* not *snowmo-bile*).

---

 **Close-Up** DIVIDING ELECTRONIC ADDRESSES (URLS)

Never insert a hyphen to divide an electronic address (URL) at the end of a line. (Readers might think the hyphen is part of the address.) MLA style recommends that you break the URL after a slash. If this is not possible, break it in a logical place—after a period, for example—or avoid the problem altogether by moving the entire URL to the next line.

---

## 36b Dividing Compound Words

A **compound word** is composed of two or more words. Some familiar compound words are always hyphenated: *no-hitter, helter-skelter.* Other compounds are always written as one word (*fireplace*) and others as two separate words (*bunk bed*). Your dictionary can tell you whether or not a particular compound requires a hyphen.

### 1 Hyphenating with Compound Adjectives

A **compound adjective** is made up of two or more words that function together as an adjective. When a compound adjective *precedes* the noun it modifies, use hyphens to join its elements.

The research team tried to use <u>nineteenth-century</u> technology to design a <u>space-age</u> project.

When a compound adjective *follows* the noun it modifies, do not use hyphens to join its elements.

> The three government-operated programs were run smoothly, but the one that was not government operated was short of funds.

*Note:* A compound adjective formed with an adverb ending in *-ly* is not hyphenated even when it precedes the noun: *Many upwardly mobile families are on tight budgets.*

Use **suspended hyphens**—hyphens followed by a space or by appropriate punctuation and a space—in a series of compounds that have the same principal elements.

> Graduates of two- and four-year colleges were eligible for the grants.

> The exam called for sentence-, paragraph-, and essay-length answers.

### ❷ Hyphenating with Certain Prefixes or Suffixes

Use a hyphen between a prefix and a proper noun or adjective.

> mid-July          pre-Columbian

Use a hyphen to connect the prefixes *all-, ex-, half-, quarter-, quasi-,* and *self-* and the suffix *-elect* to a noun.

> ex-senator          self-centered          president-elect

Also hyphenate to avoid certain hard-to-read combinations, such as two *i*'s (*semi-illiterate*) or more than two of the same consonant (*shell-less*).

### ❸ Hyphenating in Compound Numerals and Fractions

Hyphenate compounds that represent numbers below one hundred (even if they are part of a larger number).

> the twenty-first century    three hundred sixty-five days

Also hyphenate the written form of a fraction when it modifies a noun.

> a two-thirds share of the business

# CHAPTER 37

# Using Abbreviations

Generally speaking, **abbreviations** are not appropriate in college writing except in tables, charts, and works-cited lists. Some abbreviations are acceptable only in scientific, technical, or business writing or only in a particular discipline. If you have questions about the appropriateness of a particular abbreviation, consult a style manual in your field.

---

**Close-Up** ABBREVIATIONS IN ELECTRONIC COMMUNICATIONS

Like emoticons and acronyms, which are popular in personal email and instant messages, shorthand abbreviations and symbols—such as GR8 (great) and 2NITE (tonight)—are common in text messages. Although they are acceptable in informal electronic communication, such abbreviations are not appropriate in college writing or in business communication.

---

## 37a Abbreviating Titles

Titles before and after proper names are usually abbreviated.

Mr. Homer Simpson          Rep. John Lewis
Henry Kissinger, PhD       Dr. Martin Luther King, Jr.

Do not, however, use an abbreviated title without a name.

   *doctor*
The ~~Dr.~~ diagnosed hepatitis.

## 37b Abbreviating Organization Names and Technical Terms

Well-known businesses and government, social, and civic organizations are frequently referred to by capitalized initials.

See
27a
These <u>abbreviations</u> fall into two categories: those in which the initials are pronounced as separate units (EPA, MTV) and **acronyms**, in which the initials are pronounced as a word (NATO, FEMA).

To save space, you may use accepted abbreviations for complex technical terms that are not well known, but be sure to spell out the full term the first time you mention it, followed by the abbreviation in parentheses.

> Citrus farmers have been using ethylene dibromide (EDB), a chemical pesticide, for more than twenty years. Now, however, EDB has contaminated water supplies.

## Close-Up   ABBREVIATIONS IN MLA DOCUMENTATION

See
11a2
<u>MLA documentation style</u> requires abbreviations of publishers' company names—for example, **Columbia UP** for *Columbia University Press*—in the works-cited list. Do not, however, use such abbreviations in the text of your paper.

MLA style permits the use of abbreviations that designate parts of written works (**ch. 3, sec. 7**)—but only in the works-cited list and parenthetical documentation. Finally, MLA recommends abbreviating citations for classic literary works and for books of the Bible in parenthetical citations: **(Oth.)** (for *Othello*); **(Exod.)** for Exodus. These words should not be abbreviated in the text of your paper or in the works-cited list.

## 37c   Abbreviating Dates, Times of Day, Temperatures, and Numbers

50 BC (*BC* follows the date)
3:03 p.m. (lowercase)
AD 432 (*AD* precedes the date)
180°F (Fahrenheit)

Always capitalize *BC* and *AD*. (The alternatives *BCE*, for "before the Common Era," and *CE*, for "Common Era," are also capitalized.) The abbreviations *a.m.* and *p.m.* are used only when they are accompanied by numbers: *I'll see you in the morning* (not *in the a.m.*).

Avoid the abbreviation *no.* except in technical writing, and then use it only before a specific number: *The unidentified substance was labeled no. 52.*

## 37d Editing Misused Abbreviations

In college writing, the following are not abbreviated.

### 1 Latin Expressions

Poe wrote "The Gold Bug," "The Tell-Tale Heart," ~~etc.~~
*and so on.*

Many musicians (~~e.g.,~~ Bruce Springsteen) have been influenced by Bob Dylan.
*for example,*

### 2 Names of Days, Months, or Holidays

On ~~Sat., Dec.~~ 23, I started my ~~Xmas~~ shopping.
*Saturday, December* *Christmas*

### 3 Names of Streets and Places

He lives on Riverside ~~Dr.~~ in ~~NYC.~~
*Drive* *New York City.*

**Exceptions:** The abbreviations *U.S.* (*U.S. Coast Guard*), *St.* (*St. Albans*), and *Mt.* (*Mt. Etna*) are acceptable, as is *DC* in *Washington, DC.*

### 4 Names of Academic Subjects

~~Psych.~~ and English ~~lit.~~ are required courses.
*Psychology* *literature*

### 5 Units of Measurement

MLA style does not permit abbreviations for units of measurement and requires that you spell out words such as *inches, feet, years, miles, pints, quarts,* and *gallons.*

In technical and business writing, however, some units of measurement are abbreviated when they are preceded by a numeral.

The hurricane had winds of 35 mph.

One new hybrid gets over 50 mpg.

### 6 Symbols

The symbols =, +, and # are acceptable in technical and scientific writing but not in nontechnical college writing. The symbols % and $ are acceptable only when used with See 38b numerals (15%, $15,000), not with spelled-out numbers.

CHAPTER **38**

# Using Numbers

Convention determines when to use a **numeral** (22) and when to spell out a number (twenty-two). Numerals are commonly used in scientific and technical writing and in journalism, but they are used less often in academic or literary writing.

*Note:* The guidelines in this chapter are based on the *MLA Handbook for Writers of Research Papers,* 7th ed. (2009). **APA style**, however, requires that all numbers below ten be spelled out if they do not represent specific measurements and that the numbers ten and above be expressed in numerals. See Ch. 12

## 38a Spelled-Out Numbers versus Numerals

Unless a number falls into one of the categories listed in **38b**, spell it out *if you can do so in one or two words.*

The Hawaiian alphabet has only twelve letters.

Class size stabilized at twenty-eight students.

The subsidies are expected to total about two million dollars.

Numbers *more than two words* long are expressed in figures.

The dietitian prepared 125 sample menus.

The developer of the community purchased 300,000 doorknobs and 153,000 faucets.

Never begin a sentence with a numeral. If necessary, re-word the sentence.

**Faulty:** 250 students are currently enrolled.

**Revised:** Current enrollment is 250 students.

*Note:* When one number immediately precedes another in a sentence, spell out the first, and use a numeral for the second: *five 3-quart containers.*

## 38b Conventional Uses of Numerals

Use numerals in the following situations:

- **Addresses:** 1920 Walnut Street, Philadelphia, PA 19103
- **Dates:** January 15, 1929    1914–1919
- **Exact Times:** 9:16    10 a.m. or 10:00 a.m. (but spell out times of day when they are used with *o'clock:* ten o'clock)
- **Exact Sums of Money:** $25.11    $6,752.00
- **Divisions of Works:** Act 5    lines 17–28    page 42
- **Percentages and Decimals:** 80%    3.14

*Note:* You may spell out a percentage (*eighty percent*) if you use percentages infrequently in your paper, provided it can be expressed in two or three words. Always use a numeral (not a spelled-out number) with a % symbol.

- **Measurements with Symbols or Abbreviations:** 32°  15 cc
- **Ratios and Statistics:** 20 to 1  a mean of 40
- **Scores:** a lead of 6 to 0
- **Identification Numbers:** Route 66  Track 8  Channel 12

# Developing Strategies for Academic and Professional Success

# CHAPTER 39

# Ten Habits of Successful Students

Successful students have *learned* to be successful: they have developed specific strategies for success, and they apply those strategies to their education. If you take the time, you can learn the habits of successful students and apply them to your own college education—and, later on, to your career.

## 39a Learn to Manage Your Time Effectively

College makes many demands on your time. It is hard, especially at first, to balance studying, coursework, family life, friendships, and a job. But if you don't take control of your schedule, it will take control of you; if you don't learn to manage your time, you will always be struggling to catch up.

The calendar function in your cell phone is a valuable tool that can help you to manage your time. Since your phone is always with you, it is a good place to record school-related deadlines, appointments, and reminders (every assignment due date, study group meeting, conference appointment, and exam) as well as outside responsibilities, such as work hours and medical appointments. Be sure to enter tasks and dates as soon as you learn of them.

You can also use your calendar to help you plan a study schedule, as illustrated in Figure 39.1. You do this by blocking out times to study or to complete assignment-related tasks—such as

FIGURE 39.1 Sample cell phone calendar.

a library database search for a research paper—in addition to appointments and deadlines.

Remember: your college years can be a very stressful time, but although some degree of stress is inevitable, it can be kept in check. If you are organized, you will be better able to handle the pressures of a college workload.

## 39b Put Studying First

To be a successful student, you need to understand that studying is something you do regularly, not right before an exam. You also need to know that studying does not mean just memorizing facts; it also means reading, rereading, and discussing ideas until you understand them.

To make studying a regular part of your day, set up a study space that includes everything you need (supplies, good light, a comfortable chair) and does not include anything you do not need (clutter, distractions). Then, set up a tentative study schedule. Try to designate at least two hours each day to complete assignments due right away, to work on those due later on, and to reread class notes. When you have exams and papers, you can adjust your schedule accordingly.

Successful students often form **study groups,** and you should use this strategy whenever you can—particularly in a course you find challenging. A study group of four or five students who meet regularly (not just the night before an exam) can make studying more focused and effective as well as less stressful. By discussing concepts with your classmates, you can try out your ideas and get feedback, clarify complex concepts, and formulate questions for your instructor.

---

### CHECKLIST
### Working in a Study Group

Working collaboratively in a study group requires some degree of organization. To get the most out of your study group, you need to set some ground rules:

❑ Meet regularly.

❑ Decide in advance who will be responsible for particular tasks.

❑ Set deadlines.

❑ Listen when someone else is speaking.

*continued*

**Working in a Study Group** *(continued)*

❏ Don't reject other people's ideas and suggestions without considering them very carefully.

❏ Have one person take notes to keep a record of the group's activities.

❏ Take stock of the group's problems and progress at regular intervals.

❏ Be mindful of other students' learning styles and special needs.

## 39c   Be Sure You Understand School and Course Requirements

To succeed in school, you need to know what is expected of you; if you are not sure, ask.

When you first arrived at school, you probably received a variety of orientation materials—a student handbook, library handouts, and so on—that set forth the rules and policies of your school. (These materials may also be available online.) Read these documents carefully (if you have not already done so). If you do not understand something, ask your peer counselor or your adviser for clarification.

**ESL TIP**

If you did not attend high school in the United States, some of your instructors' class policies and procedures may seem strange to you. To learn more about the way US college classes are run, read the syllabus for each of your courses and talk to your instructors about your concerns. You may also find it helpful to talk to older students with cultural backgrounds similar to your own.

You also need to know the specific requirements of each course you take. A course **syllabus** tells you when assignments are due and when exams are scheduled. In addition, it may explain the instructor's policies about attendance and lateness, assignments and deadlines, plagiarism, and classroom etiquette. A syllabus may also explain penalties for late assignments or missed quizzes, explain how assignments are graded, tell how much each assignment is worth, or note additional requirements, such as fieldwork or group projects. Requirements vary significantly from course to course, so read each syllabus (as well as any supplementary handouts) carefully, and keep track of updates that may appear on your class's Web page.

## 39d  Be an Active Learner in the Classroom

Education is not about sitting passively in class and waiting for information and ideas to be given to you. It is up to you to be an active participant in your own education.

First, take as many small classes as you can. Small classes enable you to interact with other students and with your instructor. If a large course has recitation sections, be sure to attend them regularly, even if they are not required. Also, be sure to take classes that require writing. Good writing skills are essential to your success as a student (and as a college graduate entering the workforce), and you will need all the practice you can get.

Take responsibility for your education by attending class regularly and arriving on time. Listen attentively, and take careful, complete notes. (Try to review these notes later with other students to make sure you have not missed anything important.) Do your homework on time, and keep up with the reading. When you read an assignment, use **active reading** <sup>See Ch. 1</sup> strategies, interacting with the text (for example, underlining the text and making marginal annotations) instead of just looking at what is on the page. If you have time, read beyond the assignment, looking on the Internet and in books, magazines, and newspapers for related information.

Finally, participate in class discussions: ask and answer questions, volunteer opinions, and give helpful feedback to other students. By participating in this way, you learn to consider other points of view, to test your ideas, and to respect the ideas of others.

**ESL TIP**

Especially in small classes, US instructors usually expect students to participate in class discussion. If you feel nervous about speaking up in class, you might start by expressing your support of a classmate's opinion.

## 39e  Be an Active Learner Outside the Classroom

Taking an active role in your education is also important outside the classroom. Do not be afraid to approach your instructors; take advantage of their office hours, and keep in touch with them by email. Get to know your major adviser well, and be sure he or she knows who you are and where your academic interests lie. Make appointments, ask questions, and explore possible solutions to problems: this is how you learn.

In addition, become part of your school community. Read your school newspaper, check your college Web site regularly, and participate in activities. This involvement can help you develop new interests and friendships as well as enhance your education.

Finally, participate in the life of your community outside your school. Try to arrange an **internship,** a job that enables you to gain practical experience. (Many businesses, nonprofit organizations, and government agencies offer internships—paid or unpaid—to qualified students.) Take **service-learning** courses, if they are offered at your school, or volunteer at a local school or social agency. As successful students know, education is more than just attending classes.

## 39f    Take Advantage of College Services

Colleges and universities offer students a wide variety of support services. For example, if you are struggling with a particular course, you can go to the tutoring service offered by your school's academic support center or by an individual department. If you need help with writing or revising a paper, you can make an appointment with the writing center, where tutors will give you advice. If you are having trouble deciding on what courses to take or what to major in, you can see your academic adviser. If you are having trouble adjusting to college life, a peer counselor or (if you live in a dorm) your resident adviser may be able to help you. Finally, if you have a personal or family problem you would rather not discuss with another student, you can make an appointment at your school's counseling center, where you can get advice from professionals who understand student problems.

> **ESL TIP**
>
> Many ESL students find using their school's writing center very helpful.
> Most writing centers provide assistance with assignments for any course, and they often assist with writing job application letters and résumés. Many writing centers have tutors who specialize in working with ESL students.

Many other services are available—for example, at your school's computer center, job placement service, and financial aid office. Your academic adviser or instructors can tell you where to find the help you need, but it is up to you to make the appointment.

## **39g** Use the Library

Because so much material is available on the Internet, you may think your college library is outdated or even obsolete. But learning to use the library is an important part of your education. See 7a, 8a

The library can provide a quiet place to study—something you may need if you have a large family or noisy roommates. The library also provides access to materials that cannot be found online—rare books, special collections, audiovisual materials—as well as electronic databases that contain material you will not find on the free Internet.

Finally, the library is the place where you have access to the expert advice of your school's reference librarians. These professionals can answer questions, guide your research, and point you to sources that you might never have found on your own.

## **39h** Use Technology

Technological competence is essential to success in college. For this reason, it makes sense to develop good word-processing skills and to become comfortable with the Internet. You should already know how to send and receive See 7b, 8b email from your university account as well as how to attach files to your email. Beyond these basics, you should learn how to manage the files you download, how to evaluate Web sites, and how to use the electronic resources of your library. You might also find it helpful to know how to scan documents (containing images as well as text) and how to paste these files into your documents.

If you do not have these skills, you need to locate campus services that will help you get them. Workshops and online tutorials may be available through your school library or campus computing services, and individual assistance on software and hardware use is available in computer labs.

Part of being technologically savvy in college involves being aware of the online services your campus has to offer. For example, many campuses rely on customizable information-management systems called **portals.** Not unlike commercial services, such as Yahoo! or America Online, a portal requires you to log in with a user ID and password to access services such as locating and contacting your academic adviser and viewing your class schedule and grades.

Finally, you need to know not only how to use technology to enhance a project—for example, how to use *PowerPoint* for an <u>oral presentation</u> or *Excel* to make a <u>table</u>—but also *when* to use technology (and when not to).

See 43d, 40d1

## 39i   Make Contacts

One of the most important things you can do for yourself is to make academic and professional contacts that you can use during college and after you graduate.

Your first contacts are your classmates. Be sure you have the names, phone numbers, and email addresses of at least two students in each of your classes. These contacts will be useful to you if you miss class, if you need help understanding your notes, or if you want to start a study group.

You should also build relationships with students with whom you participate in college activities, such as the college newspaper or the tutoring center. These people are likely to share your goals and interests, and so you may want to get feedback from them as you choose a major, consider further education, and make career choices.

Finally, develop relationships with your instructors, particularly those in your major area of study. One of the things cited most often in studies of successful students is the importance of **mentors,** experienced individuals whose advice you trust. Long after you leave college, you will find these contacts useful.

## 39j   Be a Lifelong Learner

Your education should not stop when you graduate from college. To be a successful student, you need to see yourself as a lifelong learner.

Get in the habit of reading newspapers; know what is happening in the world outside school. Talk to people outside the college community so that you don't forget there are issues that have nothing to do with courses and grades. Never miss an opportunity to learn: try to get in the habit of attending plays and concerts sponsored by your school or community and lectures offered at your local library or bookstore.

And think about the life you will lead after college. Think about who you want to be and what you have to do to get there. This is what successful students do.

# CHAPTER 40

# Designing Effective Documents

**Document design** is a set of guidelines that help you determine how to design a piece of written work so that it communicates your ideas clearly and effectively. All well-designed documents share the same general characteristics: an effective format, clear headings, useful lists, and helpful visuals.

## 40a Creating an Effective Visual Format

An effective document contains visual cues that help readers find, read, and interpret information on a page.

### 1 Margins

**Margins** frame a page and keep it from looking overcrowded. Because a page with narrow (or no) margins can make a document difficult to read, margins should be at least one inch all around. If the material you are writing about is highly technical or unusually difficult, use wider margins (one and a half inches).

Except for documents such as flyers and brochures, in which you might want to isolate blocks of text for emphasis, you should **justify** (uniformly align, except for paragraph indentations) the left-hand margin.

### 2 White Space

**White space** is the area of a page that is intentionally left blank. Used effectively, white space can isolate material and focus a reader's attention on it. You can use white space around a block of text—a paragraph or a section, for example—or around visuals such as charts, graphs, and photographs.

### 3 Color

**Color** (when used in moderation) can emphasize and classify information—such as the headings in a résumé or the bars on a graph—while also making it visually appealing. Remember, however, that too many colors can distract or confuse readers.

### 4 Typeface and Type Size

**Typefaces** are distinctively designed sets of letters, numbers, and punctuation marks. The typeface you choose should be suitable for your purpose and audience. In your academic writing, avoid fancy or elaborate typefaces—*script* or **old English**, for example—that call attention to themselves and distract readers. Instead, select a typeface that is simple and direct—Cambria, Times New Roman, or Arial, for example. For most of your academic papers, use 10- or 12-point type (headings will sometimes be larger).

### 5 Line Spacing

**Line spacing** refers to the amount of space between the lines of a document. If the lines are too far apart, the text will seem to lack cohesion; if the lines are too close together, the text will appear crowded and be difficult to read. The type of writing you do can determine line spacing: the paragraphs of business letters, memos, and some reports are usually single-spaced and separated by a double space, but the paragraphs of academic papers are usually double-spaced.

## 40b   Using Headings

Headings serve some useful purposes in a text:

- Headings tell readers that a new idea is being introduced.
- Headings emphasize key ideas.
- Headings indicate how information is organized in a text.

### 1 Number of Headings

The number of headings you use depends on the document. A long, complicated document will need more headings than a shorter, less complicated one. Keep in mind that too few headings will not be of much use, but too many headings will make your document look like an outline.

### 2 Phrasing

Headings should be brief, informative, and to the point. They can be single words—**Summary** or **Introduction**, for example— or they can be phrases (always stated in <u>parallel terms</u>): **Traditional Family Patterns, Alternate Family Patterns, Modern Family Patterns**. Finally, headings can be questions (**How Do You Choose a Major?**) or statements (**Choose Your Major Carefully**).

See
24a

## 3 Indentation

Different style guides provide different guidelines concerning the placement of headings. For example, the APA style guide makes the following recommendations: first-level headings should be centered, second-level headings should be justified left, and third-level headings should be indented one-half inch. Consult the appropriate style guide for the guidelines on this issue.

## 4 Typographical Emphasis

You can emphasize important words in headings by using **boldface,** *italics,* or ALL CAPITAL LETTERS. Used in moderation, these distinctive type styles make a text easier to read. Used excessively, however, they slow readers down.

## 5 Consistency

Headings at the same level should have the same typeface, type size, spacing, and color. If one first-level heading is boldfaced and centered, all other first-level headings must be boldfaced and centered. Using consistent patterns reinforces the connection between content and ideas and makes a document easier to understand.

*Note:* Never separate a heading from the text that goes with it. If a heading is at the bottom of one page and the text that goes with it is on the next page, move the heading onto the next page along with the text.

## 40c Constructing Lists

By breaking long discussions into a series of key ideas, a list makes information easier to understand. By isolating individual pieces of information in this way, a list directs readers to important information on a page.

**CHECKLIST**
### Constructing Effective Lists
When constructing a list, follow these guidelines:
- **Indent each item.** Each item in a list should be indented so that it stands out from the text around it.

*continued*

## Constructing Effective Lists *(continued)*

❑ **Set off items with bullets or numbers.** Use **bullets** when items are not organized according to any particular sequence or priority (the members of a club, for example). Use **numbers** when you want to indicate that items are organized according to a sequence (the steps in a process, for example).

❑ **Introduce a list with a complete sentence.** Introduce a list with a complete sentence (followed by a colon) that tells readers what the list contains.

❑ **Use parallel structure.** Lists are easiest to read when all items are parallel and about the same length.

A number of factors can cause high unemployment:

- a decrease in consumer spending
- a decrease in factory orders
- a decrease in factory output

❑ **Capitalize and punctuate correctly.** If the items in a list are fragments (as in the example above), begin each item with a lowercase letter, and do not end it with a period. However, if the items in a list are complete sentences, begin each item with a capital letter and end it with a period.

❑ **Don't overuse lists.** Too many lists will give readers the impression that you are simply enumerating points instead of discussing them.

Figure 40.1 shows a page from a student's report that incorporates some of the effective design elements discussed in **40a–c.** Notice that the use of different typefaces and type sizes contributes to the document's overall readability.

FIGURE 40.1 A well-designed page from a student's report. © Cengage Learning.

## 40d Using Visuals

**Visuals,** such as tables, graphs, diagrams, and photographs, can help you convey complex ideas that are difficult to communicate with words; they can also help you attract readers' attention.

### 1 Tables

**Tables** present data in rows and columns. Tables may contain numerical data, text, or a combination of the two. Keep in mind that tables distract readers, so include only those necessary to support your points. (Note that the table in Figure 40.2 reports the student writer's original research and therefore needs no documentation.)

As the following table shows, the Madison location now employs more workers in every site than the St. Paul location.

*Reference to table provides context*

Table 1
Number of Employees at Each Location

*Heading and descriptive caption*

*Boldface and shading emphasize column headings*

| Employees | Location | |
|---|---|---|
| | Madison | St. Paul |
| Plant | 461 | 254 |
| Warehouse | 45 | 23 |
| Outlet Stores | 15 | 9 |

*Dividing lines improve readability of data*

Because this location has grown so quickly, steps must be taken to

FIGURE 40.2 Sample table from a student paper. © Cengage Learning.

### 2 Graphs

Like tables, **graphs** present data in visual form. However, whereas tables present specific numerical data, graphs convey the general pattern or trend that the data suggest. Figure 40.3 on page 340 is an example of a bar graph showing data from a source.

### 3 Diagrams

A **diagram** calls readers' attention to specific details of a mechanism or object. Diagrams are used in scientific and technical writing to clarify concepts that are difficult to explain in words. Figure 40.4 on page 340, which illustrates the sections of an orchestra, serves a similar purpose in a music education paper.

Reference to graph provides context

the demographics of college students are changing. According to a 2002 US Department of Education report entitled *Nontraditional Undergraduates*, the percentage of students who could be classified as "nontraditional" has increased over the last decade (see fig. 1).

Data

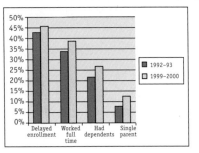

Label and citation

Fig. 1. United States, Dept. of Educ., Office of Educ. Research and Improvement, Natl. Center for Educ. Statistics; *Nontraditional Undergraduates*, by Susan Choy; 2002; *National Center for Education Statistics*; Web; 27 Feb. 2003.

**FIGURE 40.3** Sample graph from a student paper. Data © US Department of Education. © Cengage Learning.

Reference to diagram provides context

The sections of an orchestra are arranged precisely to allow for a powerful and cohesive performance. Fig. 1 illustrates the placement of individual sections of an orchestra.

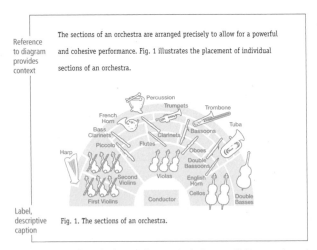

Label, descriptive caption

Fig. 1. The sections of an orchestra.

**FIGURE 40.4** Sample diagram from a student paper. © Cengage Learning.

## 4 Photographs

**Photographs** enable you to show exactly what something or someone looks like. Although it is easy to paste photographs directly into a text, you should do so only when they support or enhance your points. The photograph of a wooded trail in Figure 40.5 illustrates the student writer's description.

travelers are well advised to be prepared, to always carry water, and to dress for the conditions. Loose fitting, lightweight wicking material covering all exposed skin is necessary in summer, and layers of warm clothing are needed for cold-weather outings. Hats and sunscreen are always a good idea no matter what the temperature, although most of the trails are quite shady with huge oak trees. Fig. 1 shows a shady portion of the trail.

*Reference to photo provides context*

*Photo sized and placed appropriately within text with consistent white space above and below*

Fig. 1. Greenbelt Trail in springtime (author photo).

*Label and descriptive caption*

FIGURE 40.5 Sample photograph from a student paper. © Cengage Learning.

## CHECKLIST
## Using Visuals

When using visuals in your papers, follow these guidelines:

- ❑ Use a visual only when it contributes something important to the discussion, not for embellishment.
- ❑ Use the visual in the text only if you plan to discuss it in your paper (place the visual in an appendix if you do not).
- ❑ Introduce each visual with a complete sentence.
- ❑ Follow each visual with a discussion of its significance.
- ❑ Leave wide margins around each visual.
- ❑ Place the visual as close as possible to the section of your paper in which it is discussed.
- ❑ Label each visual appropriately.
- ❑ Document each visual borrowed from a source.

CHAPTER **41**

# Writing in a Digital Environment

Online communication is different from print communication. In order to write effectively for an online audience, you should be aware of the demands of writing in a digital environment.

## 41a Considering Audience and Purpose

The most obvious difference between electronic communication and print communication is the nature of the **audience.** Audiences for print documents simply read a discussion. Audiences for electronic documents, however, can post responses and sometimes communicate directly with the writer.

The **purpose** of electronic communication is sometimes different from that of print communication. Unlike print documents, which appear as finished products, electronic documents are often open-ended. In fact, with wikis (**see 41b3**), readers are encouraged to add or edit content and, in this way, to participate in the creation of a document.

Internet documents also tend to be shorter and more to the point than articles written for print magazines and newspapers. Because most people read Internet articles on the screen, they may be reluctant to read articles that are more than a page or two in length.

Today the line between print and electronic documents is blurring. For example, scholarly articles may be published in online-only journals, and news stories may appear both in print and online. When a print article is published online, it usually includes Web-specific elements such as links or streaming video. As online writing becomes the norm, writers need to understand its advantages and its unique features.

## 41b Writing in a Wired Classroom

Increasingly instructors are using the Internet as well as specific Web-based technology to teach writing. Some of the most popular tools that students can use to create Web-based content in an electronic writing environment are discussed here.

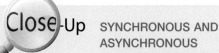

**Close-Up**  SYNCHRONOUS AND ASYNCHRONOUS COMMUNICATION

With **synchronous communication,** all parties involved in the communication process are present at the same time and can be involved in a real-time conversation. Chat rooms, discussion boards, and instant messaging are examples of synchronous communication. Synchronous communication tools are often used in distance-learning classes to create a virtual classroom environment.

With **asynchronous communication,** there is a delay between the time a message is sent and the time it is received. Asynchronous exchanges occur in emails, texts, blogs, wikis, Web forums, and discussion groups. With asynchronous communication, students can post comments or send email messages and read comments posted by their instructors or other students.

**1 Using Email**

Email enables you to exchange ideas with classmates, ask questions of your instructors, and communicate with the writing center or other campus services. You can insert email links in Web documents, and you can transfer files as email attachments from one computer to another. In many classes, writing assignments are submitted to instructors as email attachments.

**Close-Up**  EMAILS TO INSTRUCTORS

When you write emails to your instructors, you should maintain a certain level of formality. For example, you should begin your emails with "Dear Professor" not "Hey Prof" or "Doc." You should also use complete sentences and avoid emoticons, unusual fonts, and informal abbreviations.

## 2 Using Blogs

A **blog** is like an online journal. Some writing instructors encourage students to create and maintain blogs that function as online writing journals. Blogs are not limited to text; they can contain photographs, videos, music, audio, and personal artwork as well as links to other blogs or Web sites. Most course management systems, such as *Blackboard* and *Angel,* make it easy to create a blog.

## 3 Using Wikis

A **wiki** (Hawaiian for *fast*) is a Web site that allows users to add, remove, or change content. With wikis, individuals can work together on a project, adding, deleting, and modifying content as the need arises. Some writing instructors create wikis to encourage students to collaborate on reports, encyclopedia entries, or brochures. The result is a project that is the collective work of all the students who contributed to it.

## 4 Using Listservs

**Listservs** (sometimes called **discussion lists**) are electronic mailing lists. They enable individuals to communicate with groups of people interested in particular topics. Subscribers to a listserv send emails to a main email address, and these messages are automatically routed to all members of the group. Listservs can be especially useful in composition classes, permitting students to post comments on reading assignments as well as to discuss other subjects with the entire class.

## 5 Using Podcasts

A **podcast** is any broadcast—audio or visual—that has been converted to an MP3 or similar format for playback on the Internet or with an MP3 playback device. Podcasting is becoming increasingly common in college classrooms. Instructors podcast class lectures that students can access at their leisure. Instructors also use podcasts to present commentary on students' writing, to distribute supplementary material such as audio recordings or speeches, or to communicate class information or news.

### 6 Using *Twitter* and *Facebook*

Some instructors use *Twitter* as a tool to teach writing. For example, because tweets force students to be concise, some writing instructors ask students to tweet their thesis statements to the class. In addition, instructors can use *Twitter* as an easy way to get in touch with students (*Don't forget. Class cancelled tomorrow.*) and to reinforce important course concepts (*Your arguments must be supported by evidence. Look out for logical fallacies.*).

Some instructors form *Facebook* groups and post links to Web sites, documents, and other links on the group pages. Students can post questions about class assignments and discuss topics that interest them.

CHAPTER **42**

# Writing for the Workplace

Whether you are writing letters of application, résumés, memos, or email, you should always be concise, avoid digressions, and try to sound as natural as possible.

## 42a Writing Letters of Application

A **letter of application** (electronic or print) summarizes your qualifications for a particular job.

Begin your letter of application by identifying the job you are applying for and telling where you heard about it. In the body of your letter, provide the specific information that will convince readers you are qualified for the position. Conclude by stating that you have enclosed your résumé and that you will be available for an interview. (A sample letter of application appears on page 346.)

*Sample Letter of Application*

246 Hillside Drive
Urbana, IL 61801
kr237@metropolis.105.com
March 19, 2012

*Heading*

*Inside address*

Mr. Maurice Snyder, Personnel Director
Guilford, Fox, and Morris
22 Hamilton Street
Urbana, IL 61822

*Salutation (followed by a colon)*

Dear Mr. Snyder:

My college advisor, Dr. Raymond Walsh, has told me that you are interested in hiring a part-time accounting assistant. I believe that my academic background and my work experience qualify me for this position.

I am presently a junior accounting major at the University of Illinois. During the past year, I have taken courses in taxation, trusts, and business law. I am also proficient in *QuickBooks* and *Sage 50*. Last spring, I gained practical accounting experience by working in our department's tax clinic.

*Double-space* ⟶

*Single-space* ⟶

After I graduate, I hope to get a master's degree in taxation and then return to the Urbana area. I believe that my experience in taxation as well as my familiarity with the local business community will enable me to make a contribution to your firm.

I have enclosed a résumé for your review. I will be available for an interview any time after midterm examinations, which end March 23.

*Complimentary close*

Sincerely yours,

*Written signature*

*Sandra Kraft*

*Typed signature*
*Additional data*

Sandra Kraft
Enc.: Résumé

*Note:* After you have been interviewed, you should send a **follow-up email** to the person (or persons) who interviewed you. Because many applicants do not write follow-up emails, they can make a positive impression.

## 42b   Designing Résumés

A **résumé** lists relevant information about your education, job experience, goals, and personal interests.

The most common way to arrange the information in your résumé is in **chronological order,** listing your education and work experience in sequence, moving from latest to earliest job. Your résumé should be brief (one page, if possible), clear, and logically organized. Emphasize important information with italics, bullets, boldface, or different fonts. (A sample résumé appears on page 348.)

## 42c   Writing Memos

Memos communicate information within an organization. Begin your memo with a purpose statement, followed by a background section. In the body of your memo, support your main point. If your memo is short, use bulleted or numbered lists to emphasize information. If it is more than two or three paragraphs, use headings to designate individual sections. End your memo by stating your conclusions and recommendations. (A sample memo appears on page 349.)

## 42d   Writing Emails

In many workplaces, virtually all internal (and many external) communications are transmitted as email. Although personal email tends to be informal, business email observes the conventions of standard written communication.

## Close-Up   WRITING EMAILS

The following rules can help you communicate effectively in an electronic business environment:

- Write in complete sentences. Avoid slang, imprecise diction, and abbreviations.

*(continued on p. 350)*

## Sample Résumé: Chronological Order

SCHOOL                                HOME
3812 Hamilton St. Apt. 18        110 Ascot Ct.
KAREN L. OLSON        Philadelphia, PA 19104        Harmony, PA 16037
215-382-0831                          412-452-2944
olsont@dunm.ocs.drexel.edu

EDUCATION

**DREXEL UNIVERSITY**, Philadelphia, PA 19104
Bachelor of Science in Graphic Design
Anticipated Graduation: June 2014
Cumulative Grade Point Average: 3.2 on a 4.0 scale

COMPUTER SKILLS AND COURSEWORK

HARDWARE

Familiar with both Macintosh and PC systems

SOFTWARE

*Adobe Illustrator, Photoshop,* and *Type Align; QuarkXPress;
CorelDRAW; Adobe InDesign*

COURSES

Corporate Identity, Environmental Graphics, Typography, Photography, Painting and Printmaking, Sculpture, Computer Imaging, Art History

EMPLOYMENT EXPERIENCE

*THE TRIANGLE,* Drexel University, Philadelphia, PA 19104
January 2011–present
Graphics Editor. Design all display advertisements submitted to Drexel's student newspaper.

**UNISYS CORPORATION**, Blue Bell, PA 19124
June–September 2011, Cooperative Education
Graphic Designer. Designed interior pages as well as covers for target marketing brochures. Created various logos and spot art designed for use on interoffice memos and departmental publications.

**CHARMING SHOPPES, INC.**, Bensalem, PA 19020
June–December 2010, Cooperative Education
Graphic Designer/Fashion Illustrator. Created graphics for future placement on garments. Did some textile designing. Drew flat illustrations of garments to scale in computer. Prepared presentation boards.

**DESIGN AND IMAGING STUDIO**, Drexel University, Philadelphia, PA 19104
October 2009–June 2010
Monitor. Supervised computer activity in studio. Answered telephone. Assisted other graphic design students in using computer programs.

ACTIVITIES AND AWARDS

*The Triangle,* Graphics Editor: 2011–present
Kappa Omicron Nu Honor Society, vice president: 2011–present
Graphics Group, vice president: 2010–present
Dean's List: spring 2011, fall and winter 2012

REFERENCES AND PORTFOLIO

Available upon request.

*Sample Memo*

TO: Ina Ellen, Senior Counselor
FROM: Kim Williams, Student Tutor Supervisor
SUBJECT: Construction of a Tutoring Center
DATE: November 10, 2013

*Opening component*

This memo proposes the establishment of a tutoring center in the Office of Student Affairs.

*Purpose statement*

## BACKGROUND

Under the present system, tutors must work with students at a number of facilities scattered across the university campus. As a result, tutors waste a lot of time running from one facility to another and are often late for appointments.

## NEW FACILITY

*Body*

I propose that we establish a tutoring facility adjacent to the Office of Student Affairs. The two empty classrooms next to the office, presently used for storage of office furniture, would be ideal for this use. We could furnish these offices with the desks and file cabinets already stored in these rooms.

## BENEFITS

The benefits of this facility would be the centralizing of the tutoring services and the proximity of the facility to the Office of Student Affairs. The tutoring facility could also use the secretarial services of the Office of Student Affairs.

## RECOMMENDATIONS

*Conclusion*

To implement this project, we would need to do the following:

1. Clean up and paint rooms 331 and 333
2. Use folding partitions to divide each room into five single-desk offices
3. Use stored office equipment to furnish the center

I am certain these changes would do much to improve the tutoring service. I look forward to discussing this matter with you in more detail.

**WRITING EMAILS** *(continued)*

- Use an appropriate tone. Address readers with respect, just as you would in a standard business letter.
- Include a subject line that clearly identifies your content.
- Make your message as short as possible. Because most emails are read on the screen, long discussions are difficult to follow.
- Use short paragraphs, leaving an extra space between paragraphs.
- Use lists and internal headings to focus your discussion and to break it into manageable parts.
- Reread and edit your email after you have written it.
- Proofread carefully before sending your email.
- Make sure that your list of recipients is accurate and that you do not send your email to unintended recipients.
- Do not send your email until you are absolutely certain that your message says exactly what you want it to say.
- Do not forward an email you receive unless you have the permission of the sender.
- Watch what you write. Keep in mind that email written at work is the property of the employer, who has the legal right to access it—even without your permission.

CHAPTER **43**

# Making Oral Presentations

At school and on the job, you may sometimes be called upon to make **oral presentations.** The guidelines that follow can make the experience easier and less stressful.

## 43a Getting Started

Just as with writing an essay, the preparation phase of an oral presentation is as important as the speech itself.

*Identify Your Topic* The first thing you should do is identify the topic of your speech. Once you have a topic, you should decide how much information you will need.

*Consider Your Audience* Consider the nature of your audience. Is your audience made up of experts or of people who know very little about your topic? How much background information will you have to provide? Can you use technical terms, or should you avoid them? Do you think your audience will be interested in your topic, or will you have to create interest?

See 2b

*Consider Your Purpose* Your speech should have a specific purpose that you can sum up concisely. To help you zero in on your purpose, ask yourself what you are trying to accomplish with your presentation.

See 2a

*Consider Your Constraints* How much time do you have for your presentation? (Obviously a ten-minute presentation requires more information than a three-minute presentation.) Do you know a lot about your topic, or will you have to do research?

## 43b Planning Your Speech

In the planning phase, you develop a thesis; then, you decide what points you will discuss and divide your speech into a few manageable sections.

*Develop a Thesis Statement* As you plan your speech, you should develop a thesis statement that clearly communicates your main idea to your audience.

See 3b

*Decide on Your Points* Once you have developed a thesis, you can decide what points you will discuss. Keep in mind that listeners must understand information the first time they hear it. For this reason, your speech should focus on points that are clear and easy to follow.

*Outline the Individual Parts of Your Speech* Every speech has a beginning, a middle, and an end. Your **introduction** should introduce your subject, engage your audience's interest, and state your thesis. The **body,** or middle section, of your speech should present the points that support your thesis. It should also include the facts, examples, and other information that will convince listeners that your thesis is reasonable. Your **conclusion** should bring your speech to a definite end and reinforce your thesis.

## 43c Preparing Your Presentation Notes

Most people use some form of presentation notes when they give a speech.

*Full Text* Some people write out the full text of their speech and refer to it during their presentation. If the type is large enough, this strategy can be useful. One disadvantage of using the full text of your speech is that it is easy to lose your place; another is that you may find yourself simply reading.

*Notecards* Some people write parts of their speech—for example, a list of key points or definitions—on notecards. With some practice, you can use notecards effectively. You have to be careful, however, not to become so dependent on the cards that you lose eye contact with your audience or begin fidgeting with the cards as you speak.

*Outlines* Some people refer to an outline when they give a speech. As they speak, they can glance down at the outline to remind themselves of a point they may have forgotten. Because an outline does not contain the full text of a speech, the temptation to read is eliminated. However, if you draw a blank, an outline gives you very little help.

*iPads* Some people use an iPad as a teleprompter. In order to do this, you need a stand for your iPad and an app, such as *Teleprompt+*, that turns an iPad into a teleprompter. *Teleprompt+* allows you to scroll your speech at various speeds, to pause it with a double-tap on the screen, and to time yourself as you speak. (*Teleprompt+* will even make video recordings of your presentation and of your practice sessions.)

## 43d Preparing Visual Aids

**Visual aids** can reinforce important information and make your speech easier to understand. For a simple speech, a visual aid may be no more than a definition or a few key terms, names, or dates written on the board. For a more complicated presentation, you might need charts, graphs, diagrams, photographs, or presentation software.

*Microsoft PowerPoint,* the most commonly used **presentation software** package, enables you to prepare attractive, professional slides (see Figure 43.1). This program contains many options for backgrounds, color schemes, and special effects, and also lets you supplement your slides with sound and video.

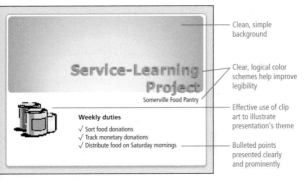

FIGURE 43.1 Effective *PowerPoint* slide. © Cengage Learning.

*Prezi,* available free on the Internet at <prezi.com>, is a presentation tool that is gaining in popularity. Many people think that *Prezi* presentations are more interesting and engaging than *PowerPoint* presentations. With *Prezi*, images and text are pasted on a large screen or "stage" instead of on individual slides (see Figure 43.2). Users can move around the stage (much the way a Skycam at a football game does) and zoom in and out, depending on what they want to emphasize. In addition, videos, such as those available on *YouTube*, can easily be pasted into *Prezi*.

FIGURE 43.2 *Prezi* presentation stage.

## Using Visual Aids in Your Presentation

| Visual Aid | Advantages | Disadvantages |
|---|---|---|
| *Computer presentations*  Bob Daemmrich/ PhotoEdit | Clear<br>Easy to read<br>Professional<br>Graphics, video, sound, and animated effects<br>Portable (disk or CD-ROM) | Special equipment needed<br>Expertise needed<br>Special software needed<br>Software might not be compatible with all computer systems |
| *Overhead projectors*  Lew Zimmerman/ istockphoto.com | Transparencies are inexpensive<br>Transparencies are easily prepared with computer or copier<br>Transparencies are portable<br>Transparencies can be written on during presentation<br>Projector is easy to operate | Transparencies can stick together<br>Transparencies can be accidentally placed upside down<br>Transparencies must be placed on projector by hand<br>Some projectors are noisy<br>Speaker must avoid tripping over power cord during presentation |
| *Document cameras (digital visualizers)*  Business Wire/Handout/ Getty Images Publicity/ Getty Images | Captures visual images in real time<br>Projects images from a sheet of paper or projects 3D objects<br>Zooms in on small text, pictures, or objects<br>Interfaces with a whiteboard or a computer<br>Has a high-definition display | Much more expensive than an overhead projector<br>Must connect to another device to display an image<br>Not yet widely available |

| Visual Aid | Advantages | Disadvantages |
|------------|-----------|---------------|
| **Slide projectors**<br><br>Andy Crawford/<br>Dorling Kindersley/<br>Getty Images | Slides are colorful<br>Slides look professional<br>Projector is easy to use<br>Order of slides can be rearranged during presentation<br>Portable (slide carousel) | Slides are expensive to produce<br>Special equipment needed for lettering and graphics<br>Dark room needed for presentation<br>Slides can jam in projector |
| **Posters or flip charts**<br><br>mbbirdy/<br>istockphoto.com | Low-tech and personal<br>Good for small-group presentations<br>Portable | May not be large enough to be seen in some rooms<br>Artistic ability needed<br>May be expensive if prepared professionally<br>Must be secured to an easel |
| **Chalkboards or whiteboards**<br><br>Jeffrey Coolidge/<br>Stone/Getty Images | Available in most rooms<br>Easy to use<br>Easy to erase or change information during presentation | Difficult to draw complicated graphics<br>Handwriting must be legible<br>Must catch errors while writing<br>Cannot face audience when writing or drawing<br>Very informal |

# 43e  Rehearsing Your Speech

Practice your speech often—at least five times. Do not try to memorize your entire speech, but be sure you know it well enough so that you can move from point to point without constantly looking at your notes. Finally, time yourself.

Make certain that your three-minute speech actually takes three minutes to deliver.

## 43f Delivering Your Speech

Keep in mind that a certain amount of nervousness is normal, so try not to focus on it too much. While you are waiting to begin, take some deep breaths to help you calm down. Once you get to the front of the room, take the time to make sure that everything you will need is there and that all your equipment is positioned properly.

When you begin speaking, pace yourself. Speak slowly and clearly, and look at the entire audience. Even though your speech is planned, it should sound natural and conversational. Use pauses to emphasize important points, and try to sound enthusiastic about your subject.

How you look will be the first thing that listeners notice about you, so dress appropriately for the occasion. (Although shorts and a T-shirt may be appropriate in some situations, they are not suitable for a classroom presentation.)

CHAPTER 44

# Writing in the Disciplines

All instructors, regardless of academic discipline, have certain expectations when they read a paper. They expect to see standard English, correct grammar and spelling, logical thinking, and clear documentation of sources. In addition, they expect to see sensible organization, convincing support, and careful editing. Despite these similarities, however, instructors in various disciplines have different expectations about a paper.

One way of putting these differences into perspective is to think of the various disciplines as communities of individuals who exchange ideas about issues that concern them. Just as in any community, scholars who write within a discipline have agreed to follow certain practices—conventions of style and vocabulary, for example. Without these conventions, it would be difficult or even impossible for them to communicate effectively with one another. If, for example, everyone writing about literature used a different documentation format or a different specialized vocabulary, the result would be chaos. To a large extent, then, learning to write in a particular discipline involves learning the conventions that govern a discourse community.

The chart on pages 358–59 sums up some of the differences among disciplines in assignments, style and format, documentation, and research methods and sources.

## Writing in the Disciplines: An Overview

### HUMANITIES

| Disciplines | Assignments | Style and Format |
|---|---|---|
| Languages | Response essay | *Style* |
| Literature | Analysis essay | Specialized vocabulary |
| Philosophy | Annotated bibliography | Direct quotations from sources |
| History | Bibliographic essay | |
| Religion | Book or film review | *Format* |
| Art history | | Little use of internal headings or visuals |
| Music | | |

### SOCIAL SCIENCES

| Disciplines | Assignments | Style and Format |
|---|---|---|
| Anthropology | Personal experience essay | *Style* |
| Psychology | | Specialized vocabulary, including statistical terminology |
| Economics | Book review | |
| Business | Case study | |
| Education | Annotated bibliography | *Format* |
| Sociology | | Internal headings |
| Political science | Literature review | Visuals (graphs, maps, flowcharts, photographs) |
| Social work | Proposal | |
| Criminal justice | | Numerical data (in tables) |
| Linguistics | | |

### NATURAL AND APPLIED SCIENCES

| Disciplines | Assignments | Style and Format |
|---|---|---|
| *Natural Sciences* | Laboratory report | *Style* |
| Biology | Observation essay | Frequent use of passive voice |
| Chemistry | Literature survey | Few direct quotations |
| Physics | Abstract | |
| Astronomy | Biographical essay | *Format* |
| Geology | | Internal headings |
| Mathematics | | Tables, graphs, and illustrations (exact formats vary) |
| *Applied Sciences* | | |
| Engineering | | |
| Computer science | | |
| Nursing | | |
| Pharmacy | | |

| Documentation | Research Methods and Sources | |
|---|---|---|
| English, languages, philosophy: MLA | Internet sources | See Ch. 11 |
| History, art history: Chicago | Library sources (print and electronic) | |
| | Interviews | See Ch. 13 |
| | Observations (museums, concerts) | |
| | Oral history | |

| Documentation | Research Methods and Sources | |
|---|---|---|
| APA | Internet sources | See Ch. 12 |
| | Library sources (print and electronic) | |
| | Surveys | |
| | Observations (behavior of groups and individuals) | |

| Documentation | Research Methods and Sources | |
|---|---|---|
| Biological sciences: CSE | Internet sources | See Ch. 14 |
| Other scientific disciplines use a variety of different documentation styles; see 14d | Library sources (print and electronic) | |
| | Observations | |
| | Experiments | |
| | Surveys | |

**Note:** For information on avoiding plagiarism across the disciplines, see 10f.

# Resources for Bilingual and ESL Writers

# CHAPTER 45

# Adjusting to the US Classroom

If you went to school outside of the United States, you may not be familiar with the way writing is taught in US composition classes.

## Close-Up   ADJUSTING TO THE US CLASSROOM

Here are some aspects of US classrooms that may be unfamiliar to you:

- **Punctuality**   Students are expected to be in their seats and ready to begin class at the scheduled time. If you are late repeatedly, your grade may be lowered.
- **Student–Instructor Relationships**   The relationship between students and instructors may be more casual or friendly than you are used to. However, instructors still expect students to abide by the rules they set.
- **Class Discussion**   Instructors typically expect students to volunteer ideas in class and may even enjoy it when students disagree with their opinions (as long as the students can make good arguments for their positions). Rather than being a sign of disrespect, this is usually considered to be evidence of interest and involvement in the topic under discussion.

## 45a   Understanding the Writing Process

Typically, US composition instructors teach writing as a See Ch. 3 **process**. This process usually includes the following components:

- **Planning and shaping your writing**   Your instructor will probably help you get ideas for your writing by assigning relevant readings, conducting class discussions, and asking you to keep a journal or engage in **freewriting** See 3a3 and **brainstorming**.

- **Writing multiple drafts**   After you write your paper for the first time, you will probably get feedback from your instructor or your classmates so that you can **revise** (improve) your paper before receiving a grade on it. Instructors expect students to use the suggestions they receive to make significant improvements to their papers. (For more information on the drafting process, **see 3d.**)

- **Looking at sample papers**   Your instructor may provide the class with sample papers of the type that he or she has assigned. Such samples can help you understand how to complete the assigned paper. Sometimes the samples are strong papers that can serve as good examples of what to do. However, most samples will have both strengths and weaknesses, so be sure you understand your instructor's opinion of the samples he or she provides.

- **Engaging in** <u>peer review</u> (sometimes called peer editing)   Your instructor may ask the class to work in small groups or in pairs to exchange ideas about an assigned paper. You will be expected to provide other students with feedback on the strengths and weaknesses of their papers. Afterward, you should think carefully about your classmates' comments about your paper and make changes to improve it. See 6h3

- **Attending conferences**   Your instructor may schedule one or more appointments with you to discuss your writing and may ask you to bring a draft of the paper you are working on. Your instructor may also be available to help you with your paper without an appointment during his or her office hours. In addition, many educational institutions have **writing centers** where tutors help students get started on their papers or improve their drafts. When you meet with your instructor or writing center tutor, bring a list of specific questions about your paper, and be sure to make careful notes about what you discuss. You can refer to these notes when you revise your paper.

 **Close-Up**   USING YOUR NATIVE LANGUAGE

Depending on your language background and skills, you may find it helpful to use your native language in some stages of your writing.

*(continued)*

## 45b  Understanding English Language Basics

Getting used to writing and editing your work in English will be easier if you understand a few basic principles:

ESL 46a

- **In English, words may change their form according to their function.** For example, verbs change form to communicate whether an action is taking place in the past, present, or future.
- **In English, context is extremely important to understanding function.** In the following sentences, for instance, the very same words can perform different functions according to their relationships to other words.

  Juan and I are taking a <u>walk</u>. (*Walk* is a noun, a direct object of the verb taking, with an article, *a*, attached to it.)

  If you <u>walk</u> instead of driving, you will help conserve the Earth's resources. (*Walk* is a verb, the predicate of the subject *you*.)

See Ch. 33

- **Spelling in English is not always phonetic and sometimes may seem illogical.** Spelling in English may be related more to the history of the word and to its origins in other languages than to the way the word is pronounced. Therefore, learning to spell correctly is often a matter of memorization, not sounding out the word phonetically. For example, "ough" is pronounced differently in *tough*, *though*, and *thought*.

- <u>Word order</u> **is extremely important in English sen-** ESL 46f **tences.** In English sentences, word order may indicate which word is the subject of the sentence and which is the object, whether the sentence is a question or a statement, and so on.

## 45c Learning to Edit Your Work

Editing your papers involves focusing on grammar, spell- See 3e ing, punctuation, and mechanics. The approach you take to editing for grammar errors should depend on your strengths and weaknesses in English.

If you learned English mostly by speaking it, if you have strong oral skills, and if you instinctively make correct judgments about English, the best approach for you may be reading your paper aloud and listening for mistakes, correcting them by deciding what sounds right. You may even find that as you read aloud, you automatically correct your written mistakes. (Be sure to transfer those corrections to your paper.) In addition to proofreading your paper from beginning to end, you might find it helpful to start from the end of the paper, reading and proofreading sentence by sentence. This strategy can keep you from being distracted by your ideas, allowing you to focus on grammar alone.

If you learned English mostly by reading, studying grammar rules, and/or translating between your native language and English, you may not feel that you have good instincts about what sounds right in English. If this is the case, you should take a different approach to editing your papers. First, identify the errors you make most frequently by looking at earlier papers your instructor has marked or by asking your instructor for help. Once you have identified your most common errors, read through your paper, checking each sentence for these errors. Try to apply the grammar and mechanics rules you already know, or check the relevant grammar explanations in **Chapter 46** for help.

After you check your paper for grammar errors, you should check again to make sure that you have used proper punctuation, capitalization, and spelling. If you have difficulty with spelling, you can use a spell checker to help you, but remember that spell checkers cannot catch every error. After you have made grammar and mechanics corrections on your own, you can seek outside help in identifying errors you might have missed. You should also keep a notebook with a list of your most frequent grammatical errors and review it often.

# CHAPTER 46

# Grammar and Style for ESL Writers

For ESL writers (as for many native English writers), grammar can be a persistent problem. Grammatical knowledge in a second language usually develops slowly, with time and practice, and much about English is idiomatic (not subject to easy-to-learn rules). This chapter is designed to provide you with the tools you will need to address some of the most common grammatical errors made by ESL writers.

## 46a Using Verbs

### 1 Subject-Verb Agreement

<sup>See</sup> A1.3 English **verbs** change their form according to person, number, and tense. The verb in a sentence must agree with the subject in person and number. **Person** refers to *who* <sup>See</sup> 23a4 or *what* is performing the action of the verb (for example, *myself, you,* or someone else), and **number** refers to *how many* people or things are performing the action (one or more than one).

<sup>See</sup> 17a   In English, the rules for **subject-verb agreement** are very important. Unless you use the correct person and number in the verbs in your sentences, you will confuse your English-speaking audience by communicating meanings you do not intend.

### 2 Tense

In English, the form of a verb changes according to when the action of the verb takes place—in the past, present, or future. One problem that many nonnative speakers of English have with English verb tenses results from the large number of <sup>See</sup> 18a **irregular verbs** in English. For example, the first-person singular present tense of *be* is not "I be" but "I am," and the past tense is not "I beed" but "I was."

## Close-Up CHOOSING THE SIMPLEST VERB FORMS

Some nonnative English speakers use verb forms that are more complicated than they need to be. They may do this because their native language uses more complicated verb forms than English does or because they "overcorrect" their verbs into complicated forms. Specifically, nonnative speakers tend to use progressive and perfect verb forms instead of simple verb forms. To communicate your ideas clearly to an English-speaking audience, choose the simplest possible verb form.

### 3 Auxiliary Verbs

The **auxiliary verbs** (also known as **helping verbs**) *be, have,* and *do* are used to create some present, past, and future forms of verbs in English: "Julio *is taking* a vacation"; "I *have been* tired lately"; "He *does* not *need* a license." The auxiliary verbs *be, have,* and *do* change form to reflect the time frame of the action or situation and to agree with the subject; however, the main verb remains in simple present or simple past form.

## Close-Up AUXILIARY VERBS

Only auxiliary verbs, not the verbs they "help," change form to indicate person, number, and tense.

> **Present:** We have to eat.
>
> **Past:** We had to eat. (*not* "We had to ate.")

Modal auxiliaries (such as *can* and *should*) do not change form to indicate tense, person, or number.

See
A1.3

### 4 Negative Verbs

The meaning of a verb may be made negative in English in a variety of ways, chiefly by adding the words *not* or *does not* to the verb (is, is *not*; can ski, *cannot* ski; drives a car, *does not* drive a car).

## Close-Up  CORRECTING DOUBLE NEGATIVES

A **double negative** is an error that occurs when the meaning of a verb is made negative not just once but twice in a single sentence.

Henry doesn't have ^any^ ~~no~~ friends. (*or* Henry ^has^ ~~doesn't have~~ no friends.)

I looked for articles in the library, but there ^were^ weren't none. (*or* I looked for articles in the library, but there weren't ^any^ ~~none~~.)

**5** Phrasal Verbs

Many verbs in English are composed of two or more words that are combined to create a new idiomatic expression—for example, *check up on, run for, turn into,* and *wait on.* These verbs are called **phrasal verbs.** It is important to become familiar with phrasal verbs and their definitions so you will recognize these verbs as phrasal verbs instead of as verbs that are followed by prepositions.

*Separable Phrasal Verbs* Often, the words that make up a phrasal verb can be separated by a direct object. In these **separable phrasal verbs,** the object can come either before or after the preposition. For example, "<u>Ellen</u> <u>turned down</u> the job offer" and "<u>Ellen</u> <u>turned</u> the job offer <u>down</u>" are both correct. However, when the object is a pronoun, the pronoun must come before the preposition. Therefore, "<u>Ellen</u> <u>turned</u> it <u>down</u>" is correct; "<u>Ellen</u> <u>turned down</u> it" is incorrect.

## Close-Up  SEPARABLE PHRASAL VERBS

| Verb | Definition |
|---|---|
| call off | cancel |
| carry on | continue |
| cheer up | make happy |
| clean out | clean the inside of |

| cut down | reduce |
|---|---|
| figure out | solve |
| fill in | substitute |
| find out | discover |
| give back | return something |
| give up | stop doing something or stop trying |
| leave out | omit |
| pass on | transmit |
| put away | place something in its proper place |
| put back | place something in its original place |
| put off | postpone |
| start over | start again |
| talk over | discuss |
| throw away/out | discard |
| touch up | repair |

*Inseparable Phrasal Verbs* Some phrasal verbs—such as *look into* and *break into*—consist of words that can never be separated. With these **inseparable phrasal verbs,** you do not have a choice about where to place the object; the object must always follow the preposition. For example, "Anna cared for her niece" is correct, but "Anna cared her niece for" is incorrect.

## Close-Up  INSEPARABLE PHRASAL VERBS

| Verb | Definition |
|---|---|
| come down with | develop an illness |
| come up with | produce |
| do away with | abolish |
| fall behind in | lag |
| get along with | be congenial with |
| get away with | avoid punishment |
| keep up with | maintain the same achievement or speed |
| look up to | admire |
| make up for | compensate |
| put up with | tolerate |
| run into | meet by chance |
| see to | arrange |
| show up | arrive |
| stand by | wait or remain loyal to |
| stand up for | support |
| watch out for | beware of or protect |

## 6 Voice

See 18d  Verbs may be in either active or passive **voice**. When the subject of a sentence performs the action of the verb, the verb is in **active voice.** When the action of the verb is performed on the subject, the verb is in **passive voice.**

> Karla and Miguel <u>purchased</u> the plane tickets. (active voice)
>
> The plane tickets <u>were purchased</u> by Karla and Miguel. (passive voice)

Because your writing will usually be clearer and more concise if you use the active voice, you should use the passive voice only when you have a good reason to do so. For example, in scientific writing, it is common for writers to use the passive voice in order to convey the idea of scientific objectivity (lack of bias).

## 7 Transitive and Intransitive Verbs

Many nonnative English speakers find it difficult to decide whether or not a verb needs an object and in what order direct and indirect objects should appear in a sentence. Learning the difference between transitive verbs and intransitive verbs can help you with such problems.

A **transitive verb** is a verb that takes a direct object: "<u>My father asked</u> a question" (subject + verb + direct object). In this example, *asked* is a transitive verb; it needs an object to complete its meaning.

An **intransitive verb** is a verb that does not take an object: "<u>The doctor smiled</u>" (subject + verb). In this example, *smiled* is an intransitive verb; it does not need an object to complete its meaning.

A transitive verb may be followed by a direct object or by both an indirect object and a direct object. (An indirect object answers the question "To whom?" or "For whom?") The indirect object may come before or after the direct object. If the indirect object follows the direct object, the preposition *to* or *for* must precede the indirect object.

> s    v     do
>
> <u>Keith wrote</u> a letter. (subject + verb + direct object)

> s    v     io    do
>
> <u>Keith wrote</u> his friend a letter. (subject + verb + indirect object + direct object)

> s    v     do    io
>
> <u>Keith wrote</u> a letter *to* his friend. (subject + verb + direct object + *to/for* + indirect object)

Some verbs in English look similar and have similar meanings, except that one verb is transitive and the other is intransitive. For example, *lie* is intransitive, *lay* is transitive; *sit* is intransitive, *set* is transitive; *rise* is intransitive, *raise* is transitive. Knowing whether a verb is transitive or intransitive can help you with troublesome verb pairs like these and also help you place the words in the correct order.

*note:* It is also important to know whether a verb is transitive or intransitive because only transitive verbs can be used in the passive voice. To determine whether a verb is transitive or intransitive—that is, to determine whether or not it needs an object—consult the example phrases in a dictionary. See 18d

## 8 Infinitives and Gerunds

In English, two verb forms may be used as nouns: **infinitives,** which always begin with *to* (as in *to work, to sleep, to eat*), and **gerunds,** which always end in *-ing* (as in *working, sleeping, eating*).

To bite into this steak requires better teeth than mine. (infinitive used as a noun)

Cooking is one of my favorite hobbies. (gerund used as a noun)

Sometimes the gerund and the infinitive form of the same verb can be used interchangeably. For example, "He continued *to sleep*" and "He continued *sleeping*" convey the same meaning. However, this is not always the case. Saying, "Marco and Lisa stopped *to eat* at Julio's Café" is not the same as saying, "Marco and Lisa stopped *eating* at Julio's Café." In this example, the meaning of the sentence changes depending on whether a gerund or infinitive is used.

## 9 Participles

In English, verb forms called **present participles** and **past participles** are frequently used as adjectives. Present participles usually end in *-ing*, as in *working, sleeping,* and *eating*, and past participles usually end in *-ed, -t,* or *-en*, as in *worked, slept,* and *eaten*.

According to the Bible, God spoke to Moses from a burning bush. (present participle used as an adjective)

Some people think raw fish is healthier than cooked fish. (past participle used as an adjective)

A **participial phrase** is a group of words consisting of the participle plus the noun phrase that functions as the object or complement of the action being expressed by the participle. To avoid confusion, the participial phrase must be placed as close as possible to the noun it modifies.

> Having visited San Francisco last week, Jim and Lynn showed us pictures from their vacation. (The participial phrase is used as an adjective that modifies *Jim and Lynn*.

## 10 Verbs Formed from Nouns

In English, nouns can sometimes be used as verbs, with no change in form (other than the addition of an -*s* for agreement with third-person singular subjects or the addition of past tense endings). For example, the nouns *chair, book, frame,* and *father* can all be used as verbs.

> She <u>chairs</u> a committee on neighborhood safety.
>
> We <u>booked</u> a flight to New York for next week.
>
> I will <u>frame</u> my daughter's diploma after she graduates.
>
> He <u>fathered</u> several children before he was thirty.

## 46b Using Nouns

See 33g <u>Nouns</u> name things: people, animals, objects, places, feelings, ideas. If a noun names one thing, it is **singular;** if a noun names more than one thing, it is **plural.**

### 1 Recognizing Noncount Nouns

Some English nouns do not have a plural form. These are called **noncount nouns** because what they name cannot be counted. (**Count nouns** name items that can be counted, such as *woman* or *desk*.)

## Close-Up NONCOUNT NOUNS

The following commonly used nouns are noncount nouns. These words have no plural forms. Therefore, you should never add -*s* or -*es* to them.

| | |
|---|---|
| advice | homework |
| clothing | information |
| education | knowledge |
| equipment | luggage |
| evidence | merchandise |
| furniture | revenge |

## 2 Using Articles with Nouns

English has two kinds of **articles,** *indefinite* and *definite.*

Use an **indefinite article** (*a* or *an*) with a noun when readers are not familiar with the noun you are naming—for example, when you are introducing the noun for the first time. To say "James entered *a* building" signals to the audience that you are introducing the idea of the building for the first time. The building is indefinite, or not specific, until it has been identified.

The indefinite article *a* is used when the word following it (which may be a noun or an adjective) begins with a consonant or with a consonant sound: *a tree, a onetime offer.* The indefinite article *an* is used if the word following it begins with a vowel (*a, e, i, o,* or *u*) or with a vowel sound: *an apple, an honor.*

Use the **definite article** (*the*) when the noun you are naming has already been introduced, when the noun is already familiar to readers, or when the noun to which you refer is specific. To say "James entered *the* building" signals to readers that you are referring to the same building you mentioned earlier. The building has now become specific and may be referred to by the definite article.

## Close-Up   USING ARTICLES WITH NOUNS

There are two exceptions to the rules governing the use of articles with nouns:

1. **Plural nouns** do not require indefinite articles: "I love horses," not "I love a horses." (Plural nouns do, however, require definite articles: "I love the horses in the national park near my house.")
2. **Noncount nouns** may not require articles: "Love conquers all," not "A love conquers all" or "The love conquers all."

**3** Using Other Determiners with Nouns

**Determiners** are words that function as <u>adjectives</u> to limit or qualify the meaning of nouns. In addition to articles, **demonstrative pronouns, possessive nouns and pronouns, numbers** (both **cardinal** and **ordinal**), and other words indicating amount or order can function in this way.

---

## Close-Up   USING OTHER DETERMINERS WITH NOUNS

- **Demonstrative pronouns** (*this, that, these, those*) communicate the following:

  1. the relative nearness or farness of the noun from the speaker's position (*this* and *these* for things that are *near, that* and *those* for things that are *far*): *this* book on my desk, *that* book on your desk; *these* shoes on my feet, *those* shoes in my closet.

  2. the number of things indicated (*this* and *that* for *singular* nouns, *these* and *those* for *plural* nouns): *this* (or *that*) flower in the vase, *these* (or *those*) flowers in the garden.

- **Possessive nouns** and **possessive pronouns** (*Ashraf's, his, their*) show who or what the noun belongs to: *Maria's* courage, *everybody's* fears, the *country's* natural resources, *my* personality, *our* groceries.

- **Cardinal** numbers (*three, fifty, a thousand*) indicate how many of the noun you mean: *seven* continents. **Ordinal** numbers (*first, tenth, thirtieth*) indicate in what order the noun appears among other items: *third* planet.

- Words other than numbers may indicate **amount** (*many, few*) and **order** (*next, last*) and function in the same ways as cardinal and ordinal numbers: *few* opportunities, *last* chance.

---

## 46c   Using Pronouns

See
A1.2 Any English noun may be replaced by a <u>pronoun</u>. For example, *doctor* may be replaced by *he* or *she*, *books* by *them*, and *computer* by *it*.

**1** Pronoun Reference

See
19c <u>Pronoun reference</u> is very important in English sentences, where the noun the pronoun replaces (the **antecedent**) must

be easily identified. In general, you should place the pronoun as close as possible to the noun it replaces so the noun to which the pronoun refers is clear. If this is impossible, use the noun itself instead of replacing it with a pronoun.

**Unclear:** When Tara met Emily, she was nervous. (Does *she* refer to Tara or to Emily?)

**Clear:** When Tara met Emily, Tara was nervous.

**Unclear:** Stefano and Victor love his DVD collection. (Whose DVD collection—Stefano's, Victor's, or someone else's?)

**Clear:** Stefano and Victor love Emilio's DVD collection.

## 2 Pronoun Placement

Never use a pronoun immediately after the noun it replaces. For example, do not say, "Most of my classmates *they* are smart"; instead, say, "Most of my classmates are smart."

The only exception to this rule occurs with an **intensive pronoun,** which ends in -*self* and emphasizes the preceding noun or pronoun: "Marta *herself* was eager to hear the results."

## 3 Indefinite Pronouns

Unlike **personal pronouns** (*I, you, he, she, it, we, they, me, him, her, us,* and *them*), **indefinite pronouns** do not refer to a particular person, place, or thing. Therefore, an indefinite pronoun does not require an antecedent. **Indefinite pronoun subjects** (*anybody, nobody, each, either, someone, something, all, some*), like personal pronouns, must <u>agree</u> in number <sup>See</sup> 17b with the sentence's verb.

      *has*
Nobody ~~have~~ failed the exam. (*Nobody* is a singular subject and requires a singular verb.)

## 4 Appositives

Appositives are nouns or noun phrases that identify or rename an adjacent noun or pronoun. An appositive usually follows the noun it identifies or renames, but can sometimes precede it.

My parents, Mary and John, live in Louisiana. (*Mary and John* identifies *parents*.)

**note:** The <u>case</u> of a pronoun in an appositive depends on <sup>See</sup> 19a the case of the word it describes.

If an appositive is *not* necessary to the meaning of the sentence, use commas to set off the appositive from the rest of the sentence. If an appositive *is* necessary to the meaning of the sentence, do not use commas.

> His aunt Trang is in the hospital. (*Trang* is necessary to the meaning of the sentence because it identifies which aunt is in the hospital.)

> Akta's car, a 1994 Jeep Cherokee, broke down last night. (*a 1994 Jeep Cherokee* is not necessary to the meaning of the sentence.)

### 5 Pronouns and Gender

A pronoun must agree in **gender** with the noun to which it refers.

> My *sister* sold *her* old car.

> Your *uncle* is walking *his* dog.

*Note:* In English, most nonhuman nouns are referred to as *it* because they do not have grammatical gender. However, exceptions are sometimes made for pets, ships, and countries. Pets are often referred to as *he* or *she*, depending on their gender, and ships and countries are sometimes referred to as *she*.

## 46d Using Adjectives and Adverbs

See A1,
4–5;
Ch. 20

**Adjectives and adverbs** are words that **modify** (describe, limit, or qualify) other words.

### 1 Position of Adjectives and Adverbs

**Adjectives** in English usually appear *before* the nouns they modify. A native speaker of English would not say, "*Cars red and black* are involved in more accidents than *cars blue or green*" but would say instead, "*Red and black cars* are involved in more accidents than *blue or green cars*."

However, adjectives may appear *after* linking verbs ("The name seemed *familiar*."), *after* direct objects ("The coach found them *tired* but *happy*."), and *after* indefinite pronouns ("Anything *sad* makes me cry.").

**Adverbs** may appear before or after the verbs they describe, but they should be placed as close to the verb as possible: not "I *told* John that I couldn't meet him for lunch *politely*," but "I *politely told* John that I couldn't meet him for lunch" or "I *told* John *politely* that I couldn't meet him for lunch." When an adverb describes an adjective or another adverb, it usually comes *before* that adjective or adverb: "The essay has *basically sound* logic"; "You must express yourself *absolutely clearly*." Never place an adverb between the verb and the direct object.

**Incorrect:**  Rolf drank *quickly* the water.

**Correct:**  Rolf drank the water *quickly* (or, Rolf *quickly* drank the water).

**2** Order of Adjectives

A single noun may be modified by more than one adjective, perhaps even by a whole list of adjectives. Given a list of three or four adjectives, most native speakers would arrange them in a sentence in the same order. If, for example, shoes are to be described as *green* and *big*, numbering *two*, and of the type worn for playing *tennis*, a native speaker would say "two big green tennis shoes." Generally, the adjectives that are most important in completing the meaning of the noun are placed closest to the noun.

---

## Close-Up  ORDER OF ADJECTIVES

1. Articles (*a, the*), demonstratives (*this, those*), and possessives (*his, our, Maria's, everybody's*)
2. Amounts (*one, five, many, few*), order (*first, next, last*)
3. Personal opinions (*nice, ugly, crowded, pitiful*)
4. Sizes and shapes (*small, tall, straight, crooked*)
5. Age (*young, old, modern, ancient*)
6. Colors (*black, white, red, blue, dark, light*)
7. Nouns functioning as adjectives to form a unit with the noun (*soccer* ball, *cardboard* box, *history* class)

---

## 46e  Using Prepositions

In English, **prepositions** (such as *to, from, at, with, among, between*) give meaning to nouns by linking them with other words and other parts of the sentence. Prepositions convey several different kinds of information:  See A1.6

● Relations to **time** (*at* nine o'clock, *in* five minutes, *for* a year)

- Relations of **place** (*in* the classroom, *at* the library, *beside* the chair) and **direction** (*to* the market, *onto* the stage, *toward* the freeway)
- Relations of **association** (go *with* someone, the tip *of* the iceberg)
- Relations of **purpose** (working *for* money, dieting *to* lose weight)

### ❶ Commonly Used Prepositional Phrases

In English, the use of prepositions is often idiomatic rather than governed by grammatical rules. In many cases, therefore, learners of English as a second language need to memorize which prepositions are used in which phrases.

In English, some prepositions that relate to time have specific uses with certain nouns, such as days, months, and seasons:

- *On* is used with days and specific dates: *on* Monday, *on* September 13, 1977.
- *In* is used with months, seasons, and years: *in* November, *in* the spring, *in* 1999.
- *In* is also used when referring to some parts of the day: *in* the morning, *in* the afternoon, *in* the evening.
- *At* is used to refer to other parts of the day: *at* noon, *at* night, *at* seven o'clock.

## Close-Up  DIFFICULT PREPOSITIONAL PHRASES

The following phrases (accompanied by their correct prepositions) sometimes cause difficulties for ESL writers:

| | | |
|---|---|---|
| according *to* | *at* least | relevant *to* |
| apologize *to* | *at* most | similar *to* |
| appeal *to* | refer *to* | subscribe *to* |
| different *from* | | |

### ❷ Commonly Confused Prepositions

The prepositions *to, in, on, into,* and *onto* are very similar to one another and are therefore easily confused:

- *To* is the basic preposition of direction. It indicates movement toward a physical place: "She went *to* the restaurant"; "He went *to* the meeting." *To* is also used to form the infinitive of a verb: "He wanted *to deposit* his paycheck before noon"; "Irene offered *to drive* Maria to the baseball game."

- *In* indicates that something is within the boundaries of a particular space or period of time: "My son is *in* the garden"; "I like to ski *in* the winter"; "The map is *in* the car."
- *On* indicates position above or the state of being supported by something: "The toys are *on* the porch"; "The baby sat *on* my lap"; "The book is *on* top of the magazine."
- *Into* indicates movement to the inside or interior of something: "She walked *into* the room"; "I threw the stone *into* the lake"; "He put the photos *into* the box." Although *into* and *in* are sometimes interchangeable, note that usage depends on whether the subject is stationary or moving. *Into* usually indicates movement, as in "I jumped *into* the water." *In* usually indicates a stationary position relative to the object of the preposition, as in "Mary is swimming *in* the water."
- *Onto* indicates movement to a position on top of something: "The cat jumped *onto* the chair"; "Crumbs are falling *onto* the floor." Both *on* and *onto* can be used to indicate a position on top of something (and therefore they can sometimes be used interchangeably), but *onto* specifies that the subject is moving to a place from a different place or from an outside position.

## Close-Up   PREPOSITIONS IN IDIOMATIC EXPRESSIONS

Many nonnative speakers use incorrect prepositions in idiomatic expressions. Compare the incorrect expressions in the left-hand column below with the correct expressions in the right-hand column.

| Common Nonnative Speaker Usage | Native Speaker Usage |
| --- | --- |
| according *with* | according *to* |
| apologize *at* | apologize *to* |
| appeal *at* | appeal *to* |
| believe *at* | believe *in* |
| different *to* | different *from* |
| *for* least, *for* most | *at* least, *at* most |
| refer *at* | refer *to* |
| relevant *with* | relevant *to* |
| similar *with* | similar *to* |
| subscribe *with* | subscribe *to* |

## 46f Understanding Word Order

Word order is extremely important in English sentences. For example, word order may indicate which word is the subject of a sentence and which is the object, or it may indicate whether a sentence is a question or a statement.

### 1 Standard Word Order

Like Chinese, English is an "SVO" language, or one in which the most typical sentence pattern is "subject-verb-object." (Arabic, by contrast, is an example of a "VSO" language.)

### 2 Word Order in Questions

Word order in questions can be particularly troublesome for speakers of languages other than English because there are so many different ways to form questions in English.

---

## Close-Up   WORD ORDER IN QUESTIONS

1. To create a **yes/no question** from a statement whose verb is a form of *be* (*am, is, are, was, were*), move the verb so it precedes the subject.

   Rasheem <u>is</u> in his laboratory.
   <u>Is</u> Rasheem in his laboratory?

   When the statement is *not* a form of *be*, change the verb to include a form of *do* as a helping verb, and then move that helping verb so it precedes the subject.

   Rasheem <u>researched</u> the depletion of the ozone level.
   <u>Did</u> Rasheem <u>research</u> the depletion of the ozone level?

2. To create a **yes/no question** from a statement that includes one or more helping verbs, move the first helping verb so it precedes the subject.

   Rasheem <u>is researching</u> the depletion of the ozone layer.
   <u>Is</u> Rasheem <u>researching</u> the depletion of the ozone layer?

   Rasheem <u>has been researching</u> the depletion of the ozone layer.
   <u>Has</u> Rasheem <u>been researching</u> the depletion of the ozone layer?

3. To create a **question asking for information,** replace the information being asked for with an **interrogative** word (*who, what, where, why, when, how*) at the beginning of the question, and invert the order of the subject and verb as with a yes/no question.

Rasheem <u>is</u> in his laboratory.

Where <u>is</u> Rasheem?

Rasheem <u>is researching</u> the depletion of the ozone layer.

What <u>is</u> Rasheem <u>researching</u>?

Rasheem <u>researched</u> the depletion of the ozone level.

What <u>did</u> Rasheem <u>research</u>?

If the interrogative word is the subject of the question, however, do *not* invert the subject and verb.

Who <u>is researching</u> the depletion of the ozone level?

4. You can also form a question by adding a **tag question** (such as *won't he?* or *didn't I?*) to the end of a statement. If the verb of the main statement is *positive,* then the verb of the tag question is *negative;* if the verb of the main statement is *negative,* then the verb of the tag question is *positive.*

Rasheem <u>is researching</u> the depletion of the ozone layer, <u>isn't</u> he?

Rasheem <u>doesn't</u> intend to write his dissertation about the depletion of the ozone layer, <u>does</u> he?

# Grammar Review

## A1  Parts of Speech

The **part of speech** to which a word belongs depends on its function in a sentence.

### 1  Nouns

**Nouns** name people, animals, places, things, ideas, actions, or qualities.

A **common noun** names any of a class of people, places, or things: *artist, judge, building, event, city.*

A **proper noun,** always <u>capitalized</u>, refers to a particular <sup>See</sup> person, place, or thing: *Mary Cassatt, World Trade Center, Crimean War.*

A **collective noun** designates a group thought of as a unit: *committee, class, family.*

An **abstract noun** refers to an intangible idea or quality: *love, hate, justice, anger, fear, prejudice.*

### 2  Pronouns

**Pronouns** are words used in place of nouns. The noun for which a pronoun stands is called its **antecedent.**

If you use a <u>quotation</u> in your paper, you must document <u>it</u>. (Pronoun *it* refers to antecedent *quotation.*)

Although different types of pronouns may have the same form, they are distinguished from one another by their function in a sentence.

A **personal pronoun** stands for a person or thing: *I, me, we, us, my, mine, our, ours, you, your, yours, he, she, it, its, him, his, her, hers, they, them, their, theirs.*

The firm made Debbie an offer, and <u>she</u> couldn't refuse <u>it</u>.

See
17a4,
17b3

An <u>indefinite pronoun</u> does not refer to any particular person or thing, so it does not require an antecedent. Indefinite pronouns include *another, any, each, few, many, some, nothing, one, anyone, everyone, everybody, everything, someone, something, either,* and *neither.*

<u>Many</u> are called, but <u>few</u> are chosen.

A **reflexive pronoun** ends with -*self* and refers to a recipient of the action that is the same as the actor: *myself, yourself, himself, herself, itself, oneself, themselves, ourselves, yourselves.*

They found <u>themselves</u> in downtown Pittsburgh.

**Intensive pronouns** have the same form as reflexive pronouns. An intensive pronoun emphasizes a preceding noun or pronoun.

Darrow <u>himself</u> was sure his client was innocent.

A **relative pronoun** introduces an adjective or noun clause in a sentence. Relative pronouns include *which, who, whom, that, what, whose, whatever, whoever, whomever,* and *whichever.*

Gandhi was the man <u>who</u> led India to independence. (introduces adjective clause)

<u>Whatever</u> happens will be a surprise. (introduces noun clause)

An **interrogative pronoun** introduces a question. Interrogative pronouns include *who, which, what, whom, whose, whoever, whatever,* and *whichever.*

<u>Who</u> was at the door?

A **demonstrative pronoun** points to a particular thing or group of things. *This, that, these,* and *those* are demonstrative pronouns.

<u>This</u> is one of Shakespeare's early plays.

A **reciprocal pronoun** denotes a mutual relationship. The reciprocal pronouns are *each other* and *one another. Each other* indicates a relationship between two individuals; *one another* denotes a relationship among more than two.

Cathy and I respect <u>each other</u> despite our differences.

Many of our friends do not respect <u>one another</u>.

**3** Verbs

Verbs can be classified into two groups: *main verbs* and *auxiliary verbs*.

*Main Verbs* **Main verbs** carry most of the meaning in a sentence or clause. Some main verbs are action verbs.

He <u>ran</u> for the train. (physical action)

He <u>thought</u> about taking the bus. (emotional action)

Other main verbs are linking verbs. A **linking verb** does not show any physical or emotional action. Its function is to link the subject to a **subject complement,** a word or phrase that renames or describes the subject.

Carbon disulfide <u>smells</u> bad.

**Frequently Used Linking Verbs**

| | | | | |
|---|---|---|---|---|
| appear | believe | look | seem | taste |
| be | feel | prove | smell | turn |
| become | grow | remain | sound | |

*Auxiliary Verbs* **Auxiliary verbs** (also called **helping verbs**), such as *be* and *have,* combine with main verbs to form **verb phrases.** Auxiliary verbs indicate tense, voice, or mood.

[auxiliary] [main verb]    [auxiliary] [main verb]

The train <u>has started</u>. We <u>are leaving</u> soon.

[verb phrase]              [verb phrase]

Certain auxiliary verbs, known as **modal auxiliaries,** indicate necessity, possibility, willingness, obligation, or ability.

**Modal Auxiliaries**

| | | | |
|---|---|---|---|
| can | might | ought [to] | will |
| could | must | shall | would |
| may | need [to] | should | |

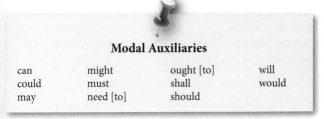

*Verbals* **Verbals,** such as *known* or *running* or *to go,* are verb forms that act as adjectives, adverbs, or nouns. A verbal can never serve as a sentence's main verb unless it is used with one or more auxiliary verbs (*He is running*). Verbals include *participles, infinitives,* and *gerunds.*

## PARTICIPLES

Virtually every verb has a **present participle,** which ends in *-ing* (*loving, learning*) and a **past participle,** which usually ends in *-d* or *-ed* (*agreed, learned*). Some verbs have <u>irregular</u> past participles (*gone, begun, written*). Participles may function in a sentence as adjectives or as nouns.

See 18a

> Twenty brands of <u>running</u> shoes were on display. (participle serves as adjective)

> The <u>wounded</u> were given emergency first aid. (participle serves as noun)

## INFINITIVES

An **infinitive** is made up of *to* and the base form of the verb (*to defeat*). An infinitive may function as an adjective, an adverb, or a noun.

> Ann Arbor was clearly the place <u>to be.</u> (infinitive serves as adjective)

> Carla went outside <u>to think.</u> (infinitive serves as adverb)

> <u>To win</u> was everything. (infinitive serves as noun)

## GERUNDS

**Gerunds,** like present participles, end in *-ing.* However, gerunds always function as nouns.

> <u>Seeing</u> is <u>believing.</u>
> Andrew loves <u>skiing.</u>

## 4 Adjectives

**Adjectives** describe, limit, qualify, or in some other way modify nouns or pronouns.

**Descriptive adjectives** name a quality of the noun or pronoun they modify.

> After the game, they were <u>exhausted.</u>

> They ordered a <u>chocolate</u> soda and a <u>butterscotch</u> sundae.

When articles, pronouns, numbers, and the like function as adjectives, limiting or qualifying nouns or pronouns, they are referred to as <u>determiners</u>.

ESL
46b3

## 5 Adverbs

**Adverbs** describe the action of verbs or modify adjectives or other adverbs (or complete phrases, clauses, or sentences). They answer the questions "How?" "Why?" "When?" "Under what conditions?" and "To what extent?"

He walked <u>rather hesitantly</u> toward the front of the room.

Let's meet <u>tomorrow</u> for coffee.

Adverbs that modify other adverbs or adjectives limit or qualify the words they modify.

He pitched an <u>almost</u> perfect game yesterday.

*Interrogative Adverbs* The **interrogative adverbs** (*how, when, why,* and *where*) introduce questions.

<u>How</u> are you doing?

<u>Why</u> did he miss class?

*Conjunctive Adverbs* **Conjunctive adverbs** act as <u>transitional words</u>, joining and relating independent clauses.

See
4b

### Frequently Used Conjunctive Adverbs

| | | | |
|---|---|---|---|
| accordingly | furthermore | meanwhile | similarly |
| also | hence | moreover | still |
| anyway | however | nevertheless | then |
| besides | incidentally | next | thereafter |
| certainly | indeed | nonetheless | therefore |
| consequently | instead | now | thus |
| finally | likewise | otherwise | undoubtedly |

## 6 Prepositions

A **preposition** introduces a noun or pronoun (or a phrase or clause that functions in the sentence as a noun), linking it to other words in the sentence. The word or word group that the preposition introduces is its **object**.

prep   obj      prep  obj

They received a postcard <u>from</u> Bobby telling <u>about</u> his trip.

### Frequently Used Prepositions

| | | | |
|---|---|---|---|
| about | beneath | inside | since |
| above | beside | into | through |
| across | between | like | throughout |
| after | beyond | near | to |
| against | by | of | toward |
| along | concerning | off | under |
| among | despite | on | underneath |
| around | down | onto | until |
| as | during | out | up |
| at | except | outside | upon |
| before | for | over | with |
| behind | from | past | within |
| below | in | regarding | without |

## 7 Conjunctions

**Conjunctions** connect words, phrases, clauses, or sentences.

*Coordinating Conjunctions* **Coordinating conjunctions** (*and, or, but, nor, for, so, yet*) connect words, phrases, or clauses of equal weight.

Should I order chicken <u>or</u> fish?

Thoreau wrote *Walden* in 1854, <u>and</u> he died in 1862.

*Correlative Conjunctions* Always used in pairs, **correlative conjunctions** also link items of equal weight.

<u>Both</u> Hancock <u>and</u> Jefferson signed the Declaration of Independence.

<u>Either</u> I will renew my lease, <u>or</u> I will move.

### Frequently Used Correlative Conjunctions

| | |
|---|---|
| both . . . and | neither . . . nor |
| either . . . or | not only . . . but also |
| just as . . . so | whether . . . or |

*Subordinating Conjunctions* Words such as *since, because,* and *although* are **subordinating conjunctions**. A subordinating conjunction introduces a dependent (subordinate) clause, connecting it to an independent (main) clause to form a <u>complex sentence</u>.

See 21a2

> <u>Although</u> people may feel healthy, they can still have medical problems.

> It is best to diagram your garden <u>before</u> you start to plant.

### 8 Interjections

**Interjections** are words used as exclamations to express emotion: *Oh! Ouch! Wow! Alas! Hey!*

## A2 Sentences

### 1 Basic Sentence Elements

A **sentence** is an independent grammatical unit that contains a <u>subject</u> (a noun or noun phrase) and a <u>predicate</u> (a verb or verb phrase) and expresses a complete thought.

> <u>The quick brown fox</u> <u>jumped over the lazy dog</u>.

> <u>It</u> <u>came from outer space</u>.

### 2 Basic Sentence Patterns

A **simple sentence** consists of at least one subject and one predicate. Simple sentences conform to one of five patterns.

*Subject + Intransitive Verb (s + v)*

>      s         v
> <u>Stock prices</u> <u>may fall</u>.

*Subject + Transitive Verb + Direct Object (s + v + do)*

>   s        v        do
> <u>Van Gogh</u> <u>created</u> *The Starry Night*.

>     s      v   do
> <u>Caroline</u> <u>saved</u> Jake.

*Subject + Transitive Verb + Direct Object + Object Complement (s + v + do + oc)*

>  s  v      do   oc
> <u>I</u> <u>found</u> the exam easy.

>      s        v    do     oc
> <u>The class</u> <u>elected</u> Bridget treasurer.

*Subject + Linking Verb + Subject Complement (s + v + sc)*

$\quad\quad$ s $\quad\quad\quad$ v $\quad$ sc
The injection <u>was</u> painless.

$\quad\quad$ s $\quad\quad\quad\quad\quad\quad$ v $\quad\quad\quad\quad$ sc
David Cameron <u>became</u> Prime Minister.

*Subject + Transitive Verb + Indirect Object + Direct Object (s + v + io + do)*

$\quad\quad$ s $\quad\quad$ v $\quad\quad$ io $\quad\quad$ do
<u>Cyrano</u> <u>wrote</u> Roxanne a poem. (Cyrano wrote a poem *for* Roxanne.)

$\quad\quad$ s $\quad\quad$ v $\quad$ io $\quad$ do
Hester <u>gave</u> Pearl a kiss. (Hester gave a kiss *to* Pearl.)

## 3 Phrases and Clauses

*Phrases* A **phrase** is a group of related words that lacks a subject or predicate or both and functions as a single part of speech. It cannot stand alone as a sentence.

- A **verb phrase** consists of a **main verb** and all its auxiliary verbs. (Time *is flying*.)
- A **noun phrase** includes a noun or pronoun plus all related modifiers. (I'll climb *the highest mountain*.)
- See A1.6 A **prepositional phrase** consists of a <u>preposition</u>, its object, and any modifiers of that object. (They considered the ethical implications *of the animal experiment*.)
- See A1.3 A **verbal phrase** consists of a <u>verbal</u> and its related objects, modifiers, or complements. A verbal phrase may be a **participial phrase** (*encouraged by the voter turnout*), a **gerund phrase** (*taking it easy*), or an **infinitive phrase** (*to evaluate the evidence*).
- An **absolute phrase** usually consists of a noun and a participle, accompanied by modifiers. It modifies an entire independent clause rather than a particular word or phrase. (*Their toes tapping*, they watched the auditions.)

*Clauses* A **clause** is a group of related words that includes a subject and a predicate. An **independent** (main) **clause** can stand alone as a sentence, but a **dependent** (subordinate) **clause** cannot. It must always be combined with an indepen- See 21a2 dent clause to form a <u>complex sentence</u>.

[Lucretia Mott was an abolitionist.] [She was also a pioneer for women's rights.] (two independent clauses)

[Lucretia Mott was an abolitionist] [who was also a pioneer for women's rights.] (independent clause, dependent clause)

Dependent clauses may be *adjective, adverb,* or *noun* clauses:

- **Adjective clauses,** sometimes called **relative clauses,** modify nouns or pronouns and always follow the nouns or pronouns they modify. They are introduced by relative pronouns—*that, what, which, who,* and so on—or by the adverbs *where* and *when.*

  Celeste's grandparents, who were born in Romania, speak little English.

- **Adverb clauses** modify verbs, adjectives, adverbs, entire phrases, or independent clauses. They are always introduced by subordinating conjunctions.

  Mark will go wherever there's a party.

- **Noun clauses** function as subjects, objects, or complements. A noun clause may be introduced by a relative pronoun or by *whether, when, where, why,* or *how.*

  What you see is what you get.

## 4 Types of Sentences

A **simple sentence** is a single independent clause. A simple sentence can consist of just a subject and a predicate.

Jessica fell.

Or, a simple sentence can be expanded with modifying words and phrases.

On Halloween, Jessica fell in love with the mysterious Henry Goodyear.

A compound sentence consists of two or more simple See 21a1 sentences linked by a coordinating conjunction (preceded by a comma), by a semicolon (alone or followed by a transitional word or phrase), by correlative conjunctions, or by a colon.

[The moon rose in the sky], and [the stars shone brightly].

[José wanted to spend a quiet afternoon]; however, [his aunt dropped by unexpectedly.]

See 21a2

A **complex sentence** consists of one independent clause and at least one dependent clause.

> independent clause      dependent clause
> [It was hard for us to believe] [that anyone could be so cruel].

A **compound-complex sentence** is a compound sentence —made up of at least two independent clauses—that also includes at least one dependent clause.

> [My mother always worried] [when my father had to work late], and [she could rarely sleep more than a few minutes at a time].

## Close-Up   CLASSIFYING SENTENCES

Sentences can also be classified according to their function:

- **Declarative sentences** make statements; they are the most common.
- **Interrogative sentences** ask questions, usually by inverting standard subject-verb order (often with an interrogative word) or by adding a form of *do* (*Is Maggie at home? Where is Maggie? Does Maggie live here?*).
- **Imperative sentences** express commands or requests, using the second-person singular of the verb and generally omitting the pronoun subject *you* (*Go to your room. Please believe me.*).
- **Exclamatory sentences** express strong emotion and end with an exclamation point (*The killing must stop now!*).

# Usage Review

This usage review lists words and phrases that writers often find troublesome.

**a, an** Use *a* before words that begin with consonants and words with initial vowels that sound like consonants: *a* person, *a* historical document, *a* one-horse carriage, *a* uniform. Use *an* before words that begin with vowels and words that begin with a silent *h: an* artist, *an* honest person.

**accept, except** *Accept* is a verb that means "to receive"; *except* as a preposition or conjunction means "other than" and as a verb means "to leave out": The auditors will *accept* all your claims *except* the last two. Some businesses are *excepted* from the regulation.

**advice, advise** *Advice* is a noun meaning "opinion or information offered"; *advise* is a verb that means "to offer advice to": The broker *advised* her client to take his attorney's *advice*.

**affect, effect** *Affect* is a verb meaning "to influence"; *effect* can be a verb or a noun—as a verb it means "to bring about," and as a noun it means "result": We know how the drug *affects* patients immediately, but little is known of its long-term *effects*. The arbitrator tried to *effect* a settlement between the parties.

**all ready, already** *All ready* means "completely prepared"; *already* means "by or before this or that time": I was *all ready* to help, but it was *already* too late.

**all right, alright** Although the use of *alright* is increasing, current usage calls for *all right*.

**allusion, illusion** An *allusion* is a reference or hint; an *illusion* is something that is not what it seems: The poem makes an *allusion* to the Pandora myth. The shadow created an optical *illusion*.

**a lot** *A lot* is always two words.

**among, between** *Among* refers to groups of more than two things; *between* refers to just two things: The three parties agreed *among* themselves to settle the case. There will be a brief intermission *between* the two acts. (Note that *amongst* is British, not American, usage.)

**amount, number** *Amount* refers to a quantity that cannot be counted; *number* refers to things that can be counted: Even a small *amount* of caffeine can be harmful. Seeing their commander fall, a large *number* of troops ran to his aid.

**an, a** See **a, an.**

**and/or** In business or technical writing, use *and/or* when either or both of the items it connects can apply. In college writing, however, avoid the use of *and/or*.

**as, like** *As* can be used as a conjunction (to introduce a complete clause) or as a preposition; *like* should be used as a preposition only: In *The Scarlet Letter,* Hawthorne uses imagery *as* (not *like*) he does in his other works. After classes, Fred works *as* a manager of a fast food restaurant. Writers *like* Carl Sandburg appear once in a generation.

**at, to** Many people use the prepositions *at* and *to* after *where* in conversation: *Where* are you working *at*? Where are you going *to*? This usage is redundant and should not appear in college writing.

**awhile, a while** *Awhile* is an adverb; *a while*, which consists of an article and a noun, is used as the object of a preposition: Before we continue, we will rest *awhile* (modifies the verb *rest*). Before we continue, we will rest for *a while* (object of the preposition *for*).

**bad, badly** *Bad* is an adjective, and *badly* is an adverb: The school board decided that *Adventures of Huckleberry Finn* was a *bad* book. American automobile makers did not do *badly* this year. After verbs that refer to any of the senses or after any other linking verb, use the adjective form: He looked *bad*. He felt *bad*. It seemed *bad*.

**being as, being that** These awkward phrases add unnecessary words, thereby weakening your writing. Use *because* instead.

**beside, besides** *Beside* is a preposition meaning "next to"; *besides* can be either a preposition meaning "except" or "other than" or an adverb meaning "as well": *Beside* the tower was a wall that ran the length of the city. *Besides* its industrial uses, laser technology has many other applications. Edison invented not only the lightbulb but the phonograph *besides*.

**between, among** See **among, between.**

**bring, take**  *Bring* means "to transport from a farther place to a nearer place"; *take* means "to carry or convey from a nearer place to a farther place": *Bring* me a souvenir from your trip. *Take* this message to the general, and wait for a reply.

**can, may**  *Can* denotes ability; *may* indicates permission: If you *can* play, you *may* use my piano.

**cite, site**  *Cite* is a verb meaning "to quote as an authority or example"; *site* is a noun meaning "a place or setting"; it is also a shortened form of *Web site:* Jeff *cited* five sources in his research paper. The builder cleared the *site* for the new bank. Marisa uploaded her *site* to the Web.

**climactic, climatic**  *Climactic* means "of or related to a climax"; *climatic* means "of or related to climate": The *climactic* moment of the movie occurred unexpectedly. If scientists are correct, the *climatic* conditions of Earth are changing.

**complement, compliment**  *Complement* means "to complete or add to"; *compliment* means "to give praise": A double-blind study would *complement* their preliminary research. My instructor *complimented* me on my improvement.

**conscious, conscience**  *Conscious* is an adjective meaning "having one's mental faculties awake"; *conscience* is a noun that means the moral sense of right and wrong: The patient will remain *conscious* during the procedure. His *conscience* would not allow him to lie.

**continual, continuous**  *Continual* means "recurring at intervals"; *continuous* refers to an action that occurs without interruption: A pulsar is a star that emits a *continual* stream of electromagnetic radiation. (It emits radiation at regular intervals.) A small battery allows the watch to run *continuously* for five years. (It runs without stopping.)

**could of, should of, would of**  The contractions *could've*, *should've*, and *would've* are often misspelled as the nonstandard constructions *could of, should of,* and *would of.* Use *could have, should have,* and *would have* in college writing.

**couple, couple of**  *Couple* means "a pair," but *couple of* is often used colloquially to mean "several" or "a few." In your college writing, specify "four points" or "two examples" rather than using "a couple of."

**criterion, criteria**  *Criteria,* from the Greek, is the plural of *criterion,* meaning "standard for judgment": Of all the *criteria* for hiring graduating seniors, class rank is the most important *criterion.*

**data**   *Data* is the plural of the Latin *datum*, meaning "fact." In colloquial speech and writing, *data* is often used as the singular as well as the plural form. In college writing, use *data* only for the plural: The *data* discussed in this section *are* summarized in Appendix A.

**different from, different than**   *Different than* is widely used in American speech. In college writing, use *different from*.

**disinterested, uninterested**   *Disinterested* means "objective" or "capable of making an impartial judgment"; *uninterested* means "indifferent or unconcerned": The American judicial system depends on *disinterested* jurors. Finding no treasure, Hernando de Soto was *uninterested* in going farther.

**don't, doesn't**   *Don't* is the contraction of *do not; doesn't* is the contraction of *does not*. Do not confuse the two: My dog *doesn't* (not *don't*) like to walk in the rain. (Note that contractions are generally not acceptable in college writing.)

**economic, economical**   *Economic* refers to the economy—to the production, distribution, and consumption of goods. *Economical* means "avoiding waste" or "careful use of resources": There was strong *economic* growth this quarter. It is *economical* to have roommates in this city.

**effect, affect**   See **affect, effect.**

**e.g.**   *E.g.* is an abbreviation for the Latin *exempli gratia*, meaning "for example" or "for instance." In college writing, do not use *e.g.* Instead, use for *example* or *for instance*.

**emigrate from, immigrate to**   To *emigrate* is "to leave one's country and settle in another"; to *immigrate* is "to come to another country and reside there." The noun forms of these words are *emigrant* and *immigrant*: My great-grandfather *emigrated from* Warsaw along with many other *emigrants* from Poland. Many people *immigrate to* the United States for economic reasons, but *immigrants* still face great challenges.

**eminent, imminent**   *Eminent* is an adjective meaning "standing above others" or "prominent"; *imminent* means "about to occur": Oliver Wendell Holmes Jr. was an *eminent* jurist. In ancient times, a comet signaled *imminent* disaster.

**enthused**   *Enthused*, a colloquial form of *enthusiastic*, should not be used in college writing.

**etc.**   *Etc.,* the abbreviation of *et cetera*, means "and the rest." Do not use it in your college writing. Instead, use *and so on*—or, better yet, specify what *etc.* stands for.

**everyday, every day** *Everyday* is an adjective that means "ordinary" or "commonplace"; *every day* means "occurring daily": In the Gettysburg Address, Lincoln used *everyday* language. She exercises almost *every day.*

**everyone, every one** *Everyone* is an indefinite pronoun meaning "every person"; *every one* means "every individual or thing in a particular group": *Everyone* seems happier in the spring. *Every one* of the packages had been opened.

**except, accept** See **accept, except.**

**explicit, implicit** *Explicit* means "expressed or stated directly"; *implicit* means "implied" or "expressed or stated indirectly": The director *explicitly* warned the actors to be on time for rehearsals. Her *implicit* message was that lateness would not be tolerated.

**farther, further** *Farther* designates distance; *further* designates degree: I have traveled *farther* from home than any of my relatives. Critics charge that welfare subsidies encourage *further* dependence.

**fewer, less** Use *fewer* with nouns that can be counted: *fewer* books, *fewer* people, *fewer* dollars. Use *less* with quantities that cannot be counted: *less* pain, *less* power, *less* enthusiasm.

**firstly (secondly, thirdly, . . .)** Archaic forms meaning "in the first . . . second . . . third place." Use *first, second, third* instead.

**further, farther** See **farther, further.**

**good, well** *Good* is an adjective, never an adverb: She is a *good* swimmer. *Well* can function as an adverb or as an adjective. As an adverb, it means "in a good manner": She swam *well* (not *good*) in the meet. *Well* is used as an adjective meaning "in good health" with verbs that denote a state of being or feeling: I feel *well.*

**got to** *Got to* is not acceptable in college writing. To indicate obligation, use *have to, has to,* or *must.*

**hanged, hung** Both *hanged* and *hung* are past participles of *hang. Hanged* is used to refer to executions; *hung* is used to mean "suspended": Billy Budd was *hanged* for killing the master-at-arms. The stockings were *hung* by the chimney with care.

**he, she** Traditionally, *he* has been used in the generic sense to refer to both males and females. To acknowledge the equality of the sexes, however, avoid the generic *he.* Use plural pronouns whenever possible. **See 26c2.**

**historic, historical**  *Historic* means "important" or "momentous"; *historical* means "relating to the past" or "based on or inspired by history": The end of World War II was a *historic* occasion. *Historical* records show that Quakers played an important part in the abolition of slavery.

**hopefully**  The adverb *hopefully,* meaning "in a hopeful manner," should modify a verb, an adjective, or another adverb. Do not use *hopefully* as a sentence modifier meaning "it is hoped." Rather than "*Hopefully,* scientists will soon discover a cure for AIDS," write "*People hope* scientists will soon discover a cure for AIDS."

**i.e.**  *I.e.* is an abbreviation for the Latin *id est,* meaning "that is." In college writing, do not use *i.e.* Instead, use its English equivalent.

**if, whether**  When asking indirect questions or expressing doubt, use *whether*: He asked *whether* (not *if* ) the flight would be delayed. The flight attendant was not sure *whether* (not *if* ) it would be delayed.

**illusion, allusion**  See **allusion, illusion.**

**immigrate to, emigrate from**  See **emigrate from, immigrate to.**

**implicit, explicit**  See **explicit, implicit.**

**imply, infer**  *Imply* means "to hint" or "to suggest"; *infer* means "to conclude from": Mark Antony *implied* that the conspirators had murdered Caesar. The crowd *inferred* his meaning and called for justice.

**infer, imply**  See **imply, infer.**

**irregardless, regardless**  *Irregardless* is a nonstandard version of *regardless.* Use *regardless* or *irrespective* instead.

**is when, is where**  These constructions are faulty when they appear in definitions: A playoff is (not *is when* or *is where*) an additional game played to establish the winner of a tie.

**its, it's**  *Its* is a possessive pronoun; *it's* is a contraction of *it is: It's* no secret that the bank is out to protect *its* assets.

**kind of, sort of**  The use of *kind of* and *sort of* to mean "rather" or "somewhat" is colloquial. These expressions should not appear in college writing: It is well known that Napoleon was rather (not *kind of* ) short.

**lay, lie**  See **lie, lay.**

**leave, let**  *Leave* means "to go away from" or "to let remain"; *let* means "to allow" or "to permit": *Let* (not *leave*) me give you a hand.

**less, fewer**  See **fewer, less.**

**let, leave**   See **leave, let.**

**lie, lay**   *Lie* is an intransitive verb (one that does not take an object) meaning "to recline." Its principal forms are *lie, lay, lain, lying:* Each afternoon she would *lie* in the sun and listen to the surf. *As I Lay Dying* is a novel by William Faulkner. By 1871, Troy had *lain* undisturbed for two thousand years. The painting shows a nude *lying* on a couch.

  *Lay* is a transitive verb (one that takes an object) meaning "to put" or "to place." Its principal forms are *lay, laid, laid, laying:* The Federalist Papers *lay* the foundation for American conservatism. In October 1781, the British *laid* down their arms and surrendered. He had *laid* his money on the counter before leaving. We watched the stonemasons *laying* a wall.

**life, lifestyle**   *Life* is the span of time that a living thing exists; *lifestyle* is a way of living that reflects a person's values or attitudes: Before he was hanged, Nathan Hale said, "I only regret that I have but one *life* to lose for my country." The writer Virginia Woolf was known for her unconventional *lifestyle.*

**like, as**   See **as, like.**

**loose, lose**   *Loose* is an adjective meaning "not rigidly fastened or securely attached"; *lose* is a verb meaning "to misplace": The marble facing of the building became *loose* and fell to the sidewalk. After only two drinks, most people *lose* their ability to judge distance.

**lots, lots of, a lot of**   These words are colloquial substitutes for *many, much,* or *a great deal of.* Avoid their use in college writing: The students had *many* (not *lots of* or *a lot of* ) options for essay topics.

**man**   Like the generic pronoun *he, man* has been used in English to denote members of both sexes. This usage is being replaced by *human beings, people,* or similar terms that do not specify gender. **See 26c2.**

**may, can**   See **can, may.**

**may be, maybe**   *May be* is a verb phrase: *maybe* is an adverb meaning "perhaps": She *may be* the smartest student in the class. *Maybe* her experience has given her an advantage.

**media, medium**   *Medium,* meaning "a means of conveying or broadcasting something," is singular; *media* is the plural form and requires a plural verb: The *media have* distorted the issue.

**might have, might of**   *Might of* is a nonstandard spelling of the contraction of *might have* (*might've*). Use *might have* in college writing.

**number, amount** See **amount, number.**

**OK, O.K., okay** All three spellings are acceptable, but this term should be avoided in college writing. Replace it with a more specific word or words: The lecture was *adequate* (not *okay*), if uninspiring.

**passed, past** *Passed* is the past tense of the verb *pass; past* means "belonging to a former time" or "no longer current": The car must have been going eighty miles per hour when it *passed* us. In the envelope was a bill marked *past* due.

**percent, percentage** *Percent* indicates a part of a hundred when a specific number is referred to: "*10 percent* of his salary." *Percentage* is used when no specific number is referred to: "a *percentage* of next year's receipts." In technical and business writing, it is permissible to use the % sign after percentages you are comparing. Write out the word *percent* in college writing.

**plus** As a preposition, *plus* means "in addition to." Avoid using *plus* as a substitute for *and:* Include the principal, *plus* the interest, in your calculations. Your quote was too high; *moreover* (not *plus*), it was inaccurate.

**precede, proceed** *Precede* means "to go or come before"; *proceed* means "to go forward in an orderly way": Robert Frost's *North of Boston* was *preceded* by an earlier volume. In 1532, Francisco Pizarro landed at Tumbes and *proceeded* south.

**principal, principle** As a noun, *principal* means "a sum of money (minus interest) invested or lent" or "a person in the leading position"; as an adjective, it means "most important"; a *principle* is a noun meaning a rule of conduct or a basic truth: He wanted to reduce the *principal* of the loan. The *principal* of the high school is a talented administrator. Women are the *principal* wage earners in many American households. The Constitution embodies certain fundamental *principles.*

**quote, quotation** *Quote* is a verb. *Quotation* is a noun. In college writing, do not use *quote* as a shortened form of *quotation:* Scholars attribute these *quotations* (not *quotes*) to Shakespeare.

**raise, rise** *Raise* is a transitive verb, and *rise* is an intransitive verb—that is, *raise* takes an object, and *rise* does not: My grandparents *raised* a large family. The sun will *rise* at 6:12 tomorrow morning.

real, really   *Real* means "genuine" or "authentic"; *really* means "actually." In college writing, do not use *real* as an adjective meaning "very."

reason is that, reason is because   *Reason* should be used with *that* and not with *because,* which is redundant: The *reason* he left is *that* (not *because*) you insulted him.

regardless, irregardless   See **irregardless, regardless.**

rise, raise   See **raise, rise.**

set, sit   *Set* means "to put down" or "to lay." Its principal forms are *set* and *setting:* After rocking the baby to sleep, he *set* her down carefully in her crib. After *setting* her down, he took a nap.

Ψ *Sit* means "to assume a sitting position." Its principal forms are *sit, sat,* and *sitting:* Many children *sit* in front of the television five to six hours a day. The dog *sat* by the fire. We were *sitting* in the airport when the flight was canceled.

shall, will   *Will* has all but replaced *shall* to express all future action.

should of   See **could of, should of, would of.**

simple, simplistic   *Simple* means "plain, ordinary, or uncomplicated"; *simplistic* means "overly or misleadingly simplified": Because she had studied, Tanya thought the test was *simple.* His explanation of how the Internet works is *simplistic.*

since   Do not use *since* for *because* if there is any chance of confusion. In the sentence "*Since* President Nixon traveled to China, trade between China and the United States has increased," *since* could mean either "from the time that" or "because." To be clear, use *because.*

sit, set   See **set, sit.**

so   Avoid using *so* as a vague intensifier meaning "very" or "extremely." Follow *so* with *that* and a clause that describes the result: She was *so* pleased with their work *that* she took them out to lunch.

sometime, sometimes, some time   *Sometime* means "at some time in the future"; *sometimes* means "now and then"; *some time* means "a period of time": The president will address Congress *sometime* next week. All automobiles, no matter how reliable, *sometimes* need repairs. It has been *some time* since I read that book.

sort of, kind of   See **kind of, sort of.**

**supposed to, used to**  *Supposed to* and *used to* are often misspelled. Both verbs require the final *d* to indicate past tense.

**take, bring**  See **bring, take.**

**than, then**  *Than* is a conjunction used to indicate a comparison; *then* is an adverb indicating time: The new shopping center is bigger *than* the old one. He did his research; *then,* he wrote a report.

**that, which, who**  Use *that* or *which* when referring to a thing; use *who* when referring to a person: It was a speech *that* inspired many. The movie, *which* was a huge success, failed to impress her. Anyone *who* (not *that*) takes the course will benefit.

**their, there, they're**  *Their* is a possessive pronoun; *there* indicates place and is also used in the expressions *there* is and *there are; they're* is a contraction of *they are:* Watson and Crick did *their* DNA work at Cambridge University. I love Los Angeles, but I wouldn't want to live *there. There* is nothing we can do to resurrect an extinct species. When *they're* well treated, rabbits make excellent pets.

**themselves, theirselves, theirself**  *Theirselves* and *theirself* are nonstandard variants of *themselves.*

**then, than**  See **than, then.**

**till, until, 'til**  *Till* and *until* have the same meaning, and both are acceptable. *Until* is preferred in college writing. *'Til,* a contraction of *until,* should be avoided.

**to, at**  See **at, to.**

**to, too, two**  *To* is a preposition that indicates direction; *too* is an adverb that means "also" or "more than is needed"; *two* expresses the number 2: Last year we flew from New York *to* California. "Tippecanoe and Tyler, *too*" was William Henry Harrison's campaign slogan. The plot was *too* complicated for the average reader. Just north of *Two* Rivers, Wisconsin, is a petrified forest.

**try to, try and**  *Try and* is the colloquial equivalent of the more formal *try to:* He decided to *try to* (not *try and*) do better. In college writing, use *try to.*

**-type**  Deleting this empty suffix eliminates clutter and clarifies meaning: Found in the wreckage was an incendiary (not *incendiary-type*) device.

**uninterested, disinterested**  See **disinterested, uninterested.**

**unique** Because *unique* means "the only one," not "remarkable" or "unusual," never use constructions like *the most unique* or *very unique*.

**until** See *till, until, 'til*.

**used to** See *supposed to, used to*.

**utilize** In most cases, replace *utilize* with *use* (*utilize* often sounds pretentious).

**wait for, wait on** To *wait for* means "to defer action until something occurs." To *wait on* means "to act as a waiter": I am *waiting for* (not *on*) dinner.

**weather, whether** *Weather* is a noun meaning "the state of the atmosphere"; *whether* is a conjunction used to introduce an alternative: The *weather* will improve this weekend. It is doubtful *whether* we will be able to ski tomorrow.

**well, good** See *good, well*.

**were, we're** *Were* is a verb; *we're* is the contraction of *we are*: The Trojans *were* asleep when the Greeks attacked. We must act now if *we're* going to succeed.

**whether, if** See **if, whether.**

**which, who, that** See **that, which, who.**

**who, whom** When a pronoun serves as the subject of its clause, use *who* or *whoever;* when it functions in a clause as an object, use *whom* or *whomever:* Sarah, *who* is studying ancient civilizations, would like to visit Greece. Sarah, *whom* I met in France, wants me to travel to Greece with her. **See 19b2.**

**who's, whose** *Who's* means "who is" or "who has"; *whose* indicates possession: *Who's* going to take calculus? *Who's* already left for the concert? The writer *whose* book was in the window was autographing copies.

**will, shall** See **shall, will.**

**would of** See **could of, should of, would of.**

**your, you're** *Your* indicates possession; *you're* is the contraction of *you are*: You can improve *your* stamina by jogging two miles a day. *You're* certain to be the winner.

# Index

*Note:* Page numbers in blue indicate definitions.

## A

Peer review, 12–13, 67–69
  audience in, 12–13
  comments in, 13, 19, 67–69
  drafts in, 12–13
  in revision process, 13, 19,
    68–69, 363
*ercent, percentage*, 400
Percentage, numerals in, 325
Perfect tenses, 243–44
Period(s), 281–82
  in abbreviations, 281
  with ellipses, 306–07
  at end of sentence, 281
  in indirect questions, 281, 283
  to mark divisions in electronic
    addresses, 282, 319
  to mark divisions in literary
    works, 114–15, 282
  with other punctuation, 281,
    297, 299, 306–07
  with quotation marks, 299
  in revising comma splices,
    228–29
  in revising fused sentences,
    228–29
  in revising run-on sentences,
    228–29
Periodical(s), 74–75. *See also*
    Journal articles; Magazine
    articles; Newspaper articles
  missing, tracking down, 79
Periodical articles. *See also*
    Article(s) (publications);
    Journal articles; Magazine
    articles; Newsletter articles;
    Newspaper articles
  previewing, 2
Periodical indexes, 74–75
Person, 267, 366
  agreement in, 234, 267, 366
  shift in, 267
Personal communication. *See also*
    Business letters; Email
  APA in-text citations, 163
  APA reference list, 170
  audience in, 11
  Chicago-style endnotes and
    bibliographies, 199–200, 204
  journal writing, 15
  MLA works-cited list, 129, 134
  purpose in, 10
  text messages, 262
Personal home pages, MLA works-
    cited list, 134
Personal pronouns, 375, 383
Personal titles. *See* Titles of people

Persuasive writing, 10
Pharmacy, writing in, overview,
    358–59
Philosophic movements, capital-
    izing names of, 314
Philosophy
  specialized database, 77
  writing in, overview, 358–59
Photocopies, managing, 54–55
Photographs
  in document design, 340–41
  integrating into research
    paper, 66
  MLA works-cited list, 130, 136
  sample, 341
Phrasal verbs, 368–69
Phrase(s), 390. *See also* Transitional
    words and phrases; *specific
    types of phrase*
  commas with, 286, 288
  contradictory, commas with, 288
  deadwood, eliminating, 263
  key, repeating, 270
  misplaced, relocating, 272
  modifying, between subject and
    verb, 234–35
  noun, 266
  phrase fragments, 231
  plagiarism avoidance, 102, 103
  in series, 269
  between subject and verb, 234–35
  types of, 390
  in varying sentence openings,
    262
  wordy, eliminating, 264
Phrase fragments
  appositive, 231
  prepositional phrase, 231
  revising, 231
  verbal phrase, 231
Physics
  style manual, 225
  writing in, overview, 358–59
Place names
  abbreviating, 281, 282
  capitalizing, 313
  numerals in, 325
  prepositions and relation to, 378
Plagiarism, 98–104
  avoiding, 53, 54, 58, 98–104
  detecting, 98
  differentiating words and
    phrases, 102, 103
  intentional, 98, 99–100
  revising to eliminate, 100–01
  unintentional, 44, 98, 99

# Correction Symbols

bbr — Incorrect abbreviation: 37a–c; *editing misuse*, 37d

dj — Incorrect adjective: 46d; 20a–b; *comparative/superlative forms*, 20c

dv — Incorrect adverb: 46d; 20b; *comparative/superlative forms*, 20c

gr — Faulty agreement: *subject/verb*, 17a; *pronoun/antecedent*, 17b

ud — Audience not clear: *identifying audience*, 2b

wk — Awkward: 23a–c

a — Incorrect case: 19a; *case in special situations*, 19b

ap — Incorrect capitalization: 34a–b

oh — Lack of coherence: *paragraphs*, 4b

on — Be more concise: 22a–c

s — Comma splice: *correcting*, 15b

— Inappropriate diction: *appropriate words*, 26a; *inappropriate language*, 26b; *offensive language*, 26c

ead — Deadwood: 22a1

et — Use concrete details: 26a3–4

ev — Inadequate development: 4c

m — Dangling modifier: 25c

oc — Incorrect or inadequate documentation: *MLA*, 11a; *APA*, 12a; *Chicago*, 13a; *CSE*, 14a

xact — Use more exact word: 26a

rag — Sentence fragment: *correcting*, 16b

s — Fused sentence: *correcting*, 15b

al — Use italics: 35a–c; *for emphasis or clarity*, 35d

og — Incorrect or faulty logic: 23c

ix — Mixed construction: 23b

am — Misplaced modifier: 25a

ns — Incorrect manuscript form: *MLA*, 11b; *APA*, 12b; *Chicago*, 13b; *CSE*, 14b

um — Incorrect use of numeral or spelled-out number: 30b; 38a–b

p — Punctuation error: **Pt. 6**

par or ¶ — New paragraph: 4a–d

no ¶ — No paragraph: 4a–d

¶ coh — Paragraph not coherent: 4b

¶ dev — Paragraph not developed: 4c

¶ un — Paragraph not unified: 4a

plan — Lack of planning: 3a; 43b

purp — Purpose not clear: *determining purpose*, 2a; *purpose checklist*, p. 11

ref — Incorrect pronoun reference: 19c

rep — Unnecessary repetition: *eliminating*, 22b

rev — Revise: 3d; 6h

run-on — Run-on sentence: *correcting*, 15b

shift — Unwarranted shift: 23a

sp — Spelling error: 33a–g

sxt — Sexist or offensive language: 26c

thesis — Unclear or unstated thesis: 3b; 6d; 6g

var — Lack of sentence variety: 21a–c

w — Wordiness: *eliminating*, 22a

✓ — Apostrophe: 30a–c

[ ] — Brackets: 32d

: — Colon: 32a1–3; *editing misuse*, 32a4

^ — Comma: 28a–f; *editing misuse*, 28g

— — Dash: 32b

. . . — Ellipsis: 32f

! — Exclamation point: 27c

// — Faulty parallelism: *using parallelism*, 24a; *revising*, 24b

- — Hyphen: 36a–b

( ) — Parentheses: 32c

. — Period: 27a

? — Question mark: 27b; *editing misuse*, 27b

" " — Quotation marks: 31a–c; *with other punctuation*, 31d; *editing misuse*, 31e

; — Semicolon: 29a–b; *editing misuse*, 29c

/ — Slash: 32e

# Contents